The Soviet Bloc
in the IMF and the IBRD

The Soviet Bloc
in the IMF and the IBRD

Valerie J. Assetto

Westview Press / Boulder and London

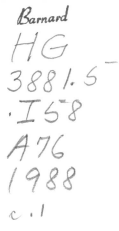

Westview Special Studies in International Economics

This Westview softcover edition is printed on acid-free paper and bound in softcovers that carry the highest rating of the National Association of State Textbook Administrators, in consultation with the Association of American Publishers and the Book Manufacturers' Institute.

Published in 1988 in the United States of America by Westview Press, Inc.; Frederick A. Praeger, Publisher; 5500 Central Avenue, Boulder, Colorado 80301

Library of Congress Cataloging-in-Publication Data
Assetto, Valerie J.
   The Soviet Bloc in the IMF and the IBRD.
   (Westview special studies in international economics)
   Bibliography: p.
   Includes index.
   1. International Monetary Fund—Europe, Eastern.
2. World Bank—Europe, Eastern. 3. Loans, Foreign—
Europe, Eastern. I. Title. II. Title: Soviet bloc
in the I.M.F. and the I.B.R.D. III. Series.
HG3881.5.I58A76 1988   332.1'52   86-7800
ISBN 0-8133-7236-4

Printed and bound in the United States of America

The paper used in this publication meets the requirements of the American National Standard for Permanence of Paper for Printed Library Materials Z39.48-1984.

6   5   4   3   2   1

To my family:
Val, Joan, Gary, Richard, Gayle, and Stephen

Contents

Tables

Acknowledgments

Several persons and organizations contributed to the successful completion of this project. The International Research and Exchanges Board (IREX) supported the early stages of the research through a Preparatory Fellowship and an Exchange Fellowship. Dr. Charles M. Loeffler and Ms. Patsy Smith also contributed their expertise in the construction of earlier versions of the manuscript. Colorado State University provided assistance for final production of the manuscript. Ms. Gayle Assetto, Ms. Terry Lane, and Mr. Emmett Lombard also contributed their time toward the completion of the final manuscript. Finally, I wish to express my heartfelt gratitude to Dr. Stephen P. Mumme, Colorado State University, for his continuous encouragement, support, advice, and assistance. I assume complete responsibility, however, for the analysis and material contained within.

Valerie J. Assetto

1

Perspectives on
IMF and IBRD Lending

One of the most significant developments in the post-war international economic system is the startling increase in the level of financial assistance provided by private and public agencies. Both bilateral and multilateral financial institutions have attempted to satisfy the need of modern nation-states for substantial amounts of financial assistance. Aid agencies and commercial banking institutions in the developed states of North America and Western Europe supply large amounts of funds to the rest of the world but the largest *single* sources of official international financial assistance, particularly to developing nations, are two specialized agencies of the United Nations, the International Monetary Fund (IMF) and the International Bank for Reconstruction and Development (IBRD or World Bank). These two agencies provide the bulk of multilateral economic assistance and balance of payments financing in the present international economy.

The purpose of this study is to examine the impact of political, non-economic factors in IMF and IBRD operations and decisions to lend using the Eastern European members of both organizations as case studies. Numerous critics of the Bank and Fund such as Cheryl Payer contend that political factors permeate the self-proclaimed technical decisions of the Bank and Fund, to the detriment of the socialist and developing countries. This analysis investigates that claim by focusing on the influence of political factors, such as ideology, on the relationship of two international financial organizations, the IMF and IBRD, and a particular class of their members, the socialist states of Eastern Europe.

The constitutions and bylaws of international agencies for economic assistance typically prohibit the inclusion in decisions to lend of any but economic or technical criteria. Yet, as will be shown, various political criteria do, in fact, affect certain lending decisions. While the decision to finance a highway in a remote area or to bolster a declining balance of payments position in a member country involves the use of numerous economic criteria, such as GNP and inflation, several political criteria may also enter into the decision-making process of international assistance organizations, either directly or indirectly. For example, political inputs may have influence when the assessment of the potential borrower's ability to repay a loan is based upon political criteria such as the borrower's regime type or when the lender attempts to control economic policy-making by the borrower. The magnitude of the funds dispensed by international lenders bestows upon these organizations this potential for influence on the decision-making processes of the borrower.[1]

The specialized agencies of the United Nations have been frequent targets of the charge of "politicization" from both ends of the political spectrum. The implicit criticism here is that "the agencies are being used as forums for political debate rather than the functional tasks for which they were founded"[2] and that they are engaging in activities which are predicated upon political criteria. However, as Lyons, et al., note, U.N. agencies are inherently political in their origins and activities (p. 83) and thus it is almost inevitable that these agencies would be subject to such criticism. The Bank and the Fund are not exceptions.

The forms that political factors may take and the points in the lender's decision-making processes in which political inputs enter influence how these factors impact upon the operations of international economic organizations. It is the central thesis of this analysis that political factors may appear in the lending decisions of the IMF and the IBRD only under certain circumstances which are determined by the attributes and policies of the borrower and only at certain stages of the decision-making process.

There are numerous reasons why the weight of political inputs in the lending policies and decisions of the international lending agencies is of critical importance to borrowers. Official statements by these international economic organizations offer a borrower few guidelines for assessing its position with respect to political criteria. Some clues to political criteria may be derived from the constitutions or regulations of these agencies, but more often political inputs are well-disguised. Knowledge of the impacts of political criteria on the level and conditions of loans from international financial organizations can assist a borrower immeasurably in preparing a stabilization or development program or a set of projects which international lenders are likely to fund. A borrower may even be able to develop a loan application strategy using the results from the analysis of the impact of political criteria to anticipate and avoid major conflicts with the lender.[3]

Analysis of the impact of political criteria in the lending policies of international economic organizations may also enable the borrower and the lender to minimize the unexpected effects of lender policies on the borrower's political and economic system. This factor could be critical to a country which is trying to preserve its unique political and economic system in the face of what it perceives to be intense international hostility. The subtle influence of the lender's ideology or procedural biases can often divert the borrower from its intended goals, although this may or may not be an intentional consequence of the lender's policies. Recognition of such a possibility gives the borrower (or the lender) the opportunity to counteract any undesirable influences which may result from the lender's operations, either in a case-by-case fashion or as part of a comprehensive set of reforms.

The decision to focus this study on the lending policies of the Fund and the Bank underscores several important aspects of international development assistance. Theoretically, multilateral aid yields less potential for political influence than does bilateral aid. It follows, therefore, that an international lending agency should be able to restrict the basis for its decisions more easily to economic criteria than would an agency or organization of a single lending state. An international organization is composed of many states whose political criteria for lending may conflict with and/or cancel one another, whereas bilateral aid subjects the borrower to the lending criteria of a single state. In the case of the Fund and the Bank, the fact that these organizations' members exhibit a wide variety of political and economic values and structures, which theoretically should increase tolerance of deviance, further reduces the potential for influence of political criteria in lending decisions to those countries.

The presence of political inputs in Bank and Fund lending policy to their members, therefore, should not be readily apparent given the nature of multilateral aid, and in fact, the appearance of such political considerations would be considered undesirable by both the organizations and their members as contrary to the purpose of multilateral aid. Indeed, the *Articles of Agreement* for both organizations specifically prohibit each organization from considering political factors in their decisions to lend and from "intervening in the domestic social or political polices of members."[4]

As increasing numbers of countries are forced to seek assistance from these organizations by the crisis in the international commercial finance market, the complaints of "politicization" are likely to increase proportionate to the increase in the role and activity of the Fund and the Bank. The very nature of the functions of these two organizations, which can be conceived of as regulatory (and perhaps even redistributive) in a broad sense, invites such claims, and not unexpectedly, the Fund's lending policies (conditionality) have been a "perennial source of controversy"[5] in the past. In part this is a consequence of the inherently political role assigned to the Fund in which the Fund must monitor the smooth functioning of the international monetary system through its supervision of members' economic policies whose selection is, in itself, a political act. Thus, the Fund is organized to perform tasks which require it to assume quasi-governmental, regulatory functions on an international scale.[6]

Aspects of the Fund's structure, such as weighted voting and the selection of its governing bodies, also contribute to perceptions of political bias,[7] as Fred L. Smith notes below:

> That the IMF's fate has rested with the political process has been totally appropriate, for the IMF is itself a political institution. It is managed by politically appointed individuals from member nations, and the political interests of its members influence its decisions.[8]

The intrusion of political variables into Bank and Fund lending policies can have immense impact on the direction of economic policy in member states. These two organizations work closely together on matters of general policy, policy evaluation research, and provision of technical assistance to members. As a result, the Fund and the Bank are alleged to have developed a "broad identity of views"[9] based on a common set of assumptions and theories about economic behavior. It is not surprising that critics such as Payer and Körner, et al., allege that the Bank and Fund's organizational ideologies closely resemble the capitalist, market philosophies of their major members. The sheer volume of funds dispersed by these two organizations make them almost indispensable to the economies of most developing nations.[10] These organizations' increasing interest in non-traditional capitalist or socialist economic systems can be traced not only to an increased interest in the development process but also to a growing concern that the heavy indebtedness of developing states, including the Soviet Bloc, will lead eventually to widespread defaults in commercial and government loans which could have a disastrous effect in the international economy (Hayter, pp. 74, 32). It is feasible to expect, therefore, that the Bank and the Fund will seek to create and maintain an environment in which the probability of default will be low. This issue becomes a political one if and when the Bank and Fund adopt a specific economic ideology in the construction of that environment.

Bank and Fund impact in member economies is amplified by the respect that these two organizations command in international financial circles. Both organizations are leaders in facilitating loans to member states from both governmental and commercial sources. Fund and Bank approval of the policies of a member nation is often used as indicator to other lenders in their decisions to lend (Hayter, p. 79). These "other lenders" may be national governments, commercial banks or other international organizations. The World Bank is a leader in composing aid consortia, groups of lenders which coordinate their efforts to lend to a particular state or region.[11] Fund approval of one of its stand-by arrangements "has come to be regarded as the lending international judgment on the soundness of a member's policies;"[12] consequently, the Fund serves, in a sense, as an international credit bureau for potential lenders. In fact, a loan from the Fund can also be a catalyst for additional assistance from commercial and government lenders.[13]

The Bank and the Fund perform a vital function in development and stabilization processes. The presence of political inputs in the decision-making process of these organizations can affect the extension of credit from both private and international lenders, and technical assistance provided by these two agencies may influence the development choices made by a state. Thus, Fund and Bank opinion may influence the entire scope of assistance to a member state. The debt coordinating functions of the Bank and Fund, therefore, constitute an effective method for imposing sanctions against recalcitrant borrowers,[14] and this lends even greater weight to the importance and potential hazards of IMF and IBRD decision-making.

In this study, the five Eastern European members of the Bank and the Fund are used as a crucial test of Bank and Fund impartiality. It is reasoned that if political factors *do* intervene in IMF and IBRD lending decisions, they would be most obvious in the case of communist countries, for reasons explained below. The term communist or Soviet Bloc is defined as limited to the Eastern European states of Czechoslovakia, Hungary, Poland, Romania, and Yugoslavia. These five states were all original members of the Bloc immediately following World War II and are distinguished by their common cultural heritage and historical relationship with the Soviet Union from other contemporary members of the Bloc, such as Vietnam or Ethiopia, whose policy options and resource bases are often quite different.

Communist states have often served as alternative role models for Third World members of the Bank and Fund. An administrative, centrally-planned economy is one option open to a state which desires to develop rapidly. Soviet and Eastern European experiences in the post-war period have demonstrated the viability of this option, as one variant or another, despite the recent stagnation of the 1980s. Bank and Fund treatment of Communist countries could also serve as an indicator to non-Communist members of the range of experimentation permitted by the IMF and IBRD.

Between 1949 and 1984, only five Communist states joined the IMF and IBRD: Czechoslovakia, Hungary, Poland, Romania, and Yugoslavia. Of these five, only Yugoslavia was a member of both organizations for the entire period under investigation. Poland and Czechoslovakia withdrew prior to 1955 (although Poland reentered the Fund in 1986), and Romania and Hungary did not join until 1972 and 1982, respectively.

For the purposes of this study, all five states are considered developing states. This is consonant with the classification assigned to these states by the IMF and IBRD (see *Annual Reports* for 1985) and thus, all four current Eastern European members of the IBRD still qualify for Bank loans despite their rather high GNP per capita figures. These countries differ from the more recent members of the Soviet Bloc in the Bank and Fund in the longevity, or perhaps stability, of their political systems. If one accepts the classification of these countries as constructed by the Bank and Fund, one must place these countries among the most-developed of the Third World, i.e., among the newly industrializing countries (NICs). Yet four of the five states have suffered severe economic difficulties during some portion of the 1949–1984 period of the sort which is typical of a developing state on the threshold of self-sustaining development such as structural imbalances, high debt service ratios, and dependence on a relatively narrow range of products for export revenues. The states of Eastern Europe also do not differ significantly from other Bank and Fund members (particularly the NICs) in their dependence on the First World states for investment capital and balance of payments financing.

Soviet Bloc members of the Bank and the Fund in their roles as developing economies share many of the same difficulties with the Fund and Bank as do other developing members of these organizations. The hostility to communism and the Soviet Union of the powerful Western members of both organizations only strengthens the potential impact of political inputs in decisions to lend to communist members. If political variables have any effect on Bank and Fund decisions, this effect should be even stronger in the decisions of the Bank and Fund to lend to their Eastern European members. With the partial exception of Yugoslavia and perhaps Hungary, the Eastern European states rely on the central-planning, state-directed model as the foundation for the structure of their economies. This is in direct contrast to the free market philosophy espoused by the Bank and Fund and is another potential source of friction with both organizations.

These states, therefore, are the focus of this study for two reasons; the Eastern European members of the Bank and the Fund can be considered a part of the group of economically developing states, and the nature of their political and economic systems can be expected to provoke hostility, or at least suspicion, from the capitalist-oriented members and staff in both organizations. Conceivably, this hostility could manifest itself in Bank and Fund decisions to lend. Thus, given the very broad and fundamental differences in economic philosophy which separate the two groups, it is reasonable to expect that if political factors *do* enter into Bank and Fund decision-making, they would be obvious in the two organizations' interactions with the communist states of Eastern Europe. The Soviet Bloc is thus a crucial test case of the role of political factors in Bank and Fund procedures.

The following sections construct the context for Bank and Fund lending to the Soviet Bloc by analyzing the views of supporters and critics of these organizations. A synthesis of these views is then presented which incorporates these analyses into a comprehensive formulation of IMF and IBRD lending. This formulation serves as the basis for the remaining examination of the Soviet Bloc in the IMF and IBRD.

Lending in the IMF and the IBRD

Most states rely on the multilateral financial assistance supplied by international economic organizations. If pronouncements by these international organizations are correct, reliance on Bank and Fund assistance assures the borrower of assistance provided according to well-defined technical criteria determined in an objective, unbiased manner. Acceptance of assistance by a member, according to the Fund and the Bank, should involve little or no loss of sovereignty on the part of the borrower. Yet, charges of politicization, particularly with reference to the IMF, suggest that perhaps this is not the case. This section examines two opposing interpretations of Fund and Bank lending decisions with respect to the inclusion of political criteria. A third perspective is offered which provides a means for integrating both approaches into a coherent explanation of IMF and IBRD operations and serves as the basis for analyzing the experiences of the Eastern European states in the IMF and IBRD.

There are two contending schools of opinions among scholars about the role of political factors in the lending policies of international financial institutions. These alternative views may be labelled the technocratic and the political approaches. The primary source of disagreement between the two views rests in the relative weight that each group ascribes to political and economic inputs in the lending process. The technocratic approach to the study of international economic organizations consists of analyses which assign a dominant role to economic inputs and economic performance in the lending decisions of international financial organizations. Analysts who adopt the technocratic approach contend that political factors have little or no effect on decisions to lend. These scholars believe that economic problems and their solutions can be formulated using strictly objective, economic criteria. Technocratic refers, then, to the type of analyses which emphasize the economic or technical nature of lending policy and decisions.

The second, political critique, approach disputes this claim. Analysts who follow the political approach contend that political factors eclipse economic factors in the lending policies of the Bank and the Fund. In this view, political criteria dominate the decision-making process in international financial organizations. The political approach argues that economic problems and solutions cannot be stripped of their political origins and content. The values and goals behind economic policy-making are essentially political, and therefore, are also normative.

The Technocratic Approach

The group of scholars representing the technocratic approach to international financial assistance stresses the importance of the economic and technical variables of development. In addition, this group argues that it is possible to make decisions to lend solely with reference to "objective economic" criteria. This approach regards the intrusion of political considerations into the decision-making process of international financial institutions as inexpedient and to be avoided at all costs. This functional approach does not ignore politics; it deliberately seeks to circumvent the controversies attendant on political decisions and procedures.[15] In this way, functionalists argue, international cooperation, and implicitly progress, could be hastened and achieved at a lower cost.

The tenets of the functionalist model of international organization provide the basis of the technocratic approach to international economic assistance. Functionalists firmly believe that the economic (welfare) components of the development process are separable from the political (power) components of the process.[16] Adherents of this task-oriented approach affirm that the technical, non-political aspects of development can be isolated and that organizations which are limited to such functionally specific aspects will maximize international welfare and promote peaceful international exchange.[17] Through a learning process, proponents of the functionalist model such as David Mitrany and Ernst Haas state that the cooperative problem-solving approach utilized in functionally specific international organizations such as the Bank and Fund will lead governments from the pursuit of "power-oriented" goals to more "welfare-oriented action" (Haas, *Beyond*, p. 47). This "spill-over" mechanism (Haas, *Beyond*, p. 48) will continue to expand cooperation into other functional areas, free of political conflict,[18] until essentially political tasks are also performed cooperatively. This is basically an indirect approach to international cooperation and integration, "sidestepping the still blazing national loyalties" (Haas, *Beyond*, p. 11) of the present nation-state system by concentrating on very limited, technical issues. Personal loyalties will gradually attach to organizations which are performing these technical tasks (Haas, *Beyond*, p. 49) and slowly, consensus on ends and means will emerge (Haas, *Beyond*, p. 38).

Cooperation through actions or behavior and not as a result of constitutional planning is a key element of functional analysis (Haas, *Beyond*, p. 12). Another important element of functionalist thought is the role of experts in performing functional activities. Haas claims that the maximum welfare "is approximated whenever a maximum of authority is exercised by technicians and administrators dedicated to the commonwealth. . . ." (Haas, *Beyond*, p. 8). In this conception, experts are apolitical, and as they are not interested in accruing political power, these experts are better able to come to agreement on international issues.[19] Lyons, et al., posit that organizations which are authorized to perform highly specialized, technical tasks, which place a premium on the technical competence of their staff and membership, and which employ decision-making rules based on contribution to the organization rather than sovereignty will encounter relatively few incidences of politicization.[20]

Neo-functionalists represent the response of functionalism to the evolution of the European Economic Community (EEC). Proponents of the neo-functionalist approach recognize that the spill-over mechanism critical to functionalist analysis may not always occur even though the international system is composed of ideal-type technocratic organizations such as the IMF. Political issues and opposition, assert the neo-functionalists, will appear at some stage of the integration process; thus, the result of the functionalist effort may conceivably be a sort of equilibrium or even spill-back.[21] If political opposition and conflict are encountered at the onset of the operations of a functionalist-type institution, then the organization's constitution must explicitly address those issues. This is contrary to functionalist thought, which ignores the role of constitutional arrangements. If political controversy is encountered at a later stage of the institution's operations, neo-functionalists suggest, machinery for the solution of political conflicts must be devised and incorporated into the organization. In either case, the neo-functionalists assert that political issues must be confronted openly whenever they arise.

Neo-functionalist analysis still retains the basic technocratic functionalist assumptions, however. This group of scholars agrees that political components can be identified and minimized by the technocratic experts who staff international economic organizations. Political issues are not encountered in the daily operations of the organization and spill-over remains the dominant mechanism. When political issues do appear, they take the form of major crises which must be resolved if further integration is to occur.

The Structure of the IMF and the IBRD

Functionalist thought had considerable impact on the architects of the United Nations group of international organizations, particularly the IMF and the IBRD. Designed in 1944 to promote international financial stability, reconstruction of war-damaged economies, and economic development, the IMF and IBRD were organized along primarily functionalist lines. According to C. Fred Bergsten, "the functional aim of each was to provide an international framework within which to manage issues where national management had become inadequate, or to handle better those issues where earlier international arrangements had failed."[22]

The tasks assigned to both organizations were limited and of a highly technical nature. This was particularly true of the IMF. The very nature of the technical functions of these two institutions required (and still requires) a highly-skilled, expert staff and knowledgeable national representatives. The organizational structure of both the Fund and the Bank was, and is, such that policy decisions are formulated by staff and representatives appointed or elected by member states. This arrangement permits continuous contact, at least in theory, with the demands and problems of members while maintaining some independence from those demands.[23] In keeping with functionalist expectations and the experiences of several other U.N. specialized agencies (Haas, *Beyond*, pp. 16–17), the essentially political problems encountered at the creation of the IMF and IBRD gradually faded as the complexity of the tasks assigned to these organizations grew.

The International Monetary Fund and the International Bank for Reconstruction and Development were created as a response to the disintegration of the international monetary system in the 1930s and the destruction of World War II. The initiative in the formation of the IMF and IBRD was taken by the United States and Great Britain.[24] In the period prior to the conference at which the IMF and IBRD were formed, the proposal to create a type of international payments union was the focus of a continuing, and occasionally heated, debate between Henry D. White from the U.S. and J. Maynard Keynes from the United Kingdom. It was these two men who provided much of the foundation and structure for the organization which became the IMF. The World Bank was almost an afterthought which began to emerge as an important issue only after substantial agreement on the payments union concept (IMF) was reached.[25]

During the period July 1 through July 21, 1944, representatives from 44 nations gathered at Bretton Woods, N.H. to discuss and create three organizations: an international payments union which would deal with international financial transfers, the balance of payments, and exchange controls (IMF); an organization to provide funds for reconstruction of war-damaged economies and future economic development (IBRD); and an organization to supplement the payments union which would regulate international trade (ITO, which for several reasons was never created). The purpose of the conference was to design a structure of international organizations which would regulate the international monetary system and thus avoid the competitive international financial policies of states which many believed were responsible for the Depression and which contributed to the outbreak of World War II. The purpose of the organizations which emerged out of the Bretton Woods conference, as stated in the *Articles of Agreement* for the Fund and the Bank, was to promote stability in the international monetary system through the promotion of free trade, stable exchange rates, and economic development.

Stabilizing the international monetary system required the cooperation of all states which participated in the system. As a result, membership in the two organizations was made as easy as possible with a corresponding goal of universality as the guideline. Criteria for membership are identical for each applicant and are kept to a minimum. To join the Fund and the Bank, the applicant must be "a 'country' that is in formal control of its external relations and that . . . is able and willing to perform the obligations of membership."[26] The Fund and the Bank reserve the right to determine the definition of "country" and whether an applicant is in control of its external relations and able to fulfill its obligations, independent of such determination by other states or international organizations (Gold, *Membership*, p. 469). Those criteria still govern the admission of new members to both organiztions, and by 1985, Fund and Bank membership had grown to 148 states.

In keeping with the desire of the participants at Bretton Woods that participation in both the IMF and IBRD be voluntary as well as universal, procedures are included in the *Articles* for the cooperation of members with non-members and for withdrawal from either organization. The withdrawal clauses in the *Articles* are unique for an international organization created immediately after World War II. Since membership in the Fund is a condition of membership in the Bank, withdrawal from the Fund also entails withdrawal from the Bank. In the Fund, there are three types of withdrawal: voluntary, on the initiative of the member; compulsory, as a result of the member's failure to perform its obligations; and an intermediate type in which the member's refusal to adopt a change in a specific value of its currency at the Fund's request leads to the member's withdrawal. There have been three cases of voluntary withdrawal from the Fund and the Bank (Poland, Cuba, and Indonesia, which later rejoined) and only one case of compulsory withdrawal (Czechoslovakia). The desire for universality in both organizations is so strong that a tremendous effort is made by the organizations to avoid situations in which withdrawal is the only alternative.

The IMF: Structure and Functions. Article I of the *Articles of Agreement* for the International Monetary Fund lists the purposes of that organization. According to Article I, the primary purpose of the Fund is to promote international monetary cooperation through consultation and collaboration of members on international monetary problems. The Fund is also directed to facilitate the growth of international trade, assist in the attainment of full employment and high levels of income, and encourage the development of productive resources in its members. In the international monetary system, the *Articles* exhort the Fund to work toward the establishment of exchange rate stability, the establishment of a multilateral system of payments, and the reduction of foreign exchange restrictions.

The Fund is also to provide assistance in moderating the effects of disequilibrium in members' balance of payments. This last function has become the primary purpose of the IMF, especially since 1972–1974 when a fixed exchange rate system was abandoned in favor of freely floating rates. The Fund is now

"a source of temporary finance for countries that [find] themselves in balance-of-payments deficit either because of their own policy mistakes or because of external economic events over which they [have] no control."[27]

In order to fulfill this important role, designers of the Fund at Bretton Woods established an authority structure which blended government representatives and experts on international monetary affairs.[28] Every member sends one representative and an alternate to serve on the highest organ of the Fund, the Board of Governors. These representatives are usually high-ranking officials in the government ministries or the central bank. The Board of Governors typically meets annually, although a subset of the Board, known as the Interim Committee, meets more frequently.

The Executive Directors "are the organ of the Fund that is in continuous session and is responsible for the conduct of the general operations of the Fund" (Gold, *Voting*, p. 55). There are 22 Executive Directors, and they are appointed (6) or elected (16) by members according to regulations specified in the *Articles* (Gold, *Voting*, p. 99; IMF, *Articles of Agreement*). Decisions of the Board of Governors and the Executive Directors are considered decisions of the entire organization and "not a decision of members or even the collectivity of members" (Gold, *Voting*, p. 89).

The Managing Director of the Fund supervises the daily operations of the Fund. He is responsible for the management of the various departments and approximately 1500 staff members (Killick, p. 131). The Managing Director is selected by the Executive Directors and is responsible to them. He is traditionally a national of a Western European member. The Fund's staff is primarily composed of well-trained experts in economics and is drawn from a wide range of countries, although nationals of the industrialized countries predominate. The Managing Director and the staff owe allegiance to the Fund alone. The departments perform administrative, technical and regional functions and are the organs through which the majority of Fund business is conducted.

Financial support for the IMF is derived primarily from member subscriptions which are payable upon entry and which are reviewed approximately every five years, or when necessary. Based on the size of this subscription, which is established with reference to economic criteria, each member is assigned a *quota*. A member's transactions and privileges in the Fund are governed by the size of its quota. Since quotas are based on the strength of a member's economy, it is no surprise that the bulk of the IMF's lendable capital is provided by the industrialized countries of Western Europe, the United States, Japan, and in the 1970s, Saudi Arabia. In addition, because access to the Fund's resources are predicated on the size of the member's quota, these same countries theoretically have access to the largest amounts of Fund assistance.

The Fund could not operate without the continued financial support of industrialized countries, and this fact is reflected in the voting strength of these members. A member's votes in the IMF are equal to 1 vote for every SDR 100,000 of quota plus 250 "basic votes," and as a result, the U.S. alone, through its financial contribution, possesses over 19 percent of the total votes in the IMF (in 1984), enough to veto any significant policy initiative.

Members "purchase" foreign currency from the Fund with their own currency. These purchases are called loans in common parlance, although in a strict sense no loan occurs since currencies are exchanged. Loans equal to more than 25 percent of a member's quota constitute the credit tranches and are subject to increasingly stringent conditions and review (conditionality). Regulations governing the interest rate, repayment period or repurchase, and the total percentage of quota a member may borrow have varied over the years in response to member needs and the state of the international economy. These regulations apply to all members equally, however.

The *Articles* of the Fund enjoin the IMF to exclude non-technical or political factors from consideration in decisions to lend and the formation of stabilization policies designed to restore balance of payments equilibrium. Performance criteria, the observance of which are required as a condition of certain types of Fund loans, are to be "formulated in arithmetic or other objective terms" so that members can be assured "that the Fund could [not] impede purchases under the Stand-by arrangement by decisions motivated by subjective or discretionary considerations."[29]

In practice, this prohibition has been translated as the priniciple of "uniformity." As defined by Fund staff member, Manuel Guitián, uniformity "requires that for any given degree of need the effort of economic adjustment sought in programs be broadly equivalent among members."[30] More specifically, the Fund is enjoined from defining policy or program requirements with reference to a particular member or category of members.[31] The purpose of program or loan conditions, according to the Fund, is not to alter a member's economic or political structure, and thus, a member's social or political policies are emphatically excluded in the *Articles of Agreement* (Article IV, Section 3(b)) from consideration (Gold, *Financial Assistance*, p. 20; Gold, *Political Considerations*, pp. 146–147). The Fund stresses that

> "The Fund approves a transaction in support of the economic policies of a government and not in support of other policies or of the government as such" (Gold, *Political Considerations*, p. 148).

Uniformity in the Fund does *not* mean, however, that the Fund blindly applies its formula and conditions regardless of the special and/or mitigating circumstances of its members. The 1979 *Review of Conditionality* explicitly instructs the IMF to "pay due regard to [members'] social, political, and economic priorities and objectives as well as their particular circumstances."[32] As Gold notes, however, this instruction does *not* compel the Fund to comply if compliance with the 1979 *Review* would violate other requirements contained within the *Articles of Agreement* (*Political Considerations*, p. 146). Killick observes that since the adoption of the revised guidelines there has been little alteration in the effects of political and social considerations on Fund lending policy (*Quest*, p. 150).

According to the Fund's own regulations, a member is *entitled* to Fund assistance if the following conditions are met:

1. the member has a clear balance of payment need

2. the member intends to use the funds in accordance with the conditions established in the *Articles of Agreement*
3. the member is eligible to receive IMF monies (i.e., is in good standing
4. a waiver is not necessary (to exceed the quota limits) (Gold, *Political Considerations*, p. 146).

To begin the lending process (purchase), the member must first request assistance from the IMF and demonstrate a need for balance of payments financing.[33] This need will be evaluated by the Fund's staff in terms of "the variability of the balance of payments and its structural trend, the availability of alternative sources of liquidity, the terms of such assistance, and the costs of adjustment" (Killick, p. 172; Guitián, *Fund Conditionality—1950-1970s*, p. 25). The goal is to restore a "viable" balance of payments which the IMF defines as "a current account deficit that can be financed, on a sustainable basis, by new capital inflows on terms that are compatible with the development and growth prospects of the country" (Guitián, *Fund Conditionality, 1950-1970*, p. 24).

The lending process in the Fund begins with a preliminary inquiry from the prospective borrower through the member's Executive Director or during the member's annual consultation with the Fund.[34] Once the request is received, the Managing Director and the staff proceed to conduct a preliminary investigation into the scope and nature of the project and prepare a briefing paper which outlines the magnitude of the problem and serves as the basis for the staff mission to the member. The mission travels to the requesting member and conducts a thorough investigation of the problem using materials supplied by the member and extensive interviews of governmental officials. In this manner, the special or peculiar circumstances of the member's situation are relayed to the staff who may or may not take such circumstances into consideration when suggesting a stabilization program and formulating a recommendation to the Managing Director (Guitián, *Fund Conditionality, 1950-1970*, p. 25).

If the mission concludes that there is a sufficient need for IMF assistance, the mission staff and members of the requesting government negotiate an appropriate "stabilization program" which is comprised of policy measures the borrower agrees to implement in return for funding which are designed to restore balance of payments equilibrium. Included in this program may be preconditions, or policies the member agrees to implement *before* the request is placed before the Executive Directors for their approval.

The program is described in the Letter of Intent in which the member formally agrees to comply with certain policy conditions and which includes quantitative measures or targets with which the program will be evaluated (performance criteria). These performance criteria are usually limited in number and macroeconomic in character. Failure to observe the criteria established in the Letter of Intent can result in the suspension of further installments of the loan, which is, in most cases, a Stand-by Agreement. The disbursal of the loan in installments is termed "phasing" and serves as a control mechanism for compliance with the terms of the agreement.

This conditionality is designed to safeguard the assets of the Fund and its members by requiring responsible policy action on the part of borrowers which is designed to alleviate the problems which resulted in the deficit. Conditionality also ensures the revolving character of the Fund lending process. With limited liquidity, the Fund must guard against irresponsible use of its assets or the domination of its lendable capital by a limited number of needy members.

The Managing Director reviews the formal Letter of Intent and then places it before the Executive Directors for approval. The Executive Directors review the agreement and as is usually the case, approve the loan. Decisions within the Executive Board are almost always consensual; it is rare that the Executive Directors deny a request. This is to be expected in that the staff is well-acquainted with the sorts of programs the Directors prefer, and informal consultation with key Executive Directors during the early stages of the negotiations are often a part of the process.[35]

Once the first installment of the Stand-by Arrangement is disbursed the member must provide the Fund with the information it needs to monitor the member's performance. If the member diverges from the stated macroeconomic targets specified in the performance criteria, the Fund can take several actions, including suspension of the remaining installments of the loan. If the member does not violate the basic intent of the program, the Fund will usually modify the agreement in consonance with the altered circumstances; in some cases this requires a renegotiation of the terms of the agreement. Significant variance from the performance targets, however, can and does result in suspension of the agreement and termination of the loan.

The IBRD: Structure and Functions. Reconstruction and development, as the IBRD's name indicates, are the primary purposes of the World Bank. By 1960, however, the reconstruction needs of Bank members had dwindled and development became the primary focus of the Bank's activities. As Article I of the Bank's *Articles of Agreement* states, the Bank is to

1. facilitate the investment of capital for productive purposes

2. promote private foreign investment and to supplement private investment through loans out of its own capital
3. to promote balanced growth of international trade and equilibrium in the balance of payments
4. to insure that adequate financing exists for the "more useful and urgent projects"
5. to pay due regard to the effect of its operations on business conditions in its members.[36]

Thus, the World Bank today is primarily a development institution which provides loans for projects designed to enhance the economic productivity and development of its members.

The organizational structure of the Bank is similar to that of the Fund. Governors are appointed by member-states, and the twenty-one Executive Directors are composed of both appointed and elected Directors. The Board of Governors meets annually, while the Executive Directors meet frequently during the week to supervise the Bank's daily operations. The qualifications of Governors and Directors of the Bank are similar to those of their counterparts in the Fund; it is common for the same official to serve as a member's Governor to both the Bank and the Fund.

The voting formula in the Bank varies slightly from that employed in the Fund. Members subscribe to Bank stock, and this subscription serves as the basis for voting in the organization. Each member receives an initial 250 votes and then one vote for every share of Bank stock that it holds. The consequence of weighted voting in the IBRD is parallel to that in the Fund; the United States and Western European nations possess virtual veto power on all major decisions taken in the organization.

The Bank's capital stock is available for subscription by members at one share equal to $100,000 (IBRD, *Articles*, Article II, Section 3, p. 52). Minimum levels of subscriptions are determined by the Bank for each member; subscriptions beyond the minimum are also established by the Bank. Sources of funds for Bank loans are derived from payments on members' capital subscriptions, the Bank's own borrowing on the world market, and net earnings.[37]

The President is the chief executive of the World Bank. He is selected by the Executive Directors and serves as their chairman. By custom, he is also a U.S. national. The President supervises the staff and the daily operations of the Bank and is responsible for the smooth operation of the Bank's several functional departments. The Project Departments accept or reject proposals submitted from the Area Departments which have responsibility for the selection and development of projects in their respective geographical areas. The Economic Departments perform the economic analysis necessary for project evaluation. Other departments serve the administrative needs of the organization.

World Bank loans are designed to furnish credit for projects where the risk is considered too great for private lenders alone. Loans are extended at slightly more favorable terms than can be obtained on the commercial market. Several conditions govern the use of Bank credit. World Bank loans must be used for productive purposes and in most cases, to finance the foreign exchange needs of a project. If the borrower is not a government, the loan must be guaranteed by the borrower's government or its central bank. Bank loans may not be tied to specific purchases, but loans must be spent in any member country, usually through competitive bidding.

The borrower must be unable to finance the project with funds from private sources. This condition is intended to promote private investment and enterprise, an integral part of the Bank's purpose (see the *Articles*, Article I). The Bank's emphasis on investment conditions and the impact of a borrower's fiscal policies on those conditions is understandable given this emphasis. Bank loans are typically used to finance infrastructure projects in areas such as power and transportation, although credits for agriculture and social infrastructure (e.g., education) increased during Robert McNamara's tenure as Bank President during the 1970s.[38]

There are six phases to the World Bank's project cycle. In the first phase, identification, the idea for a project emerges from almost ongoing interaction between Bank staff, usually in the relevant Area Department, and members. The staff then assists the member in preparing a project proposal which meets the Bank's standards. The project is appraised by the various departments of the Bank which have an interest in a project of that type in order to determine its feasibility and its relevance for both Bank policy and the member's course of development. Negotiations ensue regarding the capital requirements of the project and the policy measures the member must undertake for the project to succeed.

Once the staff is confident that the project is feasible and meets the Bank's other standards, as stated in the *Articles*, the project is forwarded to the Executive Directors for approval. Bank Directors seldom vote on projects, or even policy; as in the Fund, decisions are generally based on consensus and involve extensive discussion in informal settings.[39] In addition, because of frequent interaction, the staff is not likely to forward a project which significantly deviates from the Directors' established preferences.

Once the loan is approved, the project is implemented under Bank supervision. IBRD loans carry below-market interest rates which are applied uniformly to all projects. These rates fluctuate according to world market rates and must be established by a decision of the Executive

Directors. Due to the long-term nature of Bank projects, repayment periods are lengthy. When the project is completed, the Bank performs a formal evaluation to assess the effectiveness and efficiency of the project and the use of Bank funds.[40]

Like the Fund, the Bank is specifically prohibited from the consideration of political criteria in its charter, the *Articles of Agreement*. The *Articles* for the Bank require that:

"The Bank and its officers shall not interfere in the political affairs of any member; nor shall they be influenced in their decisions by the political character of the member or members concerned. Only economic considerations shall be relevant to their decisions, and these considerations shall be weighed impartially. . . ." (Articles of Agreement IV, Section 10).

In consonance with this requirement, the Bank asserts that its decisions to lend are founded on economic criteria alone (Ayres, p. 71). Thus, similar to Fund Standby Arrangements, conditions on Bank loans should be uniform across members.

The Bank and the Fund share several important functions and increasingly, policy orientations. For example, technical assistance is an integral part of both Fund and Bank operations and an important source of economic and financial expertise. Both organizations provide a wide range of technical assistance facilities to members upon request and in addition, offer courses on a variety of topics at their headquarters in Washington, D.C. Technical assistance in the World Bank consists of aid in developing technical plans, assistance in the choice of priorities among projects, and recommendations by the staff on the administration of selected projects.[41] Fund assistance tends to concentrate in the areas of training in modern statistical methods used to generate and evaluate monetary and fiscal policies, and current developments in central banking policies and procedures.[42] Members of the Bank and Fund do not hesitate to use the technical assistance offered by both organizations and frequently send their most promising young officials for intensive training in Washington, D.C. This accords the Bank and Fund perspective on economic and development policy tremendous influence in member countries.

With respect to policy prescriptions, Fund and Bank perspectives and functions have been converging in recent years. A clear example of this is the heightened interest in both organizations in lending for programs designed to correct structural imbalances. Both the Bank and Fund have instituted lending facilities and procedures which provide large amounts of capital for medium term loans and which employ conditionality in the supervision of those loans.[43]

The traditional distinctions between the Bank and Fund remain relevant. Bank policy continues to rely on microeconomic factors, such as investment priorities, in the evaluation of projects and policy while the Fund continues to focus on macroeconomic indicators as the primary performance criteria.[44] The Fund also displays a marked preference for its traditional pattern of short-term loans for adjustment purposes. The difference in the relationship between the two organizations occurs largely in the area of staff competences and the extent of collaboration between them, which has increased sharply in recent years (Guitián, *Fund Conditionality: 1980s*, pp. 22–23; Crockett, p. 16).

Finally, in both organizations the critical criterion in lending decisions is still "creditworthiness," (IMF, *Annual Report 1979*, p. 42) which is loosely defined as the ability of a borrower to repay a loan (Gold, *Financial Assistance*, p. 30). The IMF and the IBRD interpret "creditworthiness" in such a way that their own creditors are convinced of their "cautiousness, soundness, and reliability" (Hayter, p. 84). That they have succeeded in this is conceded by one Bank critic who notes that Bank bonds "are regarded as exceptionally safe investments" in the international banking community.[45]

This review of the structure and functions of the IMF and IBRD reveals that the IMF and the IBRD can be considered highly successful functional agencies. Organized to perform limited, technical tasks and constrained from considering political criteria, these two agencies have the trust and respect of their members and the world financial community. The daily operations of both the Fund and the Bank are performed by highly-trained specialists in economics, management and engineering. In theory, issues and problems are formulated and resolved solely in economic terms. On the surface, the Bank and the Fund would seem to be model functionalist organizations.

The Political Critique

Several scholars disagree with this functionalist approach to international organization and with the application of functional explanations to international organizations for economic assistance. This group of writers, labeled here as the political critique approach, argues that politics can never be excluded from economic or technical problems and issues; therefore, the functionalist effort to build a network of cooperation on international problems through isolating technical tasks is destined to be impeded by the stubborn intrusion of political conflicts.[46]

According to the political critique, the Bank and Fund were destined to operate as political institutions due to the nature of their origins, purposes, and functions. This group contends that since their inception, these agencies for international economic assistance were never limited to merely a defined, technical task, but were created specifically to support a particular economic system—world capitalism.[47] In this context, however, the term capitalism refers primarily to a preference for a neo-liberal and/or orthodox notion of a competitive, free market system (Ayres, p. 74; David, pp. 6–11; Körner, p. 147; Williamson, p. 31). This preference, critics allege, is due in part to the belief of Bank and Fund staff in the inherent efficiency of the private market for regulating demand and supply.[48]

Correspondingly, in the sphere of international trade and finance, critics argue that the IMF and the World Bank are designed to maintain and support a system of stable exchange rates, free trade, and unimpeded private foreign investment (Payer, *World Bank*, p. 345). This is evident in the Bank's *Articles* (Article I, Section 2). The dominant philosophy of the Fund also stresses the importance of "integration into the world market" and expressly disapproves of exchange and trade restrictions (Körner, pp. 131–133; Dell, p. 609). If such allegations are true, it would appear that there is an intrinsic bias in both organizations against socialist, centrally-planned modes of economic organization.

The role of the industrialized, First World states in the Bank and Fund is yet another source of politicization in the two organizations. Britain and the United States were crucial actors in the founding of both organizations and it was those countries' values and perceptions regarding the international economy which formed the basis of the Bretton Woods system. The quota system and the related weighted voting scheme guaranteed a predominant position for the countries of Western Europe and the United States. This dependence on the developed countries for personnel, financing, and policy change has led some critics to conclude that both organizations are merely a smokescreen for neo-colonial exploitation of the Third World by the First. Cooptation of the radical and developing states into the established Bretton Woods system assures the First World of its dominance of the international monetary system (Körner, p. 43). The United States is most often identified as the key actor, particularly in the Bank, and U.S. influence on Bank and Fund loans is often alleged; indeed, Ayres describes the Bank in its first decade as "almost an appendage of the U.S. Treasury Department" (Ayres, pp. 7, 57; Payer, *World Bank*, p. 42).

The dominance of the international economy by the capitalist nations of North America and Western Europe and the role of these countries in the creation of the World Bank and the IMF prompts Teresa Hayter, an ardent critic of the World Bank, to conclude that World Bank policy (and by implication, the policies of the Fund) is an "integral part of the foreign policies of Western capitalist nations toward underdeveloped

countries" (Hayter, p. 6). Tony Killick cites "politicking" by the Executive
Directors as the primary cause for departures from uniformity in the
Fund. Both Killick and Ayres note that a member's foreign relations
with the major powers in the Bank and Fund often determine the status
of that member's loans in each organization (Killick, pp. 205, 221; Ayres,
p. 72). As Ayres states:

"Political factors seemed to enter in to a greater extent for countries that
were highly salient to the interests of the foreign policies of the most
important donor countries (most notably the United States). . . ." (p. 72).

Killick concurs and notes that "Countries lacking in geo-political importance are the chief sufferers" (p. 221). Contrary to functionalist
prescriptions, therefore, these writers argue that the international financial
agencies of the U.N. system are not formed to perform limited, value-
free *tasks* but to support a world economic *system* based on a specific
set of ideological norms.

In a different context, dependencia theory also emphasizes the role
of international financial institutions in the preservation of the capitalist
world economic system. In this view, the developed, capitalist states of
the Northern Hemisphere provide lending capital to financial assistance
organizations for distribution to states in need of such assistance.
According to dependencia analysts, the motives behind the provision
of such aid are rarely altruistic, however. Rather, funds for such assistance
are intended to promote the lender's exports or to facilitate the establishment of trading and marketing relations between the lender and the
borrower (Mittleman, p. 158; Faaland, et al.). While such aid often has
a substantial positive impact on the economy of the borrower, proponents
of the dependencia approach assert that the terms and pattern of such
loans only reinforce the reliance, or dependence, of the borrower on
decisions made by the lender.[49] Once such dependence is established,
the borrower is vulnerable to virtual political and economic blackmail
by the lender. According to the dependencia explanation, then, the
predominance of the developed, capitalist members in the decision-
making processes of the IMF and the IBRD serves to further the interests
of world capitalism and to increase the dependence of other members
on this system. Obviously, if true, this conclusion has some very serious,
if not threatening, implications for the Communist members of the Bank
and the Fund.

One of the primary directives contained in the *Articles of Agreement*
of the Bank and the Fund is to maintain a favorable environment for
private foreign investment (Article I; Payer, *World Bank*, p. 43). This has
been translated to mean the preservation of stable political systems with

governments hospitable to, and even eager for, foreign investment, particularly from the U.S. and Western Europe. Several critics have noted the apparent hostility of the Bank and Fund to revolution since revolutionary regimes are not perceived as an environment conducive to foreign investment (Körner, pp. 25, 61). Obviously, the revolutionary context and intent of Marxist-Leninist thought pose a direct challenge to this dominant organizational ideology (Hayter, p. 10; Williamson, p. 9). In addition, the role of the state in the economies of the Soviet Bloc contradicts the alleged free market bias of both organizations and contributes to the impression that the IMF and IBRD are inherently anti-socialist (Payer, *World Bank*, p. 20; Körner, p. 133).

Conversely, IMF and IBRD lending may serve to strengthen the position of the governing party in a socialist state. The effects of operations of a lending organization on the distribution of authority are analyzed by Anthony D. Moulton who concludes that World Bank lending encourages the centralization of governmental authority in a borrower by supporting the central government in its negotiations with other units in the political system.[50] According to the political approach, lending by international organizations also tends to strengthen class distinctions within the borrower (Mittleman, p. 150). James Mittleman claims that because international loans usually have the effect of reinforcing the government in power, these loans also reinforce the position of the dominant class. A "confluence of interest" then develops between the international economic organization and government officials[51] creating a domestic constituency for the international organization in a borrowing state (Moulton, pp. 1034, 1031; Payer, *World Bank*, p. 83).

The government of the borrower not only receives international support and approval of its policies, although the Fund denies that a decision to lend connotes approval (Gold, "Political Considerations," p. 148), but is also able to relegate the responsibility for problem-solving to the international organization which will also bear the blame for failure or "any resulting unpleasantness" that the solutions might cause (Hayter, p. 41). The emergence of a group of government officials committed to and dependent upon the maintenance of cordial relations with the lending agency, therefore, enhances the political as well as economic influence of that agency on the policy process in the borrower.

Other analysts of the Bank and Fund dispute the notion that these organizations are anti-*socialist*. They point to the socialist/communist members of the organizations and the fact that many of these countries have received loans from either the IMF, the IBRD, or both (Nowzad, p. 7; Killick, pp. 176, 179). Smith notes that in 1982, 16.5 percent of IMF credit was extended to communist countries including Romania and Yugoslavia (p. 55), and Ayres comments on the continuance of

Bank lending to the Eastern European states despite the fact that they had exceeded the previously established GNP per capita for "graduation" from IBRD lending (pp. 73–74). Smith concludes that the "IMF had neither the ability nor the will to critique the institutional arrangements" of its socialist members (p. 215).

Critics who dispute that the Bank and Fund are biased against particular regime types[52] point to foreign policy orientation as the explanation for Bank and Fund political preferences. In this view, it is a member's geopolitical value for the major members which determines its treatment in the Bank and Fund. Countries which are of strategic importance to the U.S. and Western Europe or whose foreign policy orientation has captured the attention of these powers are likely to encounter political criteria in Bank and Fund decisions regarding their loans (Ayres, p. 72; Körner, p. 26; Killick, pp. 200, 205, 221). From this perspective, regime type is irrelevant.

Adherents of the political critique approach question even the objective qualities of the technical questions, methods, and personnel employed in international organizations for financial assistance. The Fund itself admits that its actions may have political implications. Joseph Gold of the IMF comments that "Political relations may be affected even though the fundamental issue is unquestionably an economic one" (Gold, *Voting*, p. 93). Seemingly technical issues and policies often have hidden or unexpected political implications and consequences. Proponents of functionalism such as Ernst Haas, recognize that even experts often disagree and that functionally organized institutions compete for funds and increased scope (Haas, *Beyond*, p. 32). In his description of the early operations of the World Health Organization, Haas relates that "experts were sharply divided on the technical issues involved, and the respective technical positions that they embraced corresponded strikingly with the political positions espoused by their governments" (Haas, *Beyond*, p. 14).

Critics of the functional approach, however, claim that dissension among experts in the Bank and the Fund is merely squabbling over minor issues with respect to means. These critics assert that a basic consensus on ends and most means exists among experts in the IMF and IBRD. Due to the nature of their education and work experiences, many of these experts have a common economic philosophy and a bias toward methods based on this philosophy (Ohman, p. 31), and as a result, policy alternatives to capitalist methods and goals are rarely offered by the Bank and Fund to their borrowers.[53] The extent to which countries with centrally-planned economic structures can benefit from the expertise of these institutions, therefore, can only be marginal and, indeed, such expertise may even be harmful.

The decision-making structures of the Bank and Fund contribute to their politicization. Since all major decisions must be approved by the Board of Governors and the Executive Directors, who are selected according to political criteria, the potential for politicization is a constant factor in the decisions of both organizations. As Killick states, "Criticisms of 'the IMF' . . . thus sometimes appear misdirected, for they would be more appropriately addressed to the country representatives who decide and control Fund policy" (p. 132). Ayres notes that the practice of the Bank's Executive Directors of merely "ratifying" projects already approved by the staff and the Managing Director stemmed from "management's fears that control and guidance of the Bank by the executive directors would adversely politicize the institution" (p. 66). Major policy directions in both the Bank and the Fund are still subject to approval by the Board of Governors, thus subjecting the Bank and Fund to possible conflicts of national interest and domination by the most powerful members.[54]

Fund and Bank decision-making rules facilitate this domination of policy by the most powerful members, usually the First World states. In both organizations a member's votes are weighted according to its contribution to the organization and in both the IMF and IBRD, the countries of Western Europe and the United States possess virtual veto power over decisions. This arrangement can be viewed as merely reflecting reality in the international economy (Nowzad, p. 3; David, p. 18), or as the perpetuation of the distribution of power which existed at the inception of the Bank and Fund and not necessarily a reflection of contemporary reality (Körner, p. 45).

Bank and Fund officials, according to Baldwin, attempt to disguise the presence of political inputs behind the rhetoric of "sound banking standards" (Baldwin, p. 69), but when pressed the Bank will admit that political criteria do creep into lending decisions and lead to non-uniform treatment of members (Baldwin, p. 75; IMF, *Annual Report 1976*, p. 146; Ayres, p. 72; Killick, p. 153). The Bank endeavors to justify this apparent violation of the *Articles of Agreement* by implying in its publications "that the Articles prohibit only the pursuit of political objectives and not the weighing of political factors" in decisions to lend (Baldwin, p. 75). Critics of the Bank and Fund contend that these "political factors" often have far more influence on loan decisions than either organization would admit. Hayter declares that the Bank will not discuss lending unless and until it is satisfied with the potential borrower's general economic policies (Hayter, p. 68). Political factors may include such elements as the borrower's government, economic and social policies, and treatment of private foreign investment. According to Hayter, the Bank will refuse to lend if it considers the borrower's political characteristics to be undesirable or unacceptable (Hayter, p. 15). Operations of the Fund are vulnerable to these same sorts of criticisms.

The works by several adherents of the political critique indicate that political variables may enter the lending policies of international organizations in a more straightforward manner than is described above. David Baldwin writes that "In carrying out their duties Bank officials cannot ignore political considerations, despite a formal ban on their doing so."[55] This is because "In a world where governments can expropriate property, manipulate exchange rates, and control the currency supply, it is nonsense to speak of evaluating the economic soundness of a project without reference to government behavior" (Baldwin, p. 40). Political factors, thus, are inevitably included as criteria in the decision to lend.

The influence of political variables described above takes the form of political inputs into the decisions to lend of an international economic organization. Another political element of international lending appears in the political critique. Critics claim that international economic institutions, specifically the Bank and the Fund, actively intervene or participate in the formation of economic and social policy *in the borrower*.[56] The Fund itself states that it requires "the assurance of an opportunity to influence the member in its choice of monetary policies" (Gold, p. 474). The World Bank also declares its desires "to come to some sort of agreement on present and future policies with the countries in which it is likely to finance projects, and to have a continuing discussion of and interest in these policies" (Hayter, p. 68).

This sort of active participation in the policy process of a borrower is contrary to both functionalist prescription and the constitutions of most international economic organizations. Yet the *Articles of Agreement* of the International Monetary Fund tacitly permit such practices by providing for the application of conditionality on loans above a certain level and of a certain type (Payer, p. 35). Conditionality is defined by the Fund as "policies the Fund expects a member to follow in order to be able to use the Fund's resources" (Gold, *Conditionality*, p. 5). Although the borrower is free to choose its economic program, the Fund is often "influential in convincing the member [which] choice should be made" (Gold, *Stand-by*, p. 48; Crockett, p. 10; Williamson, p. 25). Fund influence can also extend beyond program formulation to the implementation and supervision of that program.[57]

The World Bank also acknowledges that it is standard Bank policy to require borrowers to pursue stabilizing economic policies (IBRD, *Policies*, p. 45). An analyst of the Bank's policy, L.K. Jha, declares that the practice of requiring policy reform as a condition of lending is a well-established principle within the Bank (Jha, p. 98; Hayter, p. 70).

Baldwin claims that the provision of loans is secondary in the Bank's priorities to "influencing the behavior of governments" (Baldwin, p. 78) in both their political and economic behavior (Baldwin, p. 76; IBRD, *Policies*, p. 46). As the political critique notes, however, attempts by international lending agencies to induce policy reforms in borrowers are usually well-disguised behind economic terms such as "creditworthiness" (IMF, *Annual Report 1952*, p. 42; Gold, *Stand-by*, p. 30). The *definition* of "stabilizing" economic policies with respect to centrally-planned economies becomes an intriguing and critical question here.

Critics also dispute the impartiality of Bank and Fund methods of analysis. Scholars note the "rigid" application of monetary theory to the balance of payments problems of IMF members and sharply criticize the application of a "standard package" as part of the Fund's stabilization and conditionality requirements regardless of the nature, size, and origin of the member's problem.[58] Performance criteria in the Fund and the use of cost-benefit analysis in the Bank are faulted for their selective and arbitrary application (Körner, p. 61; Payer, *World Bank*, p. 80; Dell, p. 598). Williamson questions the use of performance criteria, noting that the "*outcome* of a program is not a measure of *compliance*," and concluding that members may be penalized for violating an agreement with which they had made every effort to comply (pp. 37–39). In this case, politicization occurs in the definition and application of "standard economic procedures."

Evaluation criteria and conditionality have been the focus for much of the controversy surrounding the Bank and the Fund in the last two decades and are often cited in explanation of members' reluctance to approach the Bank and Fund.[59] Some critics have gone so far as to credit Fund conditionality as the cause of political unrest in a country which has been "forced" to implement IMF austerity as the price of balance of payments assistance.[60] In the Fund's defense, however, these same critics often note that causality in these cases is extremely difficult to assess and that the Fund's willingness to act as a "scapegoat" often masks the initiating role of the member governments in these policies and programs.[61]

The Boundaries of Assistance

In summary, two basic approaches to analyzing the role of international organizations for economic assistance can be identified. The technocratic approach takes as its basic assumption that technical, economic functions can be purged of their political overtones and implications. This makes it possible to create international organizations which are able to lend strictly according to technical criteria based on economic performance.

In this view, the impact of agency operations is targeted at the performance of borrower's economy only. The political critique argues that political inputs can never be excluded from the lending process. Thus, it follows from that assumption that international organizations are created to meet a specific *political* and economic need; these organizations embody a specific philosophical bias. Loans made by international financial organizations, therefore, are subject to influence by numerous political inputs and have serious consequences for both the economic and the political systems of borrowers.

While both the technocratic and political approaches to international economic assistance describe a part of the lending process in international financial institutions, neither is accurate in describing the whole. There are both economic and political components in every decision to lend; the prevalence of one set of components over another varies, however. As the technocratic approach suggests, a broad area of the lending process in international economic organizations exists in which objective economic criteria predominate and in which political criteria have minimal and infrequent influence. In this technocratic arena of Bank and Fund lending policy, decisions to lend are governed by procedures which rely solely on economic or technical criteria. The borrower's past economic performance is the major determinant of the size and frequency of Bank and Fund loans to that country. Economic criteria set the limits on lending in the technocratic arena of Bank and Fund lending, and the majority of Bank and Fund loans can be placed in the technocratic arena. In this arena of lending, therefore, the lending process closely approximates the functionalist description.

There is a boundary to this technocratic arena, however, beyond which political inputs or criteria dominate and explain the decisions and behavior of the lending agency. Borrowers located in the political arena of lending are characterized by levels of assistance which are significantly higher or lower than those of borrowers with similar economic conditions and performance. This abnormal amount of assistance is explained by the unusual political characteristics of the borrower. Loans to a borrower in the political arena of lender policy-making are made with reference to the borrower's political characteristics, *not* its economic performance. Political characteristics, then, set the boundary between the technocratic and political arenas of lending. The nature of the relevant political characteristics which determine where the boundary lies is defined by the principles embodied in the lender's charter, its operating philosophy, and the biases inherent in its organizational structure.

This boundary concept of international economic assistance is depicted in Table 1.1. Loans to borrowers in the technocratic arena dominate

TABLE 1.1: The Arenas of Lending

TECHNOCRATIC ARENA	POLITICAL ARENA
economic performance criteria	political characteristics criteria
$X loans to borrower #1	$Y loans to borrower #A
borrower #2	borrower #B
.	.
.	.
.	.
borrower N	borrower N

lending policies of international organizations for economic assistance. The process in this arena is characterized by economic performance criteria and is accurately described by the technocratic approach. In the political arena, however, loans are made according to political criteria (for example, regime type) and this process is accurately described by the political critique.

A borrower's political characteristics determine the arena in which it is located at a given point in time. It follows from this last statement that a borrower may be located in different arenas at different points in time due to a shift in the boundary itself or as a result of a change in the borrower's political characteristics. If the political critique is correct, the level of assistance to borrowers in the political arena is characteristically well-above or well-below the average level of assistance to borrowers in the technocratic arena. In this way policy-making in the political arena differs sharply from the technical process in the technocratic arena as it is explicitly described in the publications of the international lending agencies.

In the boundary formulation of international lending, the lender continues to control the policy-making process. The lender assembles the relevant economic and political criteria and decides which criteria are critical to the decision to lend. The lender's initial decision may be influenced by existing political and economic characteristics of the borrower, but the borrower has no control over the manner in which these characteristics are employed in a decision to lend. The lender may even try to extend its influence by attempting to alter specific policies formulated by the borrower. The opportunity for the borrower to influence the lender occurs when standards are set and specific procedures are formulated in the lender. In general, therefore, it is the lender which attempts to influence the behavior of the borrower, although on a few occasions and in a limited way, the lender's behavior can itself be altered.

Several questions emerge out of this boundary conception of international assistance. The location and content of the boundary must first be established. Do borrowing states with certain political and economic characteristics tend to receive larger loans on better terms than states which do not possess those characteristics? Relevant political and economic criteria must be identified, indicators devised, and a profile of the standard lending pattern of international economic organizations described before this question can be answered. Once the boundary is identified, it is necessary to examine the manner in which inputs in the political arena impact upon the lending policies of international organizations for economic assistance to Communist countries.

Political factors do not enter lending policies of international organizations in the same way, nor do different political criteria have equal impact on these decisions. Which factors seem to have the most influence on lending policy? Do some political inputs appear more frequently in decisions to lend than others? At what point do political inputs enter the lending process? For example, Bank lending policies may include political inputs as criteria in a general assessment of the borrower's capacity to repay the debt or as criteria in the determination of conditions to be met by the borrower in return for a loan. Attempts to move the boundary also must be investigated. What influences a lender to revise its evaluation of inputs in the political arena and thus, to shift the location of the boundary?

The next chapter establishes the framework for examining the political arena in the policy process of two international organizations for economic assistance, the IMF and the IBRD. The relevant variables and relationships are identified as the basis for subsequent analysis. In the following chapter, the performance of the Soviet Bloc states in the IMF and IBRD is surveyed for evidence of unusual levels of assistance using aggregate data obtained from IMF and IBRD sources. The remaining chapters examine the specific cases of Soviet Bloc membership for detailed descriptions of Bank and Fund lending patterns in order to detect any Bank and Fund influence on domestic policy choices. The experiences of the Soviet Bloc in the IMF and IBRD and the implications of those experiences are then summarized in the concluding chapter.

Notes

1. R. B. Sutcliffe attributes much greater influence to financial assistance. He quotes an AID official who claims that foreign aid is often used to support

friendly governments by alleviating economic stresses on the recipient. See Teresa Hayter, *Aid as Imperialism*, (Baltimore: Penguin Books Ltd., 1971), Preface.

2. Gene M. Lyons, David A. Baldwin, and Donald W. McNemar, "The 'Politicization' Issue in the U.N. Specialized Agencies," *Proceedings of the Academy of Political Science*, vol. 34, no. 4, p. 81.

3. David A. Baldwin, "The International Bank in Political Perspective," *World Politics*, vol. 18 (October 1965), p. 77.

4. Joseph Gold, "Political Considerations Are Prohibited by Articles of Agreement When the Fund Considers Requests for Use of Resources," *IMF Survey*, 1983, p. 146.

5. John Williamson, *The Lending Policies of the International Monetary Fund*, Policy Analysis in International Economics (Washington, D.C.: Institute for International Economics, 1982), p. 9.

6. Robert Solomon, "The Politics of IMF Lending: A Comment," *Cato Journal*, vol. 4, no. 1(Spring/Summer 1984), p. 246; Tony Killick, ed., *The Quest for Economic Stabilization* (New York: St. Martin's Press, 1984), p. 63.

7. Stephen D. Krasner, "The International Monetary Fund and the Third World," *International Organization*, vol. 12, no. 3, p. 687; Charles Lipson, "The International Organization of Third World Debt," *International Organization*, vol. 35, no. 4, pp. 618, 624; Williamson, p. 15.

8. Fred L. Smith, "The Politics of IMF Lending," *Cato Journal*, vol. 4, no. 1 (Spring/Summer 1984), p. 217.

9. Hayter, *Aid as Imperialism*, p. 25.

10. John P. Lewis and Ishan Kapur, "The World Bank Group, Multilateral Aid, and the 1970s," in John P. Lewis and Ishan Kapur (eds.), *The World Bank Group, Multilateral Aid, and the 1970s* (Lexington, MA: Lexington Books, 1973), p. 1.

11. Carl I. Ohman, "Comment: A Social Radicalism," in J.P. Lewis and I. Kapur (eds.), *The World Bank Group, Multilateral Aid, and the 1970s* (Lexington, MA: Lexington Books, 1973), p. 29; Ronald T. Libby, "External Co-optation of a Less-Developed Country's Policy Making: The Case of Ghana, 1969–72," *World Politics*, vol. 29, No. 1 (October 1976), p. 88; Cheryl Payer, *The World Bank: A Critical Analysis* (New York: Monthly Review Press, 1982), pp. 15–18.

12. Joseph Gold, *The Stand-by Arrangements of the International Monetary Fund* (Washington, D.C.: IMF, 1970); Peter Körner, Gero Mass, Thomas Siebold, and Rainer Tetzlaff, *The IMF and the Debt Crisis*, translated by Paul Knight (London: Zed Books, Ltd., 1986), p. 25; Williamson, p. 19; Smith, p. 217.

13. Manuel Guitián, "Fund Conditionality and the Adjustment Process: A Look into the 1980s," *Finance and Development*, vol. 18, no. 2, p. 17; Lipson, pp. 618–619.

14. Lipson, pp. 606, 629, 630; Guitián, "A Look into the 1980s," p. 17.

15. Lyons, et al., p. 83.

16. Ernst B. Haas, *Beyond the Nation-State: Functionalism and International Organization* (Stanford, CA: Stanford University Press, 1964), pp. 47, 6.

17. Haas, *Beyond the Nation-State*, pp. 47, 6.

18. David A. Kay, "On the Reform of International Institutions: A Comment," *International Organization*, vol. 30, no. 3 (Summer 1976), p. 533.

19. Haas, *Beyond the Nation-State*, p. 11.

20. Lyons, et al., p. 89.

21. Leon Lindberg and Stuart Scheingold, *Europe's Would-Be Polity: Patterns of Change in the European Community* (Englewood Cliffs, NJ: Prentice-Hall, Inc., 1970), Chapter 4, "Alternative Models of System Change," pp. 101–140.

22. C. Fred Bergsten, "Interdependence and the Reform of International Institutions," *International Organization*, vol. 30, no. 2 (Spring 1976), p. 361.

23. Haas claims that if such contact is not maintained with member governments, expert advice is likely to be ignored (*Beyond the Nation-State*, p. 49). He warns, however, that "Government designated experts are unlikely to act much differently from their governments if the focus of action and representation is universal" (*Beyond the Nation-State*, p. 49).

24. J. Keith Horsefield and Margaret G. deVries, *The International Monetary Fund, 1945–1965* (Washington, D.C.: IMF, 1969), vol. 1, Chapters 1 and 2.

25. See IBRD, *Articles of Agreement* (Washington, D.C.: U.S. Treasury, 1944) and Edward S. Mason and Robert E. Asher, *The World Bank Since Bretton Woods*, (Washington, D.C.: The Brookings Institutions, 1973) for details.

26. Joseph Gold, *Membership and Nonmembership in the International Monetary Fund* (Washington, D.C.: IMF, 1974), p. 469.

27. Solomon, p. 244; Killick, p. 129; Sidney Dell, "Stabilization: The Political Economy of Overkill," *World Development*, vol. 10, no. 8 (1982), pp. 597–612.

28. Joseph Gold, *Voting and Decisions in the International Monetary Fund* (Washington, D.C.: IMF, 1972).

29. Joseph Gold, *Financial Assistance by the International Monetary Fund: Law and Practice*, Pamphlet Series no. 27, second edition (Washington, D.C.: IMF 1980), p. 12; Bahram Nowzad, *The IMF and Its Critics* (Princeton: Princeton University Press, 1981).

30. Manuel Guitián, "Fund Conditionality and the International Adjustment Process: The Early Period, 1950–70," *Finance and Development*, vol. 17, no. 4 (1980), pp. 23–27; Gold, "Political Considerations," p. 147.

31. Gold, *Financial Assistance*, p. 13.

32. See Manual Guitián, "Fund Conditionality and the International Adjustment Process: The Changing Environment of the 1970s," *Finance and Development* vol. 18, no. 1 (1981); Guitián, "Fund Conditionality: 1950–70," p. 25; Killick, p. 150; Korner, p. 57.

33. Lipson, p. 625; Killick, pp. 185–186.

34. This description applies to the process for obtaining a Standby Agreement only. For more details, see Edward Brau, "The Consultative Process of the Fund," *Finance and Development* vol. 18, no. 4 (1981), pp. 13–16; Killick, p. 138; Korner, p. 15.

35. Andrew Crockett, "Issues in the Use of Fund Resources," *Finance and Development*, vol. 18, no. 2 (1982), p.14; Killick, p. 140; Korner, p. 47.

36. IBRD, *Articles of Agreement*, Article I, p. 1.

37. IBRD, *The World Bank:Policies and Operations* (Washington, D.C.: IBRD, 1960).

38. This discussion of Bank lending policies is taken from IBRD, *Policies and Operations*, and Hayter, pp. 48, 67.

39. Payer, *World Bank,* p. 41; Robert Ayres, *Banking on the Poor:The World Bank and World Poverty* (Cambridge, MA: The MIT Press, 1985), p. 57.

40. This description of the Bank's project cycle is taken from IBRD, *Policies and Operations,* and Payer, *World Bank,* Chapter 3.

41. IBRD, *Policies and Operations,* p. 8; Korner, p. 51.

42. IMF, *Annual Report of the Executive Board* (Washington, D.C.: IMF, 1950), p. 82; IMF, *Annual Report, 1970,* p. 146; IMF, *Technical Assistance Services of the International Monetary Fund,* Pamphlet Series no. 30 (Washington, D.C.: IMF, 1979), p. 6.

43. Wilfred L. David, *The IMF Policy Paradigm:The Macroeconomics of Stabilization, Structural Adjustment, and Economic Development* (New York: Praeger Publishers, 1985), pp. 27–28.

44. Guitián, "Fund Conditionality:1980s," p. 16.

45. Hayter, p. 85; Carl I. Ohman, "Comment: A Social Radicalism," p. 30.

46. Theodore H. Cohn, "Politics in the World Bank Group: The Question of Loans to the Asian Giants," *International Organization,* vol. 28, no. 3 (Summer 1974), pp. 533–534; Hayter, pp. 19–20; Smith, p. 219; Graham Bird and Timothy Orme, "An Analysis of Drawings on the International Monetary Fund by Developing Countries," *World Development* vol. 9, no. 6 (1981), p. 566.

47. Daniel A. Holly, "L'O.N.U., le système économique international et la politique internationale," *International Organization,* vol. 29, no. 2 (Spring 1975), pp. 470, 474, 476–478; Hayter, p. 9; James H. Mittleman, "International Monetary Institutions and Policies of Socialism and Self-Reliance: Are They Compatible?" *Social Research,* vol. 47, no. 1 (Spring 1980), p. 163; Ayres, p. 11; David, p. 5.

48. David, p. 9; Dell, p. 605; Killick, p. 173; Körner, pp. 43, 129.

49. Anibal Pinto and Jan Knâkal, "The Centre-Periphery System Twenty Years later," *Social and Economic Studies,* vol. 22, no. 1 (March 1973), p. 81; Norman Girvan, "The Development of Dependency Economics in the Caribbean and Latin America: Review and Comparison," *Social and Economic Studies,* vol. 22, no. 1 (March 1973), p. 18; Mittleman, p. 152; Lawrence B. Krause and Joseph S. Nye, "Reflections on the Economics and Politics of International Economic Organizations," *International Organization,* vol. 29, no. 1 (Winter 1975), p. 337.

50. Anthony D. Moulton, "On Concealed Dimensions of Third World Involvement in International Economic Organizations," *International Organization,* vol. 32, no. 4 (Autumn 1978), pp. 1028–1031, 1020; Ira Sharkansky and Dennis L. Dresang, "International Assistance: Its Variety, Coordination and Impact Among Public Corporations in Kenya and the East African Community," *International Organization,* vol. 28, no. 2 (Spring 1978), p. 213; Bergsten, p. 363; Hayter, pp. 54, 77; Killick, p. 198; Körner, p. 139; Smith, p. 236.

51. Mittleman, p. 160; Moulton, p. 1020; Joseph Gold, *Membership and Nonmembership in the International Monetary Fund* (Washington, D.C.: IMF, 1974), p. 163; Hayter, p. 9.

52. For thorough treatment of this issue with respect to Latin America, see Karen Remmer, "The Politics of Economic Stabilization:IMF Standby Programs in Latin America, 1954–1984," *Comparative Politics* 19(1):1–24, 1986.

53. Hayter, p. 73; John P. Lewis and Ishan Kapur, "The World Bank Group, Multilateral Aid, and the 1970s," in J.P. Lewis and I. Kapur (eds.), *The World Bank Group, Multilateral Aid, and the 1970s* (Lexington, MA: Lexington Books, 1973), p. 2; L.K. Jha, "Comment: Leaning Against Open Doors?" in *The World Bank Group, Multilateral Aid, and the 1970s*, p. 98.

54. Krasner, pp. 670–671.

55. Baldwin, p. 68.

56. Holly, p. 479; Hayter, p. 77; Mittleman, pp. 153–154; Smith, p. 221; David, pp. 11, 119; Lipson, p. 618; Krasner, p. 679.

57. IMF, *Technical Assistance Services of the International Monetary Fund*, Pamphlet Series no. 30 (Washington, D.C.: IMF, 1979), p. 2; Sharkansky and Dresang, p. 212. For a discussion of Bank influence in project implementation and supervision, see Hayter, *Aid As Imperialism*, p. 50.

58. For extensive critiques of the IMF's formulation of stabilization and austerity programs, see Nowzad, *The IMF and Its Critics*; Smith, "The Politics of IMF Lending"; Solomon, "The Politics of IMF Lending"; Williamson, *Lending Policies of the IMF*; Körner, *The IMF and the Debt Crisis*; Bird and Orme, "Analysis of Drawings"; Dell, "Stabilization"; David, "The IMF Policy Paradigm."

59. David, p. 119; Körner, p. 54; Ayres, p. 69.

60. For discussions of the consequences of IMF conditionality for political stability in borrowers, see Remmer, "The Politics of Economic Stabilization"; Mittleman, "International Monetary Institutions"; Payer, *The World Bank and The Debt Trap* (New York: Monthly Review Press, 1972); Libby, "The External Co-optation."

61. Nowzad, p. 20; Smith, p. 230; Killick, p. 4; Dell, p. 608.

2

The Soviet Bloc and
the Arenas of Lending

This study analyzes the role of political variables in the decisions to lend to Communist members of the IMF and the IBRD. The arena of lending in which political variables dominate decisions to lend is the focus of this analysis. As described in the previous chapter, a boundary exists between the technocratic arena and the political arena in policy-making in international assistance agencies. In the technocratic arena of lending, "objective" economic criteria such as GNP govern decisions to lend; conversely, political criteria such as regime type or foreign policy dominate the decisions in the political arena. The boundary is set by the lending agency and is composed of political characteristics which the lender perceives as desirable. These "desirable" political characteristics are described or reflected in the organization's charter, its structure, and its procedures; these characteristics may not be readily apparent at first inspection, however.

Both the lending organization and the borrower desire the technocratic arena to be as large as possible, with little weight assigned to political inputs, without reducing the amount of aid extended. The lender desires to adhere to its organizational imperative to ignore political criteria, and the recipient does not want to be discriminated against based on factors which it either cannot or will not alter. As a result, the location of a borrower in the political arena is not permanent as both lender and borrower strive to return to the technocractic arena. This may occur due to shifts in the borrower's political characteristics and behavior as well as shifts in the lender's emphasis on specific political criteria (i.e., shifts in the location of the boundary).

The Political Arena

As described above and in the preceding chapter, in the technocratic arena of lending a borrower's economic characteristics determine the size and frequency of its loans from the lender. The first indication that a lender has assigned a borrower to the political arena, therefore, occurs when either the size or frequency of the recipient's loans noticeably diverge from what can be expected from its economic characteristics. If this is the case, the political arena might better explain the behavior of the lender with respect to the particular borrower. Often, the borrower may not want to alter its arena assignment due to the unusually favorable treatment of the lender. The characteristics of the political arena in any given case will affect the borrower's decisions regarding its future relationship with the lender.

There are three distinct inputs into a lender's funding decisions in developing states; ascriptive, leverage and reverse influence. Ascriptive factors are derived from the domestic economic and political charac-teristics of the borrower. These factors determine to which arena the borrower is assigned by the lender. Leverage consists of actions by the lender to alter policies of a borrower in the political arena so that the political and economic characteristics of the borrower more closely approximate the lender's desired attributes as represented by the bound-ary. Leverage reflects the effort by the lender to move the borrower from the political arena to the technocratic arena. The final set of political inputs, reverse influence, appear in efforts by the lender or borrower to relocate or redefine the boundary.

Ascriptive Factors

Ascriptive inputs are the domestic economic and political attributes of the borrower. These attributes can be considered as given, although they may change slowly in response to consistent pressure from the lender. The lender considers these inputs in formulating a decision to lend prior to any action taken by the borrower. Ascriptive criteria have influence on the lender's decisions, but the form and extent of this influence is controlled by the lender *not* the borrower. Since these inputs are attributes of the borrower and not easily altered, the borrower has no control over how and when ascriptive criteria are used by the lender. This type of factor tends to have the greatest effect on the lender's decisions to extend credit to a specific borrower because these inputs are the least resistant to change. One economic criterion, economic performance, and three political criteria, regime type, type of economic structure and the international alignment of the borrower's foreign policy, are four ascriptive inputs which may be included in arena assignment and a decision to lend.

Of the ascriptive inputs into both areas, economic performance assumes less prominence in lender decisions in the political arena. Economic performance as a criterion in decisions to lend is heavily stressed by both organizations and the technocratic analysts. In consonance with functional analysis, the *Articles of Agreement* of the IMF and the IBRD regard economic performance as the sole criterion in lending decisions. In theory, therefore, the borrower's successful economic performance in the past on several variables (such as GNP and control of the money supply) has substantial impact on the lender's consideration of an application for credit (see IMF and IBRD, *Articles of Agreement*, IBRD *General Conditions on Borrowing*). Since the Bank and Fund claim to apply these economic standards to prospective borrowers in an objective manner, the extension of an unusual level of assistance to a borrower whose economic performance is similar to states which do not receive comparable levels of assistance should be an indication of the presence of non-technocratic criteria in lending decisions.

Regime type appears frequently in analyses performed by the critics of international financial institutions. Typically, "rightist" authoritarian regimes are alleged to receive the most favorable treatment in the IMF and the IBRD.[1] These regimes are usually financially conservative and supporters of capitalist solutions to economic problems, two key elements in the organizational philosophy of both the Bank and the Fund (see discussions, Chapter 1). Both Hayter and Payer provide several examples of the negative effects of populist and "leftist" regimes in the Bank and Fund decisions to lend (Hayter, p. 31).

The third ascriptive variable which has indirect influence on the lending decisions of the Bank and the Fund is the international alignment of the borrower's foreign policy. In essence, this variable attempts to capture the effect on lending of a state's position with respect to the East–West conflict. Functionalists such as Haas and Bergsten recognize that the present system of international organizations is a reflection of the international distribution of power from 1944 to the present.[2] The IMF and the IBRD were designed primarily by Western powers and are still dominated by that group of states today. The weighted voting procedure used in both the Fund and the Bank is an example of how the structure of international relationships is translated into procedures in international organizations. Consequently, it can be expected that states which align themselves with the East in East-West conflict will receive fewer and smaller loans from the Bank and the Fund (Payer, p. 43).

Another influence on Bank and Fund decisions may be the borrower's type of economic system. This is a reasonable expectation given the capitalist bias of both organizations. Several scholars note the prevalence of "profit-and-loss thinking"[3] and modern Western economic methods in the Bank's and the Fund's efforts to promote development and to liberalize trade and payments.[4] It follows, therefore, that if economic system is important to the decisions of the Bank and the Fund, member states with centrally planned economies will receive fewer and smaller loans than states with market economies.[5]

The four ascriptive factors—economic performance, regime type, type of economic system, and international alignment—do not necessarily exert the same influence on a lender's decisions. Given the nature of Bank and Fund operations it is reasonable to expect that a compatible economic system will have more weight in lending decisions than either a borrower's regime type or its international alignment position. A borrower's ability to repay its debts, attitude toward private foreign investment, and the use of accepted market solutions to economic problems are more directly related to the purposes and operations of the Fund and the Bank than the structure of a borrower's legislature or party system. This formulation is also consistent with functionalist analysis. The weight of ascriptive inputs may vary with each borrower, however, depending on the combination of the four ascriptive inputs that is present in that state. To the Bank and the Fund a desirable regime and international alignment position may combine to outweigh the presence of an undesirable economic performance or economic system in a borrower.

Leverage

Leverage occurs in the responses of lenders to specific policy behaviors or expected behaviors by the borrower. This is an attempt by the lender to influence the behavior of the borrower by releasing or withholding funds (or threatening to do so). Action of this type by a lender is basically an effort to move the borrower closer to the technocratic arena by altering policies which may have an impact on the borrower's ascriptive characteristics.

According to some analysts, the IMF and the IBRD deliberately seek leverage over the policy behavior of LDC borrowers (Hayter; Mittleman; Payer, Libby; Cohn; Moulton; Baldwin). Leverage is most frequently cited in the literature as an example of the political aspects of Bank and Fund operations (Hayter, p. 61; Cohn, p. 561). In Mittleman's analysis, program aid leverage is not only limited to policies regarding a specific project but also "can give the lender control over the borrower's entire economy" (Mittleman, p. 152). The lender's goal is eventually to bring the borrower's ascriptive characteristics within an acceptable range as perceived by the lender.

Leverage takes four distinct forms. Funds can be used to punish, reward, induce, or reinforce specific acts or policies undertaken by the borrower (Hayter, p. 18, esp. #3). Punishment is the withholding of funds due to the failure of the borrower to meet certain standards or perform certain behaviors. The refusal to lend may also be a response to the undesirable behavior of the borrower. Leverage is usually conceived of with reference to attempts by an international organization to punish a borrower. The concept of conditionality in the Fund is an example of a member's failure to observe or meet specific economic standards. As defined above, conditionality exists when a loan is made contingent upon the institution of specific policies or satisfactory performance as measured by "objective" indicators (these are performance criteria).[6] At the conclusion of loan negotiations a borrower sends the Fund a Letter of Intent in which it declares its "objectives and policies" and agrees not to request a loan if it does not meet the performance criteria.[7] Failure to meet similar performance conditions in the Bank has similar consequences, the refusal of the organization to lend or continue to lend.

The use of Bank and Fund loans to reward borrower behavior is more difficult to identify than the use of such funds as punishment. A reward is extended for a policy or action that the lender *requested* of the borrower. This is a sensitive issue for both lender and borrower. The refusal of an international organization to lend ordinarily must be justified to the borrower and often to the entire membership of the organization. Justification of an agreement to lend is not as frequently demanded and is easier to couch in acceptable economic terms.

The denial of funds, or a sharp increase in loans, may also indicate a desire by the lending agency to *induce* a borrower, or potential borrower, to consider a different policy or action. This strategy is distinguished from a punishment or reward strategy by the fact that it is NOT a response to an action of the member's; it is an attempt by the lender to induce a certain action by the borrower. This is a risky strategy for the lender to pursue because there is no guarantee to the lender that the borrower will respond to such an inducement.

Empirically, the fourth form of leverage in international lending, reinforcement, is difficult to distinguish operationally from rewards. Both are given in return for desirable behavior. The use of loans as reinforcement differs from rewards in that it is a response by the lender to behavior *initiated by the borrower*. Often the actions being reinforced are not anticipated by the lender but are nonetheless favorably received by the lender. Thus, the lender wishes such behavior to continue and extends credit to indicate its approval. The key to differentiating a loan for reinforcement purposes and one for reward is in identifying which actor initiated the action to which the loan is a response. A reward is a loan extended in return for the borrower's adoption of the lender's policy suggestion; a reinforcement loan is a response by the lender to an action initiated by the borrower.

Loans may be employed to reinforce a regime or to reinforce a particular set of policies or reforms. The Fund's Stand-by Arrangement (or loan) and program aid in the World Bank are the primary instruments of organizations for economic assistance in supporting or preserving a government favorable to the organization (Payer, p. 31; Hayter, p. 5). In the effort to reinforce a regime, however, the Bank or Fund may "create internal political difficulties for the government concerned" (Hayter, p. 80) by supporting a faction which is advocating "politically dangerous" measures (Libby, p. 70). In at least one case, Ghana, Libby alleges that this sort of reinforcement caused the ouster of a regime cordial to the Fund by the military (Libby, p. 67). In this view, the Bank and Fund will extend credit or increase existing credits to a borrower who has initiated policies which the lender believes will bring the borrower's ascriptive characteristics closer to those specified in the boundary.

The other ascriptive factors in the Bank and the Fund lending policy also affect the use of leverage in such policy. Regime type, economic structure, and international alignment supply the basis on which the lender decides to punish, reward or reinforce. The failure to meet performance criteria, the employment of non-market techniques such as nationalization of foreign-owned industry, and/or active support of the Soviet bloc in the East-West conflict will evoke a lender's decisions to punish the offending borrower by withholding funds or refusing to lend at all. The lender will reward fulfillment of performance criteria and/or the acceptance of one of its proposals by the borrower (where this can be documented) with a continuing and perhaps increased flow of credit. A borrower's decision to implement market reforms, to support the United States in the East-West conflict, and the ouster of a populist-oriented or communist regime will elicit from the lender a larger flow of credit or provoke a decision to lend where loans had not been previously extended.

Reverse Influence

Political factors also have reverse impact on decisions of international financial organizations. Organizational response and adaptation of the lender to the political and economic demands and characteristics of the borrower are considered to be examples of reverse impact. Political inputs have an effect on the lender when the lending organization responds to changes in its environment (i.e., demands from members) through alterations in its operational philosophy, organization or procedures. This adaptation occurs because of the lending organization's desire to survive and to maintain its effectiveness. Many scholars have noted the appearance of a reciprocal relationship between the Bank, the Fund and their developing members.[8] This study examines whether the relationship of these organizations and the developing states is a reciprocal one in actuality or only in appearance. The ways in which Communist states influence Bank and Fund structures and procedures is also investigated.

Reverse influence inputs affect the efforts of lenders and borrowers to alter the content or location of the technocratic-political boundary. Both lenders and borrowers desire the technocratic arena of lending to be as broad as possible. Since the lender is prohibited in its charter from the consideration of political inputs, it endeavors to reduce the number of cases in which political inputs appear. The borrower's motives are more complex. Borrowers wish to expand the technocratic arena for two reasons. In one sense, borrowers and lenders agree that lending decisions should be limited to the consideration of only economic criteria. Yet borrowers also want their special circumstances to be included in decisions to lend. Borrowers, therefore, attempt to exclude political inputs such as regime type and international alignment from lending decisions while they simultaneously work to retain economic structure as an input. The final decision on any alteration of the boundary ultimately belongs to the lending organization, but borrowers' demands can have a significant impact on that decision.

Organization theory analyzes the attempts of organizations (usually commercial firms) to control their environments. According to this theory a relationship exists between the stability and complexity of the environment and the centralization of an organization's authority structure. Every organization endeavors to stabilize its environment, and thus, reduce the uncertainty with which it must deal. To accomplish this goal, an organization must be able to adapt to changes in its environment when they occur. As the environment becomes more uncertain or complex, the organization's structure evolves into a more decentralized, or horizontal, pattern of authority and decision-making. The environment of the World Bank and the IMF consists of the international economy. In this study the definition of the Bank and Fund environment is narrowed to include only the economic problems and conditions in Communist states and the relationship of Communist states with the Bank and the Fund.

The need for more flexibility in Bank and Fund operations is often cited by analysts.[9] This concern for responsiveness reflects the increased complexity and uncertainty in the environment of both the Bank and the Fund since the late 1950s. Since that time, the majority of members and borrowers from the two institutions have been states whose economic problems and conditions differ markedly from those of the developed states in the Northern Hemisphere.

The expansion of membership in the Bank and the Fund includes not only Third World states but communist members as well. These states have problems and characteristics different from both the developed states and the developing states. Growth in the size and composition of the Bank and Fund membership is explained by functional analysis as the gradual extension of the functional activities of both organizations to other economic problems and systems in the world economy. The inclusion of "newcomers" is encouraged and even vital to the survival and success of the organizations under study (Bergsten, p. 362; Lewis and Kapur, p. 10).

Changes in individual procedures represent an effort by the lender to satisfy some special condition in a particular borrower. It is at this point in the organization's structure that ascriptive and behavioral political inputs have the largest impact. If this is the case, lending procedures will vary to accommodate special circumstances or characteristics in a borrower's regime, economic system or international alignment position. The manner and scope of this variance is also dependent upon the concomitant philosophy and structure of the organization.

Arena Placement of the Soviet Bloc

The political critique of the IMF and IBRD posits that political factors play an important role in the lending policies of the IMF and IBRD, often masking a member's underlying characteristics. If this is true and if the Bank and the Fund have a strong preference for market-oriented economic policies and structures, as the political critique asserts, then it is reasonable to expect that lending to the Soviet Bloc, with its emphasis on central planning or a mix of market and plan, will reflect that preference.

As noted above, the presence of political factors in Bank and Fund lending can be traced, at least initially, by examining the aggregate lending to members of a particular class, such as the Soviet Bloc. If the Bank and Fund are *not* lending according to technocratic, or strictly economic criteria, one would expect to see noticeably higher or lower loan receipts to members which can be distinguished by their deviance in either direction from the standard economic characteristics of Bank and Fund members in general. The following analysis examines the loan receipts of the Eastern European Soviet Bloc members of the Fund and the Bank in order to determine into what arena, technocratic or political, they can be classified. If the Soviet Bloc members receive significantly higher or lower loan receipts from these organizations, then one can conclude that factors other than purely economic variables are operating in Bank and Fund decisions to lend to these countries, and more thorough case study analysis must be conducted.

The aggregated data used in this section are those generated and employed by the Bank and the Fund. Data are obtained directly from IMF, IBRD and UN sources for the period 1949–1984. This analysis does not intend to examine the validity of the indicators with respect to the actual phenomena being measured. The focus of this study is on the decisions made by the Bank and the Fund; official Bank and Fund sources can be considered as valid since the data included in these sources are the data actually employed in Bank and Fund lending decisions. Any biases in the data would reflect actual Bank and Fund biases and therefore, would be the most accurate indicators available for these variables.

Performance of the Bloc Relative to Non-Bloc Members

The Soviet Bloc members of the IMF and IBRD do very well in a cursory examination of aggregate lending figures from both organizations.[10] Table 2.1 lists the recipients which received the top 10 percent of total Stand-by Arrangement (SBA) receipts per year of membership from 1950 to 1984. Yugoslavia, Romania, and Hungary ranked fifth, seventh, and first, respectively, of 148 members in a comparison of total 1950–1984 SBA receipts from the IMF, controlling for number of years of membership. The results for Hungary are somewhat misleading because Hungary had been a member of the Fund for only two years in 1984 and thus, its ranking is skewed by the combination of its brief tenure and the relatively larger loans which the Fund lent during the 1980s. Romania and Yugoslavia placed twelfth and fourteenth respectively in a similar examination of SBA receipts for the 1950–1980 period.

Table 2.2 portrays the relative order of members' total SBA receipts without consideration for length of membership. Again, all three Soviet Bloc states appear in the top 10 percent with Yugoslavia ranking second only to the United Kingdom. Here again, the relatively extensive lending by the Fund in the 1980s skews the results somewhat as the Fund lent more frequently and in larger amounts during that period than in the previous three decades, with many individual loans for over $1 billion in the 1980 period. A study of total SBA receipts for the 1950–1980 period reveals that Yugoslavia and Romania still appear in the top 10 percent, placing tenth and fifteenth, respectively. Thus, the Bloc states do well in the aggregate, and the 1980s period only enhanced their relative position.

TABLE 2.1: Highest 10 Percent of IMF Members' Total SBA Receipts, Controlling for Years of Membership (in millions of SDRs)

Rank	Member	Year of Entry	Total SBA per year 1952-1984	Total SBA per year 1952-1980
1	Hungary	1982	450.00	NA
2	United Kingdom	1945	329.02	366.62
3	Korea, Rep. of	1955	96.66	40.46
4	Argentina	1956	92.40	45.30
5	Yugoslavia	1945	83.64	27.38
6	Turkey	1947	79.12	29.62
7	Romania	1972	58.51	23.11
8	Portugal	1961	50.20	NA
9	Italy	1947	47.22	52.94
10	Peru	1945	42.05	28.83
11	Zambia	1965	36.17	15.85
12	Philippines	1945	35.71	18.75
13	Kenya	1964	35.43	NA
14	France	1945	35.35	39.39
15	Thailand	1949	32.32	NA

NA--Not applicable, or does not appear in top 10 percent

Source: The data from which this table is derived are contained in IMF, Annual Reports (Washington, D.C.: IMF).

TABLE 2.2: Highest 10 Percent of IMF Members' Total SBA Receipts (in millions SDRs)

Rank	Country	Total SBA 1952-1984	Total SBA 1952-1980
1	United Kingdom	12,832.0	12,832.0
2	Yugoslavia	3,262.1	880.2
3	Turkey	2,927.6	1,047.5
4	Korea, Republic of	2,803.3	1,083.8
5	Argentina	2,587.3	1,165.0
6	Italy	1,747.1	1,747.1
7	Peru	1,639.9	1,183.8
8	Philippines	1,392.7	562.7
9	France	1,378.7	1,378.7
10	Romania	1,287.3	184.8
11	Portugal	1,154.7	NA
12	Thailand	1,131.4	NA
13	Chile	1,048.1	NA
14	United States	1,000.0	1,000.0
15	Hungary	900.0	NA

NA---Not applicable, or does not appear in the top 10 percent

Source: The data from which this table is derived are contained in IMF, Annual Reports (Washington, D.C.: IMF).

Similar results appear in an examination of total World Bank receipts. Yugoslavia ranked eighth with 4.06 percent of total Bank funds lent between 1945 and 1984, and Romania placed fourteenth in aggregate total Bank loans and percentage of total Bank loans (2.18 percent) of the 146 members of the Bank in 1984 (see Table 2.3). The relative position of the two countries reverses when length of membership is controlled: Romania ranks fifth and Yugoslavia, eighth. Table 2.4 portrays the Bank loan figures for the 1945–1980 period, with Yugoslavia and Romania improving their positions slightly. By 1986, Yugoslavia had received 4.25 percent of all Bank monies lent, and Romania reached 3.01 percent.

Performance of Bloc Countries
Relative to Economic Characteristics

In aggregate terms, the Soviet Bloc members appear to do quite well in garnering loans from the Bank and the Fund. The performance of these countries also must be evaluated in terms of the relationship of size of loans and their economic characteristics before any arena assignment can be made, however. The unusual amount of Fund and Bank loans might be due to the unusual need of these countries based on their economic performance rather than on the fact that these countries belong (or belonged, in the case of Yugoslavia) to the Soviet Bloc. If the latter is the case, then these countries would still be located in the technocratic arena.

Residual analysis of standard regressions provides a technique for evaluating the expected vs. actual loan performance of the Soviet Bloc, relative to their economic need and characteristics. Since the inception of SBAs in 1952, staff members of the Fund have published accounts of the variables and economic models the Fund employs in determining whether to lend, the size of the loan, and what conditions to require as proof of satisfactory performance. J.J. Polak began this process in 1957 in an article which linked monetary analysis to analysis of balance of payments problems.[11] This article derives the basic variables used by the Fund from monetary theory and as it has evolved, the model places emphasis on the role of domestic credit and the money supply in balance of payments equilibrium. Although much discussion of the appropriateness and effectiveness of this model, both positive and negative, has ensued, Polak's identification of the basic variables involved in the Fund's decision-making process remains valid.[12]

The Bank had not been concerned with conditionality until the 1980s and thus, has not generated as much interest in its lending criteria. Discussions of the variables used in Bank decisions to lend are often

TABLE 2.3: Top 10 Percent of Members Receiving World Bank Loans: Total Loans, Percentage Total Loans, and Controlling for Years of Membership, 1950-1984 (in millions U.S. dollars)

Rank	Country	Total Bank Loans 1950-1984	Percentage of Total Bank Loans	Total Bank Loans Per Years Member 1950-1984
1	Brazil	7,931.50	10.39	208.72
2	Indonesia	6,408.07	8.39	213.60
3	Mexico	5,605.93	7.34	143.74
4	India	5,319.43	6.96	136.39
5	Turkey	4.358.83	5.71	117.80
6	Korea, Rep. of	4,271.65	5.59	147.29
7	Philippines	3.431.59	4.49	87.98
8	Yugoslavia	3,102.46	4.06	79.55
9	Colombia	3,049.38	3.99	78.18
10	Thailand	2,846.26	3.73	81.32
11	Nigeria	2,160.07	2.83	93.91
12	Egypt	2,110.53	2.76	54.11
13	Morocco	1,997.93	2.62	78.84
14	Romania	1,667.57	2.18	138.71
15	Argentina	1,414.62	1.85	37.22

Source: The data from which this table is derived are contained in IBRD, Annual Reports (Washington, D.C.: IBRD).

TABLE 2.4: Top 10 Percent of Members' World Bank Receipts: Total Bank Loans, Percentage of Total Bank Loans, and Per Years of Membership, 1950-1980 (in millions of U.S. dollars)

Rank	Country	Total Bank Loans 1950-1980	Percentage of Total Bank Loans	Total Bank Loans Per Years Member 1950-1980
1	Brazil	5,313.7	8.95	156.27
2	Mexico	4,113.6	6.93	117.53
3	Indonesia	3,056.0	5.14	117.53
4	Korea, Rep. of	2,948.5	4.96	117.94
5	India	2,770.6	4.66	79.16
6	Colombia	2,961.4	4.65	78.89
7	Yugoslavia	2,684.1	4.52	76.68
8	Turkey	2,407.4	4.05	72.95
9	Philippines	2,389.9	4.02	68.28
10	Thailand	1,960.0	3.30	63.23
11	Romania	1,502,8	2.53	187.85
12	Morocco	1,437.3	2.42	65.33
13	Nigeria	1,380.7	2.32	72.66
14	Argentina	1,350.3	2.27	56.26
15	Iran	1,210.7	2.04	34.59

Source: The data from which this table is derived are contained in IBRD, Annual Reports (Washington, D.C.: IBRD).

included in broader studies of Bank lending such as Hayter's *Aid as Imperialism* and Mason and Asher's *The World Bank Since Bretton Woods*.[13] The Bank itself indirectly alludes to its decision-making criteria in its *Annual Reports*. Because the Bank is lending for primarily development projects, it is more concerned with the projected viability of the project and the member's ability to sustain the effort over time than with the international macroeconomic position of the state in the world economy. Of course, there is a vague, middle area between the two organizations which became broader in the 1980s when both the Bank and the Fund tentatively adopted procedures designed to facilitate structural adjustment and change in their members. The fundamental distinction between the two organizations remains, however.

Regression equations were formulated with variables derived from the sources discussed above. As suggested by Polak and others,[14] the IMF is most concerned with macroeconomic variables such as the growth rate of GNP, the size of the current account deficit, changes in the level of total reserves held by the government, the money supply, domestic credit, and occasionally, the level of government spending. As Polak and others note,[15] the Fund tends to focus on changes in the amount of credit granted to firms and, particularly, the government in the 1970s and 1980s in the construction of performance criteria. This is partially due to the reliance of the Fund on monetary theory to explain movements in the balance of payments, although this is often tempered by other factors (see Nowzad, *The IMF and Its Critics*).

Contrary to the Fund, the IBRD concentrates on performance variables which measure the health of a member's economy in a more internal sense. The Bank's focus is on the ability of a member's economy to support the suggested project, and thus variables such as GNP per capita, unemployment rate, and government expenditures become important. The Bank also examines the member's fiscal policies, paying particular attention to the level and location of government subsidies on public goods and to firms. Qualitative factors also enter into the Bank's evaluation, and the Bank has resisted attempts to quantify its evaluation procedure in recent years.[16]

These variables were entered into the respective equations for the Bank and the Fund. In the Fund regression equations, Stand-by Arrangement loans served as the dependent variable due to the fact that SBAs are the facility most frequently used by members, and conditionality is most often assessed under these procedures. Total amount of loans from the World Bank was the dependent variable in the regressions for that organization. The residuals for the years that the Soviet Bloc countries received loans of either type were analyzed to determine whether Yugoslavia, Romania, and Hungary had received unusual levels of loans

TABLE 2.5: SBA Residuals: Yugoslavia, Romania, and Hungary, 1965-1984
(in millions of SDRs)

Year	Country	Actual SBA Loan	Residual from Regression	Standard Deviation from the Mean
1965	Yugoslavia	80.00	85.22	*
1967	Yugoslavia	45.00	30.73	2.84
1971	Yugoslavia	51.75	37.66	3.83
1972	Yugoslavia	83.50	71.68	7.22
1980	Yugoslavia	408.58	371.31	3.08
1981	Yugoslavia	1662.00	1624.48	13.50
1982	Romania	1102.50	1065.35	8.85
1983	Hungary	425.00	438.09	3.64
1984	Yugoslavia	370.00	312.86	2.60
1984	Hungary	425.00	400.48	3.32

*---denotes missing

Source: The data from which this table is derived are contained in IMF, Annual Reports (Washington, D.C.: IMF).

from either organization, relative to other members with similar economic characteristics. Data for the regression equations were drawn from Bank and Fund sources.[17] The results appear in Tables 2.5, 2.6, and 2.7.

It is clear that the Soviet Bloc members have not been punished for their economic and ideological deviance. In fact, a cursory glance at the results suggests that the Bloc countries have received an unusually high level of loans from both the IMF and World Bank. Yugoslavia received eight SBAs and twenty-five World Bank loans between 1962 and 1984 totalling approximately $3.2 billion and $3.1 billion respectively. As Table 2.5 demonstrates, in every year except 1962, the Yugoslav SBA exceeded the expected amount by at least 2.5 standard deviations from the mean; in 1981, the size of the SBA was over thirteen standard deviations from the mean. Clearly, IMF lending to Yugoslavia has not been solely on the basis of its economic criteria. Yugoslavia received loans from the World Bank seven times before 1967 and annually since then. Its Bank loans from 1965 to 1984 exceed 2.5 standard deviations from the mean only twice, in 1967 and in 1979.

Due to missing data, regression equations for Romania could be computed only since 1980. In that period, Romania received a $1.2 billion loan from the IMF and three loans for a total of over $1 billion from the World Bank. Romania's 1981–1982 SBA exceeded the expected value by nearly nine standard deviations from the mean, but none of

TABLE 2.6: World Bank Loan Residuals: Yugoslavia, 1965-1984 (in millions of U.S. dollars)

Year	Actual WBL	Residual from Regression	Standard Deviation from the Mean
1965	70.0	- 6.04	*
1967	10.0	- 65.45	3.80
1968	60.5	- 15.64	*
1969	46.0	- 30.04	1.13
1970	98.5	22.57	*
1971	100.0	34.04	*
1972	75.0	- 1.80	*
1973	90.4	19.06	*
1974	128.0	52.06	*
1975	263.0	180.71	2.36
1976	242.0	158.21	1.78
1977	240.0	159.20	1.73
1978	328.0	242.11	2.16
1979	385.0	431.58	3.49
1980	347.0	- 34.00	*
1981	321.0	- 41.00	*
1982	256.0	220.50	*
1983	520.0	148.00	*
1984	451.0	- 5.00	*

*---denotes less than one standard deviation from the mean

Source: The data from which this table is derived are contained in IMF, Annual Reports (Washington, D.C.: IMF).

TABLE 2.7: World Bank Loan Residuals: Romania and Hungary, 1980-1984 (in millions of U.S. dollars)

Year	Country	Actual WBL	Residual from Regression	Standard Deviation from the Mean
1980	Romania	325.00	-116.0	*
1981	Romania	360.00	- 82.0	*
1982	Romania	321.50	277.2	1.2
1983	Hungary	239.40	194.0	*
1984	Hungary	238.80	192.4	*

*---denotes less than one standard deviation from the mean

Source: The data from which this table is derived are contained in IBRD, Annual Reports (Washington, D.C.: IBRD).

its Bank loans deviated from the norm by an appreciable amount (see Table 2.7).

Hungary became a member of the Bank and the Fund in 1982 and received two SBAs for $445 million and $416 million. Both of these loans registered above 3.3 standard deviations from the mean. Like Yugoslavia and Romania, however, its two Bank loans, for $194 million and $192.4 million, were well within what was expected given Hungary's economic characteristics.

Conclusion: The Soviet Bloc and the Political Arena

It is clear that the Soviet Bloc countries have received "special" treatment from the IMF in terms of loan receipts which have exceeded what would be expected for those countries using economic criteria. These countries also deviate from what would be expected by the political critique in that the Fund does not appear to discriminate *against* these countries in its lending. It is reasonable to assume at this point that the Soviet Bloc falls within the political arena of IMF lending.

The Bank does not appear to discriminate either for or against its Soviet Bloc members. Loan receipts from this organization are within the range of what would be expected if lending occurred in the technocratic arena. There is a hidden problem with this conclusion, however. If a maximum threshold GNP per capita criterion does exist in Bank lending, then the rules governing the Bank's technocratic arena would preclude lending to any of the Soviet Bloc countries since the 1970s at the latest. Yet all three countries have received Bank loans almost annually. This suggests that while the Bank does not violate its own rules to the extent of awarding above average loans to the three Bloc members, it continues to place these countries in the political arena simply by virtue of the fact that it lends to them at all.

There is evidence to suspect, therefore, that the Soviet Bloc members of the IMF and IBRD do indeed fall within the political arena of lending in both international organizations. The remaining chapters examine why this placement occurred and the effects of lending in the political arena on economic policy in Yugoslavia, Romania, Hungary, and eventually, Poland.

Interactions of the ascriptive factors are investigated in case studies of the Soviet Bloc members of the IMF and the IBRD. As was demonstrated earlier in this chapter, these cases were selected because of their unusually high loan receipts and the nature of their domestic characteristics. The cases are, therefore, analyzed for evidence of political considerations in lending policies of the Bank or the Fund.

Data for the analysis of leverage is drawn from many sources. Statements from the press and the Bank and Fund are employed where available. Analysis by knowledgeable scholars supplements these data. Missing and inaccurate data are potentially a serious problem at this stage of the analysis. The use of leverage is difficult to establish without access to confidential documents of the Fund, the Bank, and the member governments. Access to these types of materials is difficult to obtain, but this is not unusual given the politically sensitive nature of leverage. Neither the international organization nor its borrowers want lending to appear as infringing on the member's sovereignty. The Fund, the Bank, and member governments, therefore, are reluctant to release material which might convey this impression. It is possible that the data may even be deliberately altered to disguise Bank and Fund use of leverage in a member. As a result, there may be gaps in the link between loans and behavior which can only be estimated using data from confidential interviews and other sources.

Notes

1. Cheryl Payer, *The Debt Trap: The International Monetary Fund and the Third World* (New York: Monthly Review Press, 1974), p. 43. See also Teresa Hayter, *Aid As Imperialism* (Baltimore, MD: Penguin Books Ltd., 1971).

2. James H. Mittleman, "International Monetary Institutions and Policies of Socialism and Self-Reliance: Are They Compatible?" *Social Research*, vol. 47, no. 1 (Spring 1980), p. 165.

3. See Carl I. Ohman, "Comment: A Social Radicalism," in J.P. Lewis and I. Kapur (eds.), *The World Bank Group, Multilateral Aid, and the 1970s* (Lexington, MA: Lexington Books, 1973); Ronald T. Libby, "External Co-optation of a Less-Developed Country's Policy Making: The Case of Ghana, 1969–72," *World Politics*, vol. 29, no. 1 (October 1976), p. 88; Hayter, *Aid As Imperialism*; Payer, *The Debt Trap*; Mittleman, "International Monetary Institutions."

4. See Libby, "External Co-optation," and Mittleman, "International Monetary Institutions."

5. Michael Haas, "A Functional Approach to International Organization," *Journal of Politics*, vol. 47, no. 3 (August 1975), pp. 503, 505–506; C. Fred Bergsten, "Interdependence and the Reform of International Institutions," *International Organization*, vol. 30, no. 2 (Spring 1976), p. 362.

6. Performance criteria are used to indicate the success of the borrower's economic program for which credit was extended. These performance criteria are usually formulated in mathematical terms in order to leave "minimal scope for dispute." See Joseph Gold, *The Stand-by Arrangements of the International Monetary Fund* (Washington, D.C.: IMF, 1970), p. 152.

7. Gold, *The Stand-by Arrangements*, pp. 52, 63.

8. Theodore H. Cohn, "Politics in the World Bank Group: The Question of Loans to the Asian Giants," *International Organization*, vol. 28, no. 3 (Summer

1974), p. 561; Anthony D. Moulton, "On Concealed Dimensions of Third World Involvement in International Economic Organizations," *International Organization*, vol. 32, no. 4 (Autumn 1978), pp. 1028–1034; and L.K. Jha, "Comment: Leaning Against Open Doors?" in J.P. Lewis and I. Kapur (eds.), *The World Bank Group, Multilateral Aid, and the 1970s* (Lexington, MA: Lexington Books, 1973), p. 99.

9. Hayter, pp. 55–56; Mittleman, p. 163; John P. Lewis and Ishan Kapur, "The World Bank Group, Multilateral Aid and the 1970s," in J.P. Lewis and I. Kapur (eds.), *The World Bank Group, Multilateral Aid, and the 1970s* (Lexington, MA: Lexington Books, 1973), p. 2.

10. All figures are taken from the IMF, *Annual Reports*, 1950–1984 (Washington, D.C.: IMF) and the IBRD, *Annual Reports, 1980 and 1984* (Washington, D.C.: IBRD).

11. J.J. Polak, "Monetary Analysis of Income Formation and Payments Problems," *IMF Staff Papers* 6(1957):1–40.

12. See, among others, J.J. Polak and Victor Argy, "Credit Policy and the Balance of Payments," in *The Monetary Approach to the Balance of Payments* (Washington, D.C.: IMF, 1977); Graham Bird and Timothy Orme, "An Analysis of Drawings on the International Monetary Fund by Developing Countries," *World Development* 9(6):563–568; Tony Killick, ed., *The Quest for Economic Stabilization* (New York: St. Martin's Press, 1984); Manuel Guitian, "Fund Conditionality and the International Monetary Adjustment Process: The Early Period, 1950–1970," *Finance and Development* 17(4): 23–27, 1980; Sidney Dell, "Stabilization: The Political Economy of Overkill," *World Development* 10(8):597–612, 1982; Wilfred L. David, *The IMF Policy Paradigm* (New York: Praeger Publishers, 1985); John Williamson, *The Lending Policies of the International Monetary Fund* (Washington, D.C.: institute for International Economics, 1982).

13. See, among others, Hayter, *Aid as Imperialism*; Mason and Asher, *The World Bank Since Bretton Woods*; Robert L. Ayres, *Banking on the Poor* (Cambridge, MA: The MIT Press, 1985); Cheryl Payer, *The World Bank* (New York: Monthly Review Press).

14. See note 12, above.

15. See authors listed in note 12, above.

16. Ayres, p. 70.

17. Sources included Bank and Fund *Annual Reports*; IMF, *International Financial Statistics* (Washington, D.C.: IMF); United Nations, *Statistical Yearbook* (New York: UN).

3

The Soviet Union
at Bretton Woods

There have been only five Soviet Bloc members of the Bank and the Fund. Of these five countries only one, Yugoslavia, joined the organizations at their inception in 1944. At first glance, it would seem, therefore, that any examination of the experiences of these five states in the Bank and the Fund would have little relevance for the operations of these two organizations in the rest of the world. This is not the case, however. The experiences of Soviet Bloc states are noteworthy because they provide an example of the attitude of the Bank and the Fund toward members with non-capitalist forms of economic organization, and consequently, an indication of the extent to which political considerations enter into Bank and Fund decisions to lend.

The *Articles of Agreement* of both the IMF and the IBRD prohibit consideration of the structure of a member's economy (i.e., centrally-planned, market, etc.) in a decision to lend as economic structure is essentially a member's domestic political decision.[1] It follows, then, that a state's economic ideology should have little or no impact on its relationship with the Fund and the Bank. If political considerations are indeed a part of the Bank and Fund's lending decisions, however, this fact should be apparent in these organizations' relationships with the Soviet Bloc countries. The very foundations of these countries' central planning economic ideology pose a direct challenge to what many scholars believe is the principal philosophy, or ideology, underlying all Bank and Fund actions and decisions.

Scholars such as Daniel Holly argue that the main function of both the Bank and the Fund is to promote a capitalist world economy (Holly, "L'O.N.U.," p. 470).[2] Given this orientation, it is logical to assume that the Bank and Fund would not be particularly receptive to forms of economic organization which preclude the free operation of the market and private enterprise.[3] The almost complete prohibition of both domestic and foreign private investment and the use of central planning rather than the market to regulate the economy is typical of the economic systems of states based on a communist ideology, as well as many non-Marxist socialist states.

Even if one does not accept the argument that the Bank and the Fund are consciously promoting Western-style capitalism as a way of organizing the world economy, there is a second reason why the Bank and Fund may be inherently biased against non-capitalist forms of economic organization. The staff of both the Fund and the Bank have historically come from capitalist countries, particularly at the higher levels of management and decision-making. A quick overview of the 1981 *Annual Reports* for both the Fund and the Bank reveals that over 50 percent of senior staff members in both organizations still come from the developed, capitalist countries despite professed efforts to broaden the representativeness of the staff.[4] The education and experiences of Bank and Fund staff, therefore, does not equip them, at least initially, to understand and handle the special problems encountered in state-trading, centrally-planned economies (Payer, *Debt Trap*, p. 44). As a result, Fund and Bank recommendations place heavy emphasis on market-type solutions to balance of payments and other economic problems; in fact, Cheryl Payer contends that state-trading is the last of the options preferred by the IMF as a solution to balance of payments difficulties.[5]

Another reason for Bank and Fund "caution" in dealing with Soviet Bloc countries is their reliance upon financial markets in the capitalist developed countries as buyers for Bank and Fund securities. Neither organization can afford to alarm unduly the primarily conservative buyers of their securities (which constitute a large part of Bank and Fund capital)[6] by lending at too great a risk to the organization. To the extent that these non-organizational personnel regard Bloc countries as poor risks, political considerations can be considered economic factors as well. The tremendous amount of support in capitalist financial circles for Bank and Fund operations suggests that the prudence demonstrated by the Bank and the Fund in their lending policies has been successful.[7]

The following chapters investigate the relationship between the organizations created at Bretton Woods and a special category of Soviet Bloc countries. There are basically two types of Soviet Bloc states which have been, or are, members of the Bretton Woods organizations. The first type of Bloc member conforms to the Soviet model of a communist state. In these states democratic centralism is the basis for all decision-making, in the government as well as the party. Economic decisions are made according to a central, comprehensive plan, and private enterprise is prohibited and almost nonexistent. Countries in this category also tend to be almost exclusively pro-Soviet in their foreign polities.

The second category of Bloc members in the Bank and the Fund deviate from the Soviet model in the direction of their foreign policy with respect to the East-West conflict. The foreign policy of an innovator Soviet Bloc country is independent—an effort to maintain a non-aligned or middle road between East and West. In this sense, these countries are the "mavericks" of the Soviet Bloc. A second type of deviation from Soviet norms may occur when Bloc countries adopt market-style reforms in their economies. This type of deviation, however, is more likely to be rewarded by the Bank and Fund than punished or disapproved of by the Soviet Union.

The differences between these two types of Bloc countries in the Bank and the Fund stem from many different factors. Perhaps the most significant of these factors is the amount of domestic political support the regime receives, especially at the onset of communist power. A large reserve of domestic support enables a Communist regime to forego some of the support of its Communist brethren without endangering its position at home. Other factors which can contribute to the choice of an independent course are historical, economic, and strategic. For example, the extent to which a Soviet Bloc country must rely on the Soviet Union for essential raw materials and manufactured goods will determine the costs of an anti-Soviet or non-aligned foreign policy. These costs can be borne more easily, however, if the regime enjoys extensive support at home (i.e., a population which is willing to make the necessary sacrifices for regime independence).

The experiences of Soviet Bloc members in the Bank and the Fund also fall into two categories, successful (harmonious) and unsuccessful (conflictual). The criteria which determine success are the size of loans from the Bank and the Fund and the relative absence of conflict over the methods or philosophy of economic development chosen by the member (or recipient). The following chapter investigates the cases of conflictual or unsuccessful Soviet Bloc participation in the Bretton Woods organizations. In both cases, Poland and Czechoslovakia, conflict with the Bank and the Fund was resolved only through the withdrawal of the country from membership in both organizations. The major issues examined in this chapter are the extent to which the conflict between the Soviet Bloc members and the international organizations was based on political factors and whether this conflict was related to the member's particular economic ideology. If the international organizations are abiding by their respective charters, there should be no evidence of political issues and ideology in the controversies which erupted between the Bank, the Fund and the Bloc members.

The variables examined in each case will be:

1. Type of economic decision-making practiced by the member. Are economic decisions made according to a central, administrative plan or according to market, profit and loss criteria? If supporters of the Bank and Fund are correct, this variable should be unrelated to decisions to lend to Soviet Bloc members.
2. The reasons the member joined the Bank and the Fund. This variable will establish the expectations the member had of Bank and Fund membership. The benefits the country expected to gain from membership will largely determine the costs that country is willing to incur as a result of membership.
3. The nature of the relationship between the member and the Bretton Woods organizations, including the size and frequency of loans; the position of the member relative to other members with similar economic characteristics, such as GNP, population and inflation; and the issues which initiated open conflict between the organizations and the member, if any.
4. Changes in policy as a result of Bank and Fund leverage. These can be considered part of the costs of membership. Did the Bretton Woods organizations attempt to use loans as leverage to induce, reinforce, reward, or punish the member's economic policies?
5. Special problems or effects which arose specifically from Bank and Fund interaction with the member. These problems or effects may be perceived by the member as either costs or benefits.

The Soviet Union participated at the founding of the IMF and IBRD and thus, represented the concerns and desires of centrally planned economies with respect to the structure of both organizations. Knowledge of Soviet actions at the U.N. Monetary and Financial Conference is essential in order to understand the implications of Soviet participation for later Bloc relations with the IMF and IBRD. The issues and problems raised by the Soviets and the compromises reached between the Soviet Union and the U.S. and U.K. at Bretton Woods would influence greatly the future course of Soviet Bloc membership in the Bank and Fund. A brief examination of the Soviet Union's participation at Bretton Woods, thus, sets the stage for the experiences of Yugoslavia, Romania, Hungary and Poland.

The United Nations Monetary and Financial Conference

Among the 44 countries invited to participate at the United Nations Monetary and Financial Conference held at Bretton Woods, New Hampshire in July, 1944, were the Soviet Union, Poland, and Czechoslovakia.[8] Prior to the inauguration of the conference on July 1, 1944, the Soviet

Union participated in extensive discussions with the United States and Great Britain, initiators of the Bretton Woods concept,[9] and all four countries were included in the preliminary discussions which took place in Atlantic City, N.J., just prior to the meetings in Bretton Woods.[10] It is clear from the previous discussion, then, that the architects of Bretton Woods expected to include Communist countries as an integral part of the institutions which would emerge from the conference.[11] The United States and Great Britain perceived the Bretton Woods arrangements as the only means of avoiding the division of the world into rival economic blocs, and they regarded the Soviet Union as essential to the realization of this goal (NYT 5/17/46). In an attempt to assure the universality of membership in the organizations created at Bretton Woods, specific compromises were made to accommodate the Soviet Union and other "state-trading" countries.[12]

The Soviet Union, as the only officially socialist state represented at Bretton Woods, was an active and vocal participant in the proceedings which led to the formation of the IMF and the IBRD. The issues raised by the Soviet Union at Bretton Woods, and the concessions granted to it in the *Articles of Agreement* of both organizations, established the limits and possibilities for Communist participation in the two international organizations which persisted well into the first two decades of Bank and Fund operations, despite the failure of the Soviet Union to join either organization. An examination of Soviet demands at Bretton Woods is instructive in that some of the issues raised by the Soviets reappear several times in the interactions between the Fund and the Bank and Poland and Czechoslovakia.

Soviet Goals: Special Consideration

The points emphasized by the Soviet Union at Bretton Woods centered on four main areas: special consideration for state-trading nations and for states damaged by enemy hostilities and occupation during World War II; the size of quotas; the size of the gold portion of the quota and the disposition of that gold; and the amount of information required to be provided to the Bank and Fund.[13] Although the majority of items in which the Soviet Union sought special consideration were related to its position as a war-damaged nation, two items pertained directly to its position as a state-trading economic system; calculation of monetary reserves and changes in the par value of the ruble.

The Soviet Union asked for special consideration when the Fund calculated the Soviet's monetary reserves. Since all reserves and banking activities were centralized in one state bank in the Soviet Union, the state bank needed to retain part of its reserves as working balances for its foreign trade transactions.[14]

The Soviet delegation stated that since the states also had a monopoly over foreign trade and foreign trade pricing, the par value of the ruble was arbitrary, set by the state, and therefore, without international significance.[15] Thus, the Soviets argued, there was no need for the Soviet Union to consult the Fund when changing the par value of the ruble (Article IV, Section 5(b) and (e)). In addition, Mason claims that Article IV, Section 10 of the Fund's charter, which specifically prohibits the Fund from interfering "in the political affairs of any member; nor shall [the Fund] be influenced in [its] decisions by the political character of the member or member's concerned," was included primarily to reassure the U.S.S.R. (Mason, p. 27). A similar statement was included in the Bank's charter in Article IV, Section 10.

Reconstruction Assistance

Funds for reconstruction were a primary goal of the Soviets in the Bretton Woods deliberations. In fact, Mason claims that the Soviet Union wanted reconstruction to be the first priority of the IBRD (Mason, p. 21). In the Soviets' view, Great Britain and the Soviet Union were doing whatever was necessary to win the war and in pursuance of that aim were accepting assistance on any terms offered to them. The Soviets asserted that since they were bearing the major burden of the war (in their own calculations) they had a tremendous need for reconstruction funds in order to rebuild their devastated economy (NYT 7/9/44 and 7/22/44). Consequently, the Soviet Union proposed that an additional part be included in the purpose of the IBRD (Article I) which would state that the Bank would provide capital *"for reconstruction and restoration of the economies destroyed by the hostilities and for development"* (author's emphasis).

A modified version of this statement was included in Article I of the Bank's *Articles of Agreement*. In the section of the Bank's *Articles* dealing with "General Provisions Relating to Loans and Guarantees" (Article III, Section 1), the Soviets suggested that when lending to countries damaged by the war the "Bank shall take into consideration the special position of these countries in establishing for them the most favorable rates of interest, terms and conditions of repayment of such loans" (Bretton Woods, pp. 377, 1099). This suggestion was accepted in a limited sense by the other Bretton Woods delegations (most of whom would have benefitted from the Soviets' suggestion) and incorporated in Article III, Section 1(b) where the Bank was instructed to "pay special regard to lightening the financial burden and expediting the completion of such restoration and reconstruction" (*Articles of Agreement*, 1944, p. 56).

Gold and Reconstruction

The Soviets' concern for reconstruction was evident in its position on the size of and terms of payment of the gold subscription for war-damaged nations (Article III, Section 3(d) of the Fund). The Soviet Union supported a plan which would permit the Bank and Fund to reduce or postpone by 25–50 percent the gold portion of the subscriptions of states whose "home areas [had] suffered from enemy occupation and hostilities," depending on the extent of damage suffered by the state (Article II, Section 8; Bretton Woods, pp. 23, 33, 371). As M. S. Stepanov, leader of the Soviet delegation at Bretton Woods, stated, the Soviet Union was "very anxious to cooperate" but felt "entitled to special consideration" because the war had devastated its export capacity and created a need for the Soviet Union to conserve its foreign purchasing power, and thus, its gold.[16] "Virtually all the invaded and occupied countries" present at Bretton Woods supported the Soviet position (NYT 7/13/44).

The majority of the delegations on Committee I of Commission I at Bretton Woods did not agree with this proposal, however, and the Soviet proposition lost.[17] Some concession was made to the Soviet position in Article III, Section (d), allowing the Fund to set an alternate date for determining the net official holdings of gold of war-damaged states. Net official gold holdings was then defined as excluding newly mined gold in devastated countries, another concession to the Soviet Union (NYT 7/16/44).

Another area in which the Soviets' concern for reconstruction was evident was the area of charges applied to Fund and Bank loans and Bank guarantees (Fund Article V, Section 8, and Bank Article IV, Section 4 and 5). In the Fund, the Soviet Union wanted all charges paid uniformly by all borrowers regardless of the size of the borrower's monetary reserves (Bretton Woods, pp. 1087, 1090); the proposal was not adopted. The Soviets also proposed for the Bank that during the first ten years of Bank operations charges be limited to a range between 1/2 percent to 1 percent a year (Bretton Woods, p. 918). This proposal was amended to limit charges to between 1 percent and 1 1/2 percent a year (Article IV, Section 4(a) 5(a)). In summary, then, there was some support at Bretton Woods for the reconstruction goal of the Soviet Union, but this support was tempered by the perhaps more long-range goals of other delegations.

Quotas

Quotas were another area in which the U.S.S.R. exhibited a vigorous interest. Quotas were of intense concern at Bretton Woods because a state's voting power in both the Bank and the Fund was designed as a function of its quota. The delegations at the conference seemed to agree on the proposal that every member should have a voice in the conduct of the affairs of the two organizations (Gold, *Voting*, p. 25). The formula adopted at Bretton Woods for both the Bank and Fund assigned each member one vote per $100,000 of its quota plus 250 "basic votes."[18] At first, the Soviet Union pressed to have its subscription reduced from the $1.2 billion which was initially suggested. The Soviets sought to reduce the risk they would assume as part of the Bank and Fund's lending operations (NYT 7/20/44; Lavigne, p. 37).

On July 22, 1944, toward the end of the conference, the Soviet Union surprised everyone by announcing its decision to increase its subscriptions (and consequently, its share of the risk) to the original level of $1.2 billion in both the Bank and the Fund. U.S. Secretary of the Treasury Morgenthau commented in a statement recognizing the Soviets' decision that

> "By this move, the Soviet Union has carried even further its collaboration toward the success of this conference and toward assuring international collaboration in solving the post-war problems of the world. The solution of these future problems will have the inestimable support of the Union of Soviet Socialist Republics" (Bretton Woods, p. 1108).

The Soviets themselves stated that the move was prompted by a desire to accommodate the wishes of other delegations, especially the United States (Bretton Woods, p. 1111).

Others saw the Soviets' concession as having a more pragmatic, self-interested basis. One analyst reported that unofficially there was some expectation on the part of the Soviets that their increased subscription would enable them "to receive correspondingly more consideration for the applications for loans" (NYT 7/24/44). The Soviet action was also viewed as "an important diplomatic victory" in that it strengthened the Soviets' position at the conference by demonstrating that the U.S.S.R. was willing to make concessions, also (NYT 7/24/44). An increase in Soviet quota (or subscription) also enlarged the Soviets' percentage of the total quotas in both Bretton Woods organizations, and hence, increased the Soviets' percentage of the total votes in each organization. In the Fund, the new Soviet quota of $1.2 billion gave the Soviet Union 13.64 percent of the total quota in the Fund and 12.37 percent of the total votes, placing it third after the U.S. and the U.K. The new Soviet quota also gave the Soviet Union the right to appoint an Executive Director in each organization.[19] What appeared to be a magnanimous Soviet gesture, therefore, would have brought decided advantages to the USSR if it had joined the IMF and the IBRD.

Provision of Information

The provision of economic information was perhaps the most sensitive issue at Bretton Woods in the view of the Soviet Union. The Soviets agreed in principle that economic information was vital to the success of the Fund (NYT 7/24/44), but it was the specific content of that information that concerned the Soviets. Alternative D to Fund Article VIII, Section 5 was a list of information that the Soviet Union was willing to supply to the Fund:

1. gold holdings of Central Bank and the Treasury and their changes
2. gold convertible exchange holdings of the Central Bank and the Treasury and their changes
3. movement of capital
4. foreign trade data
5. other balance of payment items
6. rate of exchange and its changes
7. additional information with the consent of the member (Bretton Woods, pp. 267, 36).

The final list of required information in the Fund's *Articles of Agreement* (Article VIII, Section 5) appears as follows:

1. Official holdings at home and abroad of (1) gold, (2) foreign exchange.
2. Holdings at home and abroad by banking and financial agencies, other than official agencies, of (1) gold, (2) foreign exchange.
3. Production of gold.
4. Gold exports and imports according to countries of designation and origin
5. Total exports and imports of merchandise, in terms of local currency values, according to countries of destination and origin.
6. International balance of payments, including (1) trade in goods and services, (2) gold transactions, (3) known capital transactions, and (4) other items.
7. International investment position, i.e., investments within the territories of the member owned abroad and investments abroad

owned by persons in its territories so far as it is possible to
furnish this information.
8. National income.
9. Price indices, i.e., indices of commodity prices in wholesale and
retail markets and of export and import prices.
10. Buying and selling rates for foreign exchange.
11. Exchange controls, i.e., a comprehensive statement of exchange
controls in effect at the time of assuming membership in the
Fund and details of subsequent changes as they occur.
12. Where official clearing arrangements exist, details of amounts
awaiting clearance in respect of commercial and financial transactions, and of the length of time during which such arrears
have been outstanding.

Comparing the two lists it is clear that the Fund required much more
detailed information than the Soviet Union was willing to supply. The
primary difference between the two lists from the viewpoint of the
U.S.S.R. was the information the Fund required on gold (nos. 1–4).
Protection of information on gold production and transactions in gold
was (and still is) regarded by the Soviet Union as necessary to its
national security, particularly during wartime (NYT 7/16/44). This
conflict was not resolved until 1954.

The Soviet Union was also opposed to the publication of official and
unofficial Fund reports to members without the consent of the member
involved (Fund Article XII, Section 8). The Soviet Union was concerned
that politically and economically sensitive information would be released
in hostile quarters to the detriment of the Soviet Union. Again, the
Soviets lost this argument (Bretton Woods, p. 1087).

Despite lingering objections,[20] the Soviet delegation signed the Bretton
Woods agreements, citing the "friendly atmosphere" and spirit of cooperation which had prevailed at the conference (Bretton Woods, p. 1111).
The leader of the Soviet delegation, M.S. Stepanov, even applauded U.S.
Secretary of the Treasury Morgenthau for his "brilliant leadership" of
the conference during the Soviet's speech to second a motion to accept
the Final Act (Bretton Woods, p. 1112). In the Soviet Union's final
statement at the Executive Plenary Session on July 20, 1944, however,
Stepanov reiterated the U.S.S.R.'s major concerns throughout the conference: international cooperation to hasten reconstruction and the preservation of "mutual respect for the interests of the participating nations
and the sovereign rights of other states" (Bretton Woods, p. 1208). In
addition, the Soviet delegation asserted that they were "reserving the
full right of the U.S.S.R. Government to make a free and independent
study of the Draft" and that their approval of the draft did not constitute

"approval of the Draft in whole or in any of its parts on behalf of the U.S.S.R. Government."[21]

Soviet Refusal of Membership

This implicit warning was not heeded by enthusiastic and optimistic supporters of the two Bretton Woods organizations, and when the deadline for joining the organizations as original members passed without the signature of the Soviet Union,[22] these supporters remained optimistic about eventual Soviet entry. The Soviet Union, in a statement explaining why it had failed to take advantage of joining as an original member, merely commented that it "did not deem it appropriate to join the institutions 'at this time'" (NYT 1/3/46). The foundation for the optimism of some Bretton Woods supporters was the Soviets' cooperative attitude during the Bretton Woods negotiations and the fact that the U.S.S.R. delegation had signed the agreements (NYT 12/14/44, 12/28/44). Clearly, the statement made by the Soviet delegation about the meaning of its signature of the Final Act was universally ignored.

In March, 1946, three months after the deadline for original membership had passed, members of the new Bank and Fund extended a new conciliatory gesture to the U.S.S.R. Countries which had participated at Bretton Woods but had failed to join were invited to be observers of the first meeting of the organizations in Savannah, Georgia in March, 1946. The U.S. indicated its intention to introduce at that meeting a proposal to extend the period for Bretton Woods participants to join as original members (NYT 3/3/46). Failure of the Soviet Union to enter the Bank and the Fund was considered by the U.S. to be a serious potential handicap to "stable and unrestricted world trade;" consequently, the U.S. sought to pressure the U.S.S.R. to join by tying Soviet membership in the Bank and Fund to U.S. aid to the Soviet Union (NYT 3/3/46, 3/8/46).

The Soviets responded by at first ignoring the invitation to Savannah and then sending a delegation to observe the proceedings which did not include a representative from Moscow (NYT 3/8/46, 3/9/46), an indication of the Soviets' negative position with respect to the new organizations. Observers began to speculate that the Soviet Union did not intend to join the Bretton Woods organizations at any time in the foreseeable future (NYT 3/9/46). Nevertheless, the Board of Governors of both the Bank and the Fund agreed to a six-month extension of the limit for joining as an original member. This was done, in part, to facilitate Soviet membership.[23]

An invitation was once again issued to the U.S.S.R. to participate at the next meeting of the two organizations in Washington, D.C. in

September, 1946 (NYT 8/28/46). The Soviets did not reply to this invitation and sent no observers to the meeting (NYT 9/27/46). The mood of the Bretton Woods supporters altered at this point and no further "overtures" were made (NYT 9/29/46). Fund officials were anxious to assure the Soviets that they would still be "received warmly" if they decided to join at a later date,[24] but Camille Gutt, newly appointed Managing Director of the Fund, was quick to express the prevailing attitude at the meeting that the failure of the Soviets to enter the Bank and the Fund "wouldn't make any great difference" (NYT 9/2/46), a marked contrast to statements made by the U.S. in March of that same year (see above). In fact, by this time

> "Some officials felt that Russia's absence from the fund would facilitate its operating by eliminating the problem which would be presented by integrating Soviet foreign-trade practices with those of capitalistic countries, and speed its organization and action by not having to wait for a 'decision from Moscow' every time a policy decision was made" (NYT 1/3/46).

The atmosphere of international cooperation which had prevailed at Bretton Woods had dissipated, and the first signs of the Cold War appeared in the IMF and IBRD.

The Soviets, on the other hand, felt that they had ample justification for refusing membership in the IMF and IBRD. First, the proposed quotas in both organizations, and the corresponding votes, did not accord any state a veto over Fund and Bank decisions and operations, an important objective in Soviet negotiations on the United Nations (Mason, p. 29; Lavigne, p. 372). A second Soviet objection revolved around the required provision of economic information (see preceding discussion), particularly information about gold reserves and gold production (NYT 1/3/46; Lavigne, p. 372). The prospect of acquiring loans for reconstruction, the primary motivation for Soviet participation at Bretton Woods, also seemed dim to Soviet officials. Bank resources appeared insufficient for the scale of Soviet post-war needs, even without the competition of other Bank members (NYT 1/6/46; Lavigne, p. 372). Even if the Bank, for example, had been able to finance Soviet reconstruction, Bank procedures would have required the Soviets to permit unwelcome, and perhaps sensitive, investigations into the Soviet economy (Mason, p. 29). Finally, the goal of the U.N. Monetary and Financial Conference, international financial stability, could be enjoyed by the Soviets without the expense of Soviet resources, due to the restricted nature and effects of Soviet foreign trade. As one analyst commented, the Soviets could benefit from stable exchange rates "just as easily as an onlooker as a participant" (NYT 1/6/46).

The costs of Fund and Bank membership, therefore, outweighed the benefits in the Soviet calculus.

Increasing Soviet Hostility

As was mentioned earlier, Cold War issues had intruded into the two international organizations by 1946. Conflicts had arisen between the Soviet Union, Great Britain, and the U.S. over a number of issues, including the United Nations, the administration of Berlin, and the Soviet occupation of Eastern Europe.[25] Soviet interest in international cooperation dwindled as these conflicts worsened and multiplied (NYT 10/7/46; Lavigne, p. 372). The prevailing atmosphere of conflict made the Soviets understandably reluctant to entrust "any large part of her economic policy [and resources] to the Bank and Fund, in which the U.S. [was] regarded as dominant and where Russia would have no veto power" to protect its interests (NYT 10/7/46).

Soviet antagonism toward the Fund and the Bank surfaced during U.N. discussions of the arrangements that would make the IMF and IBRD affiliated agencies of the U.N. system. Bank and Fund supporters, particularly the United States, sought a special agreement with the U.N. which would insulate the lending operations of those organizations from the interference of what they considered a more "politicized" institution, the U.N. In keeping with the Cold War atmosphere at the time, one observer remarked, in effect, that this was understandable since the Soviet Union and its allies were members of the U.N. and were likely to use that organization to affect policy in its affiliated agencies (NYT 8/16/47).

The U.S.S.R., joined by Norway, chose the Economic and Social Council of the U.N. General Assembly (ECOSOC) in August 1947, to begin its battle against special consideration of the IMF and the IBRD. In a four-hour debate, the Soviets argued against an agreement in which the U.N. would abdicate any rights to review and comment upon Bank and Fund lending procedures and budgets, and claimed that such an agreement would violate the U.N.'s charter. ECOSOC disagreed by a 13–3 majority.[26] The Soviets pursued the issue next in the General Assembly of the U.N. in October 1947. In addition to its previous arguments, the Soviet Union charged that a World Bank loan to the Netherlands for reconstruction purposes was actually being used to support Netherlands aggression in Indonesia (Mason, p. 58; NYT 10/14/47).

Ironically, the Soviets also objected to provisions in the U.N. agreement with the IBRD which would permit the World Bank to withhold important information (Mason, p. 58). Finally, the Soviets accused the U.S., through

its voting strength in both the Bank and the Fund, of attempting to
convert both organizations into "instruments of its own foreign policy"
(NYT 10/14/47), and therefore, the Soviets claimed, the U.S. was trying
to ensure through these special agreements that the U.N. would interfere
in this process as little as possible (NYT 10/14/47). These arguments
failed to convince the majority of the General Assembly, and the
agreements with the IMF and the IBRD were approved, with New
Zealand, the Soviet Union, Belorussia, and the Ukraine dissenting, and
Austria and Yugoslavia abstaining (NYT 10/19/47).

It is evident from the foregoing analysis that the early relationship
between the IMF, the IBRD, and the Soviet Union was a complex one
which encompassed many issues and problems. The Soviets were the
first to provoke a conflict with the IMF and the IBRD. Its refusal to join
as an original member was initially perceived by the adherents of the
Bretton Woods agreements as an unfortunate decision but not as a
hostile move in itself. It was the Soviet's persistent failure to make any
conciliatory responses to the repeated gestures of the Fund and Bank
and the intensification of the Cold War with the U.S. which eventually
provoked the animosity of those organizations, and this animosity then
began to permeate Fund and Bank relations with other Communist
countries.

Notes

1. See Fund Article IV, Section 5(f), Bank Article III, Section 5(b), and Bank
Article IV, Section 10. All references in this chapter made to the Bank and Fund
Articles of Agreement refers to the *Articles of Agreement of the International
Monetary Fund and International Bank for Reconstruction and Development*, pub-
lished by the U.S. Treasury, Washington, D.C., in 1944.

2. See also the formulation discussion in Chapter 2.

3. Daniel A. Holly, "L'O.N.U., le système économique international et la
politique internationale," *International Organization*, vol. 29, no. 2 (Spring 1975),
p. 483. Teresa Hayter, *Aid As Imperialism* (Baltimore, MD: Penguin Books Ltd.,
1971), p. 6; and Edward S. Mason and Robert E. Asher, *The World Bank Since
Bretton Woods* (Washington, D.C.: The Brookings Institution, 1973), p. 171.

4. See also Mason, Table 4.3, "Nationality Distribution of World Bank/IDA
Professional Staff by Major Groups, 1951–71," p. 68; and the World Bank and
IMF *Annual Reports*, 1950–80 (Washington, D.C.: IMF, IBRD).

5. Cheryl Payer, *The Debt Trap: The International Monetary Fund and the Third
World* (New York: Monthly Review Press, 1974), p. 34. See also Hayter, p. 28
and L. K. Jha, "Comment: Leaning Against Open Doors?" in John P. Lewis
and Ishan Kapur (eds.), *The World Bank Group, Multilateral Aid, and the 1970's*
(Lexington, MA: Lexington Books, 1973, pp. 92–101.

6. See Mason, pp. 105–149.

7. New York Times, 9/30/48. All references to New York Times articles refer only to the date of that article.

8. Poland and Czechoslovakia were not Communist at this time although, as will be seen later, many of their demands were similar to those of the U.S.S.R.

9. Horsefield, vol. 1, and Gold, *Membership and Nonmembership*, p. 129.

10. Yugoslavia was also included in the Atlantic City and Bretton Woods meetings.

11. See also Gold, *Membership*, p. 472.

12. Gold, *Membership*, p. 472; New York Times (NYT), 1/10/46.

13. See also the NYT 7/14/44; Gold, *Membership*, pp. 13–134; Marie Lavigne, "The International Monetary Fund and the Soviet Union," in *International Economics-Comparisons and Interdependence* (New York: Springer-Verlag, 1978), p. 370.

14. *Proceedings and Documents of the United Nations Monetary and Financial Conference*, Department of State Publication 2866 (Washington, D.C.: U.S. GPO, 1948), pp. 1087, 1091. This publication will henceforth be referred to as "Bretton Woods."

15. NYT 7/15/44; see also Gold, *Membership*, p. 141; Lavigne, p. 371.

16. NYT 7/21/44, 7/7/44.

17. The membership of Committee I of Commission I (on the arrangements for the IMF) were: Belgium, Brazil, Canada, China, Czechoslovakia, Cuba, France, Mexico, New Zealand, Norway, U.S.S.R., U.K. and U.S.

18. Fund *Articles* Article II, Section 3 and Article V, Section 3; Bank *Articles* Article II, Section 3 and Article V, Section 3. See also Joseph Gold, *Voting and Decisions in the International Monetary Fund* (Washington, D.C.: IMF, 1972), p. 18.

19. Gold, *Membership*, p. 136. The Executive Directors provide the day-to-day management of the Fund. Executive Directors are appointed by the members with the five largest quotas and elected by remaining members. The *Articles of Agreement* which emerged from Bretton Woods provided for a minimum of 12 Executive Directors (5 appointed and 7 elected).

20. The Soviets made final reservations on the following articles of the IBRD: Article I, Section 4; Article III, Section 1(b); and Article V, Section 11(b).

21. Bretton Woods, pp. 1208–1209. Also see NYT 7/22/44.

22. Australia, New Zealand, Venezuela, Liberia, Haiti, El Salvador, Nicaragua, and Panama also did not take advantage of joining as original members. See NYT 1/2/46.

23. Joining as an original member gave a country an advantage in that the quota agreement made at Bretton Woods would not be subject to further negotiations. Participants at Bretton Woods which did not join the Bank and Fund by the December, 1945 deadline would have to renegotiate their quotas. See NYT 3/13/46, and Gold, *Membership*, p. 132.

24. NYT 8/16/47.

25. NYT 10/5/46.

26. NYT 8/17/47. The Soviet Union and Belorussia dissented, and Czecho-slovakia and New Zealand abstained. Yugoslavia cast an assenting vote but stated its dissatisfaction with several aspects of the agreement. See Mason, p. 54.

4

Soviet Bloc Conflict in the IMF and the IBRD

Of the four countries to withdraw from membership in the IMF and IBRD prior to 1986, three were Communist. Poland and Cuba were the first countries to withdraw voluntarily from the Bank and Fund, and Czechoslovakia was (and still is) the only case of compulsory withdrawal, or expulsion, from the organizations which were created at Bretton Woods. This chapter attempts to determine whether two out of four "failures" in the Bank and the Fund were a consequence of the fact that those members were centrally-planned economies.

The issues which led to the withdrawal of Poland and Czechoslovakia were the legacy of the conflicts and compromises of Bretton Woods. The Czech and Polish cases are excellent examples of the Bank and Fund's early efforts to resolve the ambiguities in their charters with respect to the place of state-trading members in the new international economic system devised at Bretton Woods. Czech and Polish experiences set the tone of Fund and Bank relationships with Soviet-style Communist countries. The analyses which follow trace the factors which contributed to the rapid decline in relations between the IMF and IBRD and their Soviet-style Communist members.

Poland: The Destruction of Optimism

Poland was one of the 44 countries to sign the Bretton Woods agreements in 1944 and thus was one of the original members of the Fund and Bank (NYT 12/28/45). Reconstruction was clearly Poland's primary motive for participating in the formation of both organizations. A statement made at Bretton Woods by the Polish minister in Commission II (on the IBRD) clearly indicates the goals of the non-Communist Polish government. On July 13, 1944, Dr. Ludwik Grosfield noted his country's eventual need for development loans but cited the "appalling conditions caused by warfare and occupation" which made funds for reconstruction Poland's first priority.[1] In Grosfield's view, reconstruction loans from the Bank were vital to the health of the international economy so that all states would have an "even start for development" (Bretton Woods, p. 593). Poland joined the IMF and the IBRD, therefore, with the hope that those organizations would bear a significant part of its reconstruction burden.

In the process of liberation from the Nazi occupation forces, in 1945 Poland had acquired a Soviet-style Communist regime. Since the Soviet Union closely supervised all actions of the new Polish government, decision-making processes in Poland tended to follow closely the Soviet pattern of a strong Leninist party operating according to the principle of democratic-centralism. The economy was designed and administered according to a central plan which was compiled in accordance with the directives of the top of the party structure and had the force of law. The fact that the Soviet Red Army had liberated Poland from the Nazis severely limited the Poles' foreign policy options. Consequently, the Poles supported all Soviet initiatives both inside and outside the United Nations.

In keeping with the spirit of the agreements reached at Bretton Woods, several states which had suffered extensive damage from enemy occupation and hostilities during World War II were permitted in 1946 to defer part of their capital subscriptions to the IMF and the IBRD, and they were also permitted to delay the establishment of par values for their currencies.[2] Poland was among the six nations which took advantage of the war damage clause which allowed those nations that qualified to defer payment of 1/2 of 1 percent of their capital subscriptions for a period of five years (NYT 8/31/46).[3] For Poland, the amount of its quota which could be deferred was $625,000. In the early days of the Bretton Woods organizations, then, it appeared as if Poland's expectations would be realized.

The Coal Loan

Poland's interactions with the Bank were not as auspicious. In the autumn of 1946, Poland made its first request for reconstruction assistance from the Bank. The Poles requested a loan of $600 million for general reconstruction purposes but were soon informed by World Bank officials that a loan of that magnitude was beyond the capabilities of the Bank's resources. The Bank proposed a smaller loan of $125 million to be used for the devastated coal industry. This loan would not only benefit Polish recovery but, due to the shortage of coal in Western Europe, would expedite recovery in that area as well.[4] The Poles submitted a second, revised request for $128.5 million for the coal industry in the spring of 1947 (Mason and Asher, p. 170) and warned that Polish coal production would be "curtailed sharply at the end of 1948" if a loan sufficient for re-equipping its mines was not immediately forthcoming (NYT 9/19/ 47).

In addition, Poland noted that while negotiations on its loan stagnated, other members had received their first loans and were in the process of negotiating for a second loan. In a statement which reflected the frustration and discontent with the Bank on the part of Polish officials, Polish Industry Minister, Hilary Minc, declared, "We claim what is due to us. . . ." He noted that the extent of devastation suffered by Poland during the war entitled Poland to priority in receiving reconstruction assistance, yet he noted that Poland had to wait "in a long queue of applicants" and had even been passed by in the first round (NYT 9/ 14/47)! Examination of Bank records for this period indicates that this Polish claim was not an exaggeration. Several members of the Bank had received loans prior to 1950, as is shown below:

Brazil	1 loan, totaling $75 million
Chile	2 loans, $16 million
Colombia	1 loan, $5 million
El Salvador	1 loan, $16 million
Mexico	2 loans, $34.1 million
Belgium	1 loan, $16 million
Finland	2 loans, $14.8 million
Netherlands	9 loans, $222 million
Yugoslavia	1 loan, $2.7 million
Australia	1 loan, $100 million
India	2 loans, $44 million[5]

There were several reasons for the delay in the Polish loan. Bank officials were anxious to assure themselves, their members, and the international banking community that a loan to Poland was a good risk and likely to be repaid. Accordingly, the Bank was applying its definition of "sound banking standards"[6] in its analysis of the Polish economy and its prospects. The Bank's definition of "sound banking standards" contained significant political content, despite the injunction against such in Article IV, Section 10. According to Bank sources, "Political tensions and uncertainties in or among its member countries . . . have a direct effect on economic and financial conditions in those countries and upon their credit position."[7] Political criteria were, thus, included in the definition of economic criteria, permitting the Bank to avoid, or ignore, the restriction set in Article IV, Section 10. As a result, Bank

President J.J. McCloy instructed the four member fact-finding mission to Poland to include certain political conditions in its examination of the Polish economy (NYT 6/11/47).

Poland's lack of independence from the Soviet Union was the critical political criterion which influenced the Bank's decision NOT to lend to Poland any part of its $125 million request. Bank officials felt that it "could not ignore Poland's situation in the Russian sphere in considering a loan to [Poland] and . . . its ability to act independently of the Soviet in subscribing to World Bank conditions. . ." (NYT 6/11/47). The Bank questioned whether Poland would be able to find the resources to repay its loan, given Soviet hostility to the Bank.[8] Consideration of the Polish loan came to a halt when Poland failed to attend a conference of the committee of European economic cooperation to list Marshall Plan requirements (NYT 11/5/47). At this point, Poland began to be "desperately worried" that its position as a member of the Soviet Bloc would effectively preclude it from any future use of the benefits of membership in the IBRD, despite McCloy's assurances that the Bank "did not regard Communist governments as prima facie bad risks" (NYT 3/3/49, 4/28/48).

Western private financial organizations played an important role in the Bank's evaluation of the Polish loan. One analysis of the situation concluded that it was the reluctance of Western investors to invest in Bank debentures if the Bank extended a loan to Poland which was the critical factor in the Bank's decision not to lend to Poland, rather than Poland's lack of independence from the Soviet Union (NYT 11/5/47). In addition, it was a widespread belief in the Bank that U.S. investors would be unwilling to invest in World Bank bonds if the Bank proceeded with the loan to Poland or other Communist countries (NYT 11/5/47).

The U.S., in particular, vociferously expressed its disapproval of the Polish loan. In their history of the IMF, Margaret deVries and J. Keith Horsefield describe how, in the early years of the Fund, it was a common practice for members to consult the Executive Director for the United States to get his concurrence before submitting a loan application.[9] In the case of the Polish loan, the U.S. government made it quite clear that it would instruct its Executive Director to vote against the loan, and if the Bank still extended the loan, the U.S. would refuse to grant export licenses for the mining equipment necessary to the success of the Polish loan (Mason and Asher, p. 170). The weight of Western opposition, therefore, was instrumental in the collapse of loan negotiations between the World Bank and Poland.

Other Problems with the Bank

Other issues contributed to the deterioration of the relationship between the IBRD and Poland. In September, 1948, Poland joined

Czechoslovakia and Yugoslavia in criticizing the IBRD Annual Report as biased toward Western European recovery. The three countries charged that political motivations had biased the Bank's evaluations of Eastern European loans and had resulted in a bias toward financing loans to Western Europe (NYT 9/30/48). Bank President McCloy responded that Western European recovery was vital to the recovery of the international economy as a whole and that complete economic objectivity in Bank evaluations of the Eastern European economies was difficult because it was "impossible to determine where economics ends and politics begins" in post-war Eastern Europe (NYT 9/30/48). Six months later, Poland alleged that the Bank's preference for Western Europe and the Bank's reluctance to finance the coal loan amounted to "economic warfare against Eastern Europe" in which the Bank was the instrument of the U.S. (NYT 3/3/49).

Poland further claimed in a meeting of ECOSOC that IBRD loans had been used to finance the French and Netherlands wars against Vietnam and Indonesia, respectively (NYT 3/3/49). In February, 1950, Poland again joined Czechoslovakia and Yugoslavia in pressing for the representation of the PRC in the Bank and the Fund and the ouster of the Nationalist Chinese.[10] The situation between Poland and the World Bank was rapidly degenerating.

Poland's Withdrawal

On March 14, 1950, Poland ended its problems with the Bank and Fund by withdrawing voluntarily from both organizations. It was the first withdrawal of a member from either organization since they began operations in 1946. Poland accomplished its withdrawal by informing the U.S. head of mission to Poland who then communicated this information to the IMF and IBRD through diplomatic channels (NYT 3/15/50). Poland subsequently sent the Bretton Woods organizations an official letter of withdrawal which focused on three issues: the effort of the Fund to "force" devaluations upon its members, the alleged "subservience" of the Fund to the U.S., and the failure of the Fund to fulfill the spirit of Bretton Woods, i.e., to assist Poland in reconstructing its economy.[11] Poland's Ambassador to the U.S., Josef Winiewicz explained that Poland had tolerated the faults of the Bank and Fund for so long only in the hope that it could effect a change in Bank and Fund policies (NYT 3/16/50), but Poland's inability to obtain a loan after a four-year effort and recurring conflicts with both organizations convinced Polish authorities that they could have little or no effect on Bank and Fund policies. Furthermore, it appeared to the Poles that costs of membership would soon exceed the benefits; consequently, the Poles withdrew.

The response from the Bank and the Fund came quickly. The IMF and IBRD "rejected summarily" (NYT 3/16/50) the Polish charges and cited some of their problems with that member, including Poland's reluctance to set a par value for its currency and its failure to contribute 99.9 percent of its $125 million subscription (NYT 3/15/50). Officials in the IMF, IBRD, and the U.S. interpreted Poland's withdrawal as part of a Soviet effort to strengthen its control over its satellites by encouraging their withdrawal from U.N. agencies (NYT 3/15/50, 3/16/50). Camille Gutt, Managing Director of the IMF at the time of the Polish withdrawal, characterized the Polish statement as the "familiar Kremlin line" (NYT 3/17/50). Perhaps Mr. Gutt was recalling the Soviets'comments during the U.N. debate on the affiliation agreements with the IMF and IBRD (see Chapter 3). Relations with Polish members of the Fund's staff remained cordial, however, and the Fund's Board of Governors approved an exception to a Fund rule which required that staff members be nationals of Fund members in order to retain the six Polish members on the staff at the time (Horsefield, p. 263).

Summary

Poland's relationship with the IMF and the IBRD began in a positive atmosphere and slowly disintegrated into mutual accusation. Poland's paramount aim in joining the Fund and Bank was to obtain aid for the reconstruction of its economy. The Final Agreement which emerged from Bretton Woods gave Poland every expectation of achieving this goal. By 1950, however, Poland recognized that reconstruction aid was not likely to be forthcoming in the near future, when it was most critical, and therefore, its primary reason for joining the Bank had disappeared. Poland felt that the Bank's reluctance to lend to Poland was due to a factor which Poland couldn't change: its status as a Soviet satellite. This attribute of the Polish political system was a given and could not be altered without significant and damaging repercussions to Poland's existence as an independent state. As long as Poland remained in the Soviet Bloc, therefore, it appeared that it would be highly unlikely that Poland would share in the reconstruction funds being distributed by the Bank and Fund.

In this case, the Bank, in particular, used its resources both to punish Poland's behavior and to induce Poland to change its policies. The Bank's reluctance and eventual refusal to fund the proposed Polish coal loan was an attempt by the Bank to punish Poland for its failure to pay in its subscription (despite the fact that other nations were also still in arrears) and for its faithful rendering of the Soviet line, both within the Bank and Fund and in the U.N. Poland's criticisms of Bank independence and its support of the PRC were perceived by the Bank as examples of the "Soviet line." IBRD behavior was also an effort to induce Poland to make at least some visible change in its foreign policy. Thus, the Bank was quite explicit in its explanation that it was the lack of Polish independence from the Soviet Union which led to a negative evaluation of the Polish loan.

Political considerations entered the Bank's decision not to lend to Poland during the period 1946-1950 in the evaluation stage. The fact-finding team sent to Poland in the summer of 1947 was specifically instructed to consider Poland's relationship with the Soviet Union in evaluating Polish economic conditions. The Bank's new definition of creditworthiness enabled the Bank to ignore the prohibition in its charter against consideration of political factors and include Polish-Soviet relations as an economic factor in the Polish economy. During the subsequent loan negotiations in Washington, D.C., it was the hostile attitude of one member, the U.S., and Polish comments at the Annual Meeting which contributed in great measure to the Bank's decision not to finance the coal proposal.

Poland's political attributes as a member of the Soviet Bloc placed it in the political arena of Bank and Fund lending operations almost from the beginning in 1946. Ensuing Polish foreign policy reinforced Poland's position in the political arena as is evidenced by the importance of Polish lack of independence in the evaluation of, and eventual rejection of, the Polish coal loan. Transfer of Poland to the technocratic arena would have required either a major shift in Polish foreign policy (and a monumental change in Polish political reality) or a redefinition of the 1946-1950 boundary between the two arenas. Given the mutual suspicions and lack of precedents which characterized the early Cold War period, it is difficult to imagine either alternative as a realistic possibility.

Czechoslovakia: Cold War Antagonisms

Czechoslovakia actively participated in the creation of the IMF and the IBRD at both Bretton Woods and at the earlier meeting in Atlantic City, New Jersey. Although like Poland its government was not communist at the time of the U.N. Monetary and Financial Conference in 1944, Czechoslovakia shared many of the problems and concerns of the Soviet Union. Like Poland and the U.S.S.R., Czechoslovakia's initial motive for entering into the discussions at Bretton Woods was to encourage the other participants to provide for reconstruction relief for those nations which had been devastated by the war, including Czechoslovakia itself. Accordingly, Czechoslovakia supported Alternative B to the Fund's Article III, Section 3(d) which provided that war-damaged states could postpone payment of a portion of their quotas for a period not exceeding nine months (Bretton Woods, pp. 25, 233, 628). As was noted above, this alternative was accepted in part.

The Czech delegation also suggested a revision in the waiver clause (IMF, Article V, Section 4). Article V, Section 4 permitted the Fund to waive the requirements governing the maximum a member may draw from the Fund. Passage of the Czech revision would have put more funds at the disposal of the war-damaged countries. This revision instructed the Fund to take into account the *"exceptional requirements of members* and also their records of avoiding large or continuous use of the Fund's resources" (Bretton Woods, p. 555, author's emphasis). The underscored portion, which is the Czechs' revision, was not accepted by the other delegations as part of the Final Act, although subsequent Fund behavior revealed no apparent reluctance by that organization to grant waivers in the early post-war period. Eight months later the U.S. revealed another effort of the Czechs to increase available assistance for reconstruction. Apparently, the Czech delegation was instrumental in "inducing" agreement on emergency financing of "commodity exports to war-devastated nations whose essential inventories had been wiped out by the enemy" (NYT 3/14/45).

In Commission II at Bretton Woods (on the proposal for the IBRD), the Czechs continued to pursue their reconstruction goal. As part of the discussions on the purposes of the IBRD (Article I (i)(v)), Czechoslovakia submitted Alternative F which, in addition to exhorting the Bank to provide capital for sound and constructive international investment, instructed the Bank to "facilitate smooth transition from war to peace by increasing the flow of international investment" (Bretton Woods, pp. 368–369). Czechoslovakia's motives were especially apparent in their support of Alternative H to Bank Article III, Section 4. The Czechs proposed that particularly during the early post-war period the Bank make loans for reconstruction and *recovery* purposes which would give war-devastated members some "breathing space" (Bretton Woods, p. 378). This proposal resembles the Polish idea of giving war-damaged states an "even chance for development."

In spite of the relative lack of success of the Czech suggestions at Bretton Woods, the Czechs signed the Bretton Woods agreement as an original member, prior to the December 31, 1945 deadline (NYT 12/28/45). At the first meeting of the Bank and Fund in Savannah, Georgia on March 8, 1946, Dr. Jan Viktor Mladek, Czech Minister of Finance, anxiously urged other members at the Savannah meeting to recognize the "'realities' of different social and economic institutions in various countries and not to overlook these 'fundamental differences'" (NYT 3/9/46). Conceivably, this statement was one of the reasons that Czechs took a leading role with the support of the U.S., Poland, and Yugoslavia in extending the period for original membership to December, 1946, in order to give reluctant participants from Bretton Woods, particularly the U.S.S.R., more time to evaluate membership in the IMF and the IBRD (NYT 3/14/46).

Czechoslovakia and Poland joined the U.S. in promoting Washington, D.C. as the future headquarters of both the World Bank and the IMF (Horsefield, p. 130). The controversy over Bank and Fund agreements with the U.N. provided another indication of Czechoslovakia's willingness to cooperate with other Bretton Woods supporters in the early years of Bank and Fund operations. A Czech, Dr. Jan Papanek, chaired the ECOSOC special committee which agreed to the major principles of the U.N.-IMF and U.N.-IBRD accords, especially the provision in which the U.N. agreed to waive its rights to make recommendations on Bank and Fund loans (NYT 8/16/47). When the issue came to a vote in the September, 1947 session of ECOSOC, Czechoslovakia abstained (Mason and Asher, p. 54).

Czechoslovakia also benefited from some of the concessions made at Bretton Woods. Czechoslovakia was one of the six war-damaged countries permitted to defer part of their subscription payments to the Fund and the Bank for five years. In fact, Czechoslovakia was one of only two states which were given special consideration and allowed to defer the full 2 percent of its initial subscription payment under Article II, Section 8(a) (the four remaining countries deferring payments deferred only 1/2 of 1 percent) (NYT 8/31/46). As a war-damaged state, Czechoslovakia profited from two of the concessions won at Bretton Woods, and Bank and Fund membership appeared to the Czechs to be justified.

The Czechs attempted to realize their second goal, World Bank loans to restore the ravaged Czech economy, in the summer of 1946. In August, 1946, Czechoslovakia applied for a reconstruction loan of $350 million from the World Bank. It was the second application for assistance made to the Bank, and Bank officials requested Czechoslovakia to supply the necessary data (NYT 8/29/46; Mason and Asher, p. 171). As "prolonged and serious negotiations" (Mason and Asher, p. 171) continued a year later, the proposed loan was eagerly discussed in Prague newspapers with no reference to the possibility of "enslavement"—a concern expressed by the Soviet Union at Bretton Woods (NYT 4/28/47). Failure of the Czechs to furnish information with respect to their plans for spending the loan funds and strong signs of recovery in the Czech economy in 1946 hampered progress in the negotiations between the Czech government and the IBRD (NYT 3/3/48, 4/28/48).

The Beginning of Conflict

As the brief description provided above indicates, Czechoslovakia's conflicts with the Bank and Fund began soon after those organizations commenced their operations and continued until Czechoslovakia withdrew from the Bank and Fund in 1954. In the following account, Czech problems with the IMF and the IBRD are examined individually rather than chronologically since many of Czechoslovakia's conflicts with the two organizations, while occurring simultaneously, were actually separate issues. The sources of the Czech controversy in the Bank and Fund are examined in detail in the following order:

1. The Communist coup of February, 1948
2. Czech criticisms expressed during Bank and Fund annual meetings
3. Czech failure to complete its World Bank subscription
4. Revaluation of the koruna
5. Changes in the value of the Fund's account in korunas
6. Provision of required information to the IMF

A Communist coup in Czechoslovakia in February, 1948, effectively brought negotiations on the Czech loan to a standstill. Immediately after assuming power, the new Communist regime began to institute reforms which would ultimately transform the Czech political and economic system into a model Soviet-style system with democratic centralism and central planning as the organizing principles. Czech foreign policy throughout the post-war period had been staunchly pro-Soviet; therefore, Czechoslovakia after February, 1948 was an almost perfect example of a Soviet-style Communist regime.[12]

IBRD President McCloy, when asked about the status of the Czech loan after the coup, demurred by stating that although World Bank action on the loan had been "impaired" by the coup, it was still under consideration. He revealed that the Bank had been considering sending a fact-finding mission to Czechoslovakia (an essential step in the lending process) but that decision had been postponed pending a detailed investigation of post-coup Czech conditions (NYT 3/3/48).

There were significant pressures, both internal and external to the Bank, which opposed a loan to Communist Czechoslovakia. In addition to doubts about Czech independence from the Soviet Union,[13] there was some concern that a World Bank loan to post-coup Czechoslovakia "would enable her to finance the reorientation of her trade in heavy industrial goods to the East, particularly to the Soviet Union" (NYT 11/2/47). In effect, a World Bank loan would give Czechoslovakia, in this view, the ability to pay for its raw material imports from the West with money instead of exports, leaving Czechoslovakian exports free to be employed in the Soviet Union's reconstruction effort. Other sources in the West also worried that the loan would facilitate Czech nationalization of foreign-owned business interests (NYT 11/2/47). It is interesting that the Czech rejoinder to these expressions of apprehension did not include a criticism of their essentially political nature, but merely responded in kind by asserting that credits were essential to Czech trade with the West and would actually prevent the Czech economy from absorption by the East (NYT 11/2/47).

More damaging to the future of the Czech loan was the impact that the Communist coup had on individual members of the Bank whose cooperation was necessary to the success of the project, if and when it was approved. For example, inability to come to an agreement with importing countries after the February coup led Czechoslovakia to withdraw from a multi-member timber project proposal under consideration by the World Bank (Mason and Asher, p. 168). The strong, negative reaction of the U.S. to the Czech coup was even more detrimental to the prospects for a Bank loan to Czechoslovakia. Aside from Bank concern about the reaction of U.S. investors in Bank securities,[14] it was generally rumored in Washington, D.C. "that the new Prague Government . . . had far less chance than its predecessor of receiving" the loan from the Bank (NYT 2/27/48), because, as some U.S. officials privately declared, the U.S. reaction against the coup was so strong that U.S. "action to put a general barrier to all economic aid to a Prague under Communist control was quite likely" (NYT 2/27/48). In an attempt to forestall accusations of violation of its charter in the face of these obviously noneconomic objections to the Czech loan, World Bank President McCloy asserted that the definition of economic criteria included political events and political criteria when those political factors were likely to affect a member's ability to meet its obligations to the Bank.[15]

The proposed World Bank loan was not the Czechs' only source of funds stemming from its participation at Bretton Woods. According to the Fund's *Articles of Agreement*, any member in good standing with the Fund had automatic access to an amount equal to 25 percent of its quota, the gold or reserve tranche. In 1948, as the prospects of a World Bank loan rapidly disappeared, Czechoslovakia availed itself of a portion of its reserve tranche ($6 million) to meet a temporary balance of payments crisis (NYT 1/6/55; Horsefield, p. 226). Aside from declaring Czechoslovakia ineligible to use Fund resources, there was virtually nothing the IMF could have done to prevent Czech use of the reserve tranche, even if it had desired to do so.

Czech Proposals and Their Effects

Soon after Czechoslovakia's transition to a Communist government, relations between Czechoslovakia and the Bretton Woods organizations began to deteriorate. Evidence of Czech displeasure with the Bank and the Fund began to surface at the annual meetings of both organizations. At the 1948 Annual Meeting of the Bank and Fund, Czechoslovakia joined Poland and Yugoslavia in criticizing the apparent preoccupation of the Bank and Fund with the problems of Western Europe and the "insufficient attention" paid to the recovery of the Eastern European economies (NYT 9/29/48). Although Czechoslovakia gave "qualified approval" to the annual reports of the two organizations (NYT 9/29/48), it charged that both reports contained material that was "politically motivated" and that political considerations had actually entered the consideration of Eastern European applications for reconstruction assistance (NYT 9/30/48). At the 1949 annual meetings, Czechoslovakia vigorously objected to the across-the-board devaluation of currencies then being recommended by the IMF[16] and suggested public sessions to give members an opportunity to air publicly their opinions on the devaluation dispute (NYT 9/14/49). Czechoslovakia was fast becoming the outspoken leader for dissatisfied members within the IMF and IBRD.

Czechoslovakia pursued one of its special interests as a communist country in its continual championing of the PRC in the Bank and Fund between 1950 and 1954. In February, 1950, the Executive Director representing Czechoslovakia, Poland and Yugoslavia (a Czech), objected to the Governor and Executive Director for China and claimed that only the Communist government of the Peoples' Republic of China had the right to represent China in both the Bank and Fund. The issue was sent to the Board of Governors which rejected the motion.[17] With that decision, Mr. Sucharda, the Executive Director who initiated the challenge, withdrew from any further participation in the Executive Directors or annual meetings (Gold, *Membership*, pp. 67–68; Horsefield, p. 258).

The Czech delegation resubmitted the proposal to unseat the Nationalist Chinese to the entire Bank and Fund membership at the September, 1950, annual meetings. Yugoslavia, Poland, and India joined Czechoslovakia in supporting the proposal which was soundly defeated after the Philippines suggested that the motion was out of order due to its purely political nature (Horsefield, pp. 258–259; NYT 12/30/53). "Fireworks" erupted (NYT 9/11/51) when the Czech representative, Jaroslav Docekal, introduced another motion to replace the Nationalist Chinese on the premise that 500 million Chinese had rejected the Nationalists in favor of the Communist-led PRC (NYT 9/11/51). The motion was supported by Ceylon and India but was vigorously opposed by the U.S., U.K., China, and the Philippines as "wholly provocative in purpose" (NYT 9/11/51; Horsefield, p. 259). The membership of the IMF and IBRD voted, 43-3, to "postpone indefinitely" consideration of the motion, effectively defeating it (NYT 9/11/51).

During the 1951 annual meetings Czechoslovakia sought to advance further the PRC's cause. The Czechs attempted to convince other members to pass a vote of censure of the U.S. on the grounds that the U.S. trade embargo of Communist China was in violation of the Bretton Woods agreements. In retaliation the U.S. representative "reminded" the Czechs that they still owed a significant portion of their subscription to the World Bank. The Czechs' motion was referred to the Executive Directors where it died (NYT 9/13/51).

Czech dissatisfaction sounded again at the 1952 annual meetings. The Czechs repeated the charge of the Bank's "complete subservience" to U.S. foreign policy (NYT 9/5/52) and renewed their efforts to oust Taiwan. The Czechs' allies on this unsuccessful occasion were India and Burma. At the 1954 annual meetings the, by now, familiar Czech motion to expel the Nationalist Chinese was accompanied by a U.S. motion to expel Czechoslovakia (see discussion below).

By 1953, Czechoslovakia's position in the IMF and IBRD had deteriorated. In December of that year Czechoslovakia became the first country declared ineligible by the Fund to use its resources.[18] At approximately the same time, the World Bank threatened Czechoslovakia with involuntary suspension for failing to pay in the remaining portion of its subscription. The Czechs' disagreements with both the Fund and the Bank were not resolved and in December, 1954, Czechoslovakia was expelled from both organizations.

Expulsion from the IBRD

Czechoslovakia's problems with the World Bank were focused on its failure to pay in the remaining $625 thousand of its capital subscription within the five-year period allotted to it. In 1946, Czechoslovakia requested a five-year postponement of the payment of 0.5 percent of its capital subscription to the World Bank due to economic difficulties stemming from World War II (NYT 12/30/53). The Bank discussed the problem of the Czech "default" of the 0.5 percent in 1951 but took no action at that time (NYT 12/30/53). During the 1951 investigation of the Czechs' failure to meet this obligation, the Bank claimed that Czechoslovakia was in default for failing to complete its subscription within the five years as required in the Bank's *Articles* (Article II, Section 8(a)(i)). Czechoslovakia countered this claim by arguing that in terms of Article II, Section 8(a) (ii), there was no time limit specified for the payment of the remaining 0.5 percent.

Matters came to a climax at the September, 1953 meeting when Bank officials set December 31, 1953 as the deadline for payment of the subscription after which Czechoslovakia would be suspended from membership (NYT 9/10/53, 9/13/53). As of January 5, 1954, the World Bank had received no communication whatsoever from Czechoslovakia and informed Czech authorities that failure to make payment by 12/31/54 would result in expulsion (NYT 1/2/54, 1/5/54). Suspension from the Bank meant that Czechoslovakia could not participate in Bank business and could not receive any funds from that organization. Czechoslovakia had no outstanding loans or loan applications with the Bank at the time, and there were no Czech nationals employed at the Bank. The Czechs had withdrawn from active participation in the Bank in 1951 (as a result of the dispute over PRC membership) so that suspension did not significantly alter Czech plans (NYT 1/5/54). The IBRD expelled Czechoslovakia from membership on December 31, 1954, citing failure to complete its capital subscription as the reason for expulsion.

Expulsion from the IMF

At the end of May, 1953, the Czech government undertook a "drastic" revaluation of the koruna to counter inflation. The revaluation was particularly hard on bank accounts, including the Fund's account in korunas (NYT 5/31/53; Gold, *Membership*, p. 345). In addition to countering inflation, the currency reform had two, more political purposes. The revaluation of the koruna virtually eliminated the value of Czech currency held by what the regime considered to be the anti-communist middle class, the wealthy, and hoarders (NYT 5/31/53). A "new" currency was created by designating a series of exchange rates which varied from 50:1 to 5:1 old korunas to new korunas (NYT 5/31/53). The exchange rate for external or foreign transactions was also changed, appreciating from 50 korunas per $1 U.S. to 7.2 korunas per $1 U.S. All of this was accomplished without prior consultation with the Fund as was required in Article IV. The controversy which subsequently erupted between Czechoslovakia and the Fund centered on two issues: Did the change in the value of the koruna affect Czechoslovakia's international transactions with other members and was Czechoslovakia required to consult with the Fund in either case (Horsefield, p. 359)?

Czech officials argued that the change in the value of the koruna had no effect on its international transactions with other members of the Fund because Czech trade was state-controlled and not governed by world prices (Horsefield, p. 360). Thus, the prices used in Czech foreign trade were arbitrarily set through negotiations between Czechoslovakia and its trading partners and were not necessarily based on prevailing world prices. Czechoslovakia also explained that the majority of its trade transactions were also conducted solely in foreign currencies so that the value of the koruna was irrelevant. The Czechs then cited Article IV, Section 5(e) of the Fund's charter, which read:

(e) A member may change the par value of its currency without the concurrence of the Fund if the change does not affect the international transactions of members of the Fund (IMF, *Articles of Agreement*, p. 6),

to support its contention that consultation with the Fund was not necessary since, as was described above, a change in the value of the koruna was purely of internal concern (Gold, *Membership*, p. 353). In fact, Czechoslovakia argued, Section 5(e) of Article IV was "included in the *Articles* in order to make membership available to socialist economies" (Gold, *Membership*, p. 353) which needed the flexibility contained in that section to realign their economies periodically.

The Czechs claimed further that the clause "does not affect" in Article IV, Section 5(e) actually meant "does not *adversely* affect," and as none of its trading partners was complaining, Czechoslovakia assumed that none of them had been adversely affected (Horsefield, p. 360). As for the question of whether Czechoslovakia should have consulted the Fund, i.e., whether Article IV, Section 5(e) applied or not, Czechoslovakia contended that

"The Fund had only such jurisdiction as had been conferred on it by the agreement of sovereign states, and if there was doubt about the meaning of a provision, it must be interpreted in a way that favored sovereign rights" (Gold, *Membership*, p. 352).

The Fund rejected Czechoslovakia's interpretation of Article IV, Section 5(e) and noted that the absence of complaints by Czechoslovakia's trading partners did *not* indicate the absence of adverse effects. The Fund asserted that, in fact, revaluation of the koruna would have a negative impact on trade in invisibles between Czechoslovakia and other Fund members (Gold, *Membership*, p. 359). Fund officials also refuted the Czech's argument that the revaluation of the koruna fell under the provision of Article IV, Section 5(e) at all. The Fund persisted in interpreting the Czech action in light of Section 5(f) of Article IV which stated:

(f) The Fund shall concur in a proposed change . . . if it is satisfied that the change is necessary to correct a fundamental disequilibrium (in the balance of payments). In particular, provided it is so satisfied, it shall not object to a proposed change because of the domestic social or political policies of the member proposing the change (*Articles of Agreement*, p. 6).

The Fund argued that the Czech change in the koruna might have been considered a move to correct a fundamental disequilibrium in its balance of payments *if* it had not also been accompanied by a change in the relative price structure.[19] Even if the price structure had not been altered, the Fund continued, the Fund could not determine whether the devaluation was necessary to correct a fundamental disequilibrium because Czechoslovakia had not provided any economic data which the Fund could have used to evaluate the situation (Horsefield, p. 360). A request for such information was tendered to Czechoslovakia by the Fund at the end of 1953 (Horsefield, p. 360).

Czechoslovakia's revaluation of the koruna also generated several related problems in its dispute with the Fund. The change from "old money" to "new" created a definitional problem which complicated Czechoslovakia's relations with the Fund. On August 14, 1953, 2 1/2 months after the revaluation of the koruna, the Czech State Bank informed the Fund that its account in korunas had been devalued, as had all Czech bank accounts (Gold, *Membership*, p. 346). In response to the Fund's immediate and vigorous objections, Czechoslovakia restored the Fund's account in "old" money (Horsefield, p. 361). The Fund continued to object to this "ambiguous response" (Horsefield, p. 361) since the actual value of "old" korunas was unclear and thus, the Fund was unsure whether the value of its account had actually been restored.

The value of "new" korunas again came into question when the Czechs made payments on their loan charges in "new" korunas (Horsefield, p. 360). Since the Fund had not recognized, or accepted, the Czech revaluation, it considered the "new" koruna a "non-existent currency," and therefore, not acceptable as payment on loan charges (Gold, *Membership*, p. 350). As a result, Czechoslovakia was considered in default for failing to pay the last two quarterly installments of its loan charges (Gold, *Membership*, p. 346).

Revaluation of the koruna not only revealed Czech and Fund differences in the interpretation of Article IV, Section 5(e), but also created doubts about the meaning of Article VIII, Section 5, on the provision of information (*Articles of Agreement*, p. 18). As was mentioned earlier in this section, the Fund felt that it was unable to determine whether the koruna's revaluation was necessary because Czechoslovakia had not complied with Article VIII, Section 5 in furnishing the Fund with information about its economy. Czechoslovakia explained that its refusal to provide information about its economy was due to reasons of national security. Czechoslovakia also claimed that, since all Czech international trade was conducted by a single organization, providing the required information would have actually violated Section 5(b) of Article VIII which excused members from providing information "in such detail that the affairs of individuals or corporations are disclosed."[20] At four meetings of the Executive Directors, the Fund rejected the second of Czechoslovakia's defenses, and debated whether national security was indeed a sufficient justification for withholding the required information (Horsefield, p. 363).

In defense of its position, Czechoslovakia referred to an earlier case in which a member was permitted to violate one of the Fund's *Articles* on the grounds of national security. In 1950, the United States imposed restrictions on payments to the PRC and North Korea as part of its actions against those countries during the Korean War. The U.S. action was in violation of Article VIII, Section 3. The U.S. justified its position by citing the precedents set in GATT and the ITO[21] and by claiming its sovereign rights. Frank J. Southard, Jr., the U.S. appointed Executive Director, contended that

> "a financial authority such as the Board (of Governors of the IMF) was not a suitable forum for the evaluation of the need for restrictions on security grounds. He suggested that the Fund should merely note his Government's action. . . ." (Horsefield, p. 175).

The Fund yielded to the arguments of the U.S. but devised a policy to guide Fund actions toward future violations of Article VIII. The new policy required that violations of Article VIII observe the following procedure: (1) inform the Fund's Managing Director in advance of applying restrictions; (2) the Managing Director would then advise the Executive Directors of the member's decision and its reasons for applying restrictions; (3) if the member was not informed by the Fund to cease restrictions within 30 days, the member would not be considered in violation of Article VIII; and (4) the Fund reserved the right to review periodically the member's decision and to recommend changes in that decision (Horsefield, p. 276). With respect to Czechoslovakia, the Fund found that the Czech situation differed from the U.S. decision in 1950 in that the Czechs had not complied with (1) of the new policy—giving the Fund the opportunity to judge in advance whether the refusal to provide information was warranted by the circumstances (Horsefield, p. 363).

This controversy over the provision of data under IMF Article VIII, Section 5 was intimately related to growing hostility between Czechoslovakia and the United States. It was the U.S. Executive Director, F.J.

Southard, Jr., who initiated the procedure to declare Czechoslovakia ineligible to use Fund resources on September 4, 1953, claiming that Czechoslovakia had failed to fulfill its obligations to the Fund and therefore, was eligible for compulsory withdrawal (under IMF Article XV, Section 2(a); *Articles*, p. 30). Other Executive Directors appeared to view the U.S. proposal as precipitous and sought to resolve matters with Czechoslovakia. The U.S. responded by broadening its case against Czechoslovakia to include not only the Czech default on loan charges but the Czech failure to consult the Fund on the change in the value of the koruna and its refusal to provide information on its exports, imports, balance of payments, national income, and price indices (Horsefield, p. 362). On November 4, 1953, the U.S. successfully pursued the issue of Czechoslovakia's ineligibility in the Executive Directors meeting (Horsefield, p. 361).

The decision to declare Czechoslovakia ineligible on November 4, 1953 was achieved by a vote of the Fund's Board of Governors. The final tally was 86,665 votes to 0 for ineligibility, with three Governors abstaining who were entitled to cast a total of 12,700 votes (Gold, *Membership*, p. 367; Horsefield, p. 361). Since decisions in the Fund's Board of Governors were (and are) usually made according to the "sense of the meeting,"[22] the fact that the Czech ineligibility decision prompted a formal vote testified to the seriousness with which the Board of Governors regarded the issue. As in the Bank, Czechoslovakia was given until December 31, 1954 to settle the outstanding issues in its disagreements with Fund or it would be expelled (Horsefield, p. 363; NYT 9/29/54). Only Czechoslovakia and India opposed this decision; Burma, Ceylon, Finland, Iceland, Indochina, Iran, Jordan, Lebanon, and Yugoslavia abstained from voting on this measure (NYT 9/29/54).

The Czech delegate, Julius Hajck, offered data on Czech national income but claimed that Czechoslovakia hadn't calculated price indices and thus, was unable to provide such data to the Fund.[23] He then invoked national security as a reason to justify withholding the remainder of the data mentioned by the U.S. Executive Director. Mr. Hajck alleged that provision of such information "would aid the United States in pursuing its 'hostile' trade policy" toward Czechoslovakia and would contribute to the "economic cold war" then being waged against members of the Soviet bloc (Gold, *Membership*, p. 356; NYT 9/29/54). Czechoslovakia argued that international law entitled it to defend itself against such aggressive and discriminatory actions (Gold, *Membership*, p. 362). The U.S. representative continued to discount the Czechs' defenses, however, arguing that the provision of data was an obligation of membership that was essential to the operation of the Fund (NYT 9/29/54).

On September 28, 1954, on a motion by the U.S., the Board of Governors of the IMF voted to expel Czechoslovakia from membership, effective December 31, 1954, if Czechoslovakia had not fulfilled its obligations to the Fund by that time.[24] The role of the U.S. Executive Director in both motions against Czechoslovakia indicated the deteriorating state of Czech-U.S. relations, and the U.S. can certainly be considered a contributing factor to the Czechs' ultimate withdrawal from the IMF. The Czechs made no further progress in its disputes with the Fund and was consequently expelled on the date stipulated in the motion (NYT 1/6/55). The Czech government refused to recognize this action and sent a letter to the Bank and Fund withdrawing voluntarily (Horsefield, p. 363). As in the Polish case, the five Czech members of the Fund's staff were retained (Horsefield, p. 363). Eighteen months had passed since the beginning of Czechoslovakia's disputes with the IMF.

Analysis and Summary

Czechoslovakia's relations with the IMF and the IBRD were an excellent example of the influences on lending policy of political variables in the Bank and Fund's environment which were not directly related to Bank and Fund operations. Early Czech transactions with the Fund and the World Bank, prior to the coup in 1948, had been relatively free of conflict, and Czechoslovakia seemed confident that its reason for joining the two organizations would be realized. Deterioration in Czech relations with the Bretton Woods organizations occurred simultaneously with the Czech Communist coup in February, 1948 and the intensification of the Cold War between Czechoslovakia and the United States.

The issues which formed the core of Czechoslovakia's problems with the IMF and the World Bank illustrated the contradictions of including state-trading members in two international organizations created along primarily market lines. These contradictions, which surfaced during the Bretton Woods conference, had never been completely eliminated, despite Soviet input into all important discussions. The attitude toward participation of state-trading countries in the Bank and the Fund had undergone a significant shift since Bretton Woods, however, and this was evident in the way the Bank and the Fund interpreted those articles included in their charters specifically to ease state-trading membership.

Three articles of the charters of the Bretton Woods organizations which the Soviet Union had been particularly instrumental in composing were at the heart of the Czech controversy: Fund Article IV, Section 5, on changes in par values; Article VIII, Section 5, on the provision of information; and Bank and Fund *Articles*, Article III, Section 3, on the payments of subscriptions. The wording of these articles was ambiguous; this permitted the Bank and Fund to interpret these articles in a manner detrimental to Czechoslovakia in 1954, and, in all probability, contrary to the intent of Bretton Woods. The interpretation of the Bank and Fund was certainly contrary to the intent of the Soviet Union during the conference.

Czechoslovakia's problems with the Bank and Fund were concentrated around the default, provision of information, and change of exchange rate issues. Yet Czechoslovakia was not the first country to confront the Bank and Fund with these problems.[25] For example, at the time that the World Bank was investigating whether Czechoslovakia was in default on the remaining portion of its capital subscription, Nationalist China also had not paid in its entire capital subscription (NYT 12/30/53). As discussed above, the U.S. had violated one of the Fund's articles in 1950. The procedure which was devised by the Fund to deal with future violations of Article VIII did not address the principal issue from which it had arisen: the U.S. violation of Article VIII. In essence, the procedure was merely a rubber stamp for U.S. misconduct. Czechoslovakia's status as a state-trading nation further complicated the information issue. In order for the Fund to determine whether the Czech national security defense was justified, the Fund would have needed some of the very information the Czechs were withholding, and the Czechs would not release this information as long as the U.S., which the Czechs considered to be the biggest threat to their national security, had access to such information. It was a stalemate which the Fund did not seem very anxious to break.

Finally, Czechoslovakia's insistence on its sovereign right to change the value of the koruna reflected the French argument of only six years before. The French refusal to comply with the Fund's demands resulted in the automatic ineligibility of France to use Fund resources. France remained ineligible for *four* years. Czech became ineligible to use the Fund's resources after only six months and was expelled a year later, despite its concessions and continual efforts to resolve the conflict. Clearly, Czechoslovakia's problems with the Fund were not unusual, yet the consequence of those problems *was* unusual—Czechoslovakia was the only case of compulsory withdrawal from the IMF and IBRD between 1946 and 1986.

Czechoslovakia's problems with the Fund and the Bank originated in a combination of its ascriptive and behavioral characteristics. The question of the effect on the international economy of changes in the internal structure of the Czech economy was intricately connected with Czechoslovakia's ascriptive position as a state-trading economy. The Fund rejected the Czech argument that the reevaluation of the koruna did not affect its international transactions on the basis of transactions in invisibles which could only be a very small part of its trade, which is monopolized by the state. Czechoslovakia's status as a Communist country after 1948 also affected its treatment in the Bank and Fund. In the eyes of the Bank, Czechoslovakia was no longer a good credit risk, and therefore, was practically ineligible for reconstruction assistance, at least for the period in which it was most needed.

Given the issues with the Soviet Union at Bretton Woods, Czechoslovakia's (and Poland's) status as a state-trading national almost insured that Czechoslovakia would have problems with the Fund. The centralized nature of a state-trading, centrally-planned economy was inconsistent (but not necessarily incompatible) with the structure of the international economy that was envisioned at Bretton Woods. The *Articles* of the Fund, in particular, contained many regulations which pertained to market-type economies, but there were few, if any, references to procedures found in state-trading countries. Centrally-planned economies were expected to adapt themselves as best they could to the international economic system founded at the U.N. Monetary and Financial Conference, and when the inconsistencies of these arrangements in their application to centrally-planned economies became apparent, procedures were altered to make them consistent with capitalist methods, as the Czech case demonstrates.

A behavioral characteristic, Czech relations with the U.S., had the greatest impact on Czech success, or lack of success, in the Bretton Woods organizations. The mutual suspicion and hostility between Czechoslovakia and the U.S., which was perhaps the most influential member of both the Bank and the Fund at the time, generated in part the conflict which led to the Czechs' ouster. In particular, Czechoslovakia's refusal to supply certain economic information was a direct consequence of the Czechs' perception of U.S. hostility. The Cold War had once again penetrated the Fund and the Bank.

Czechoslovakia's alliance with the Soviet Union was a part of its foreign policy which Czechoslovakia could not change and in this context, should be considered as an ascriptive characteristic. Like Poland, Czechoslovakia had little choice but to maintain close and friendly relations with the Soviet Union. It is unclear today whether the Czech population would have continued to support a Communist regime without the threat of Soviet interference. In any case, Czechoslovakia could not have changed its relationship with the Soviet Union, and as a result, the Bank estimated that the probability of a Soviet-ordered Czech default was at least high enough to warrant extreme caution.

Political considerations thus entered Bank and Fund lending decisions with respect to Czechoslovakia at the evaluation, negotiation, and final decision stages, with the usual result being a decision *not* to lend. In this sense, the Bank used its refusal to extend assistance to Czechoslovakia as a means of punishing Czechoslovakia for its alliance with the Soviet Union and its hostility to the U.S. and as a means of inducing the Czechs to change at least their behavior toward the U.S. It is unlikely that Bank and Fund members and officials believed that Czech relations with the Soviet Union could have been substantially altered due to the strong position of the Czech Communist Party at that time and the presence of at least a marginal amount of support for the regime in the Czech population. Czechoslovakia, then, provides a clear example of the influence of political inputs, particularly foreign policy, into Bank and Fund decisions to lend.

The Cold War in the Bank and the Fund

The failure of the Bank and Fund to adapt to the requirements and problems of their state-trading members was due to essentially political factors. The Bretton Woods agreements provided little guidance for the fledgling organizations in their disagreements with Poland and Czechoslovakia, and as a result, what ambiguities existed in the *Articles of Agreement* were resolved in a manner consistent with the beliefs and training of Bank and Fund staff and the majority of Bank and Fund members. Even when the objective economic conditions in the Soviet-style Communist members seemed favorable, the Bank and Fund's emphasis on lending to only "good risks" worked to exclude loans to their pro-Soviet members (NYT 8/16/47) since those countries could not guarantee that Soviet actions would not interfere with their efforts to meet their obligations to the IMF and IBRD. This fact was especially true in the Polish and Czech cases in the early Bank and Fund years.

U.S. foreign policy also had an impact on Fund and Bank perceptions of their Soviet-style Communist members. Contrary to the beliefs of the IMF (Gold, *Voting*, p. 5), the Cold War *did* intrude upon the operations of the Fund and Bank through the actions of the U.S., the member with the largest subscription, quota, and votes in both organizations (NYT 8/16/47). U.S. conflicts with the Soviet Union and Czechoslovakia in the U.N. and other arenas appeared in decisions of the Bretton Woods organizations when the U.S. opposed loans to Poland and Czechoslovakia from 1948 to 1950 and pushed for the expulsion of Czechoslovakia in 1954 despite evidence that the Czechs' actions were not without precedents in the IMF and IBRD. The majority of the *Articles of Agreement* did not benefit the state-trading members of the Bank and the Fund.

The Bretton Woods agreements seem to be the only instance of reverse influence involving Poland and Czechoslovakia. The provisions on payment of subscriptions and quotas, provision of information, and reconstruction aid were altered at the specific request of the Communist countries represented at the U.N. Monetary and Financial Conference. Despite these concessions to the Soviet Bloc, at no time during the conference were any of the organizers' (the U.S. and the U.K.) fundamental principles abandoned in response to a Communist request. During the early years of Bank and Fund operations even the few concessions noted above were strictly interpreted so that the amount of influence wielded over Bank and Fund operations by Poland and Czechoslovakia was actually minimal.

Ascriptive factors appear to have had the greatest influence on Fund and World Bank policy in these two cases. The structure of their economies and their pro-Soviet foreign policy alignment firmly placed the Soviet-style members of the Bretton Woods organizations in the political arena of decision-making and hampered their attempts to gain reconstruction aid. Foreign policy and economic structure were factors which these members could not alter.

Behavioral characteristics of these Communist members reinforced their placement in the political arena. Polish and Czech relations with the leading member of the IMF and IBRD, the U.S., were at least theoretically flexible, and it was these countries' continual conflicts with the U.S. which placed them in the political arena. To some extent, however, these countries' relations with the U.S. were constrained by the wishes of their strongest ally and patron, the U.S.S.R.

It can be concluded from this analysis that it was the primarily ascriptive characteristics of the Soviet-style Communist members which led to their lack of success in the IMF and the IBRD. Economic structure and foreign policy alignment were at the root of the Polish and Czech controversies in the Fund and Bank. These were inalterable facts of Eastern European reality in the years immediately after World War II, and thus, it was highly unlikely that a shift in the boundary between the technocratic and political arenas would have occurred as a result of a change in either the ascriptive characteristics of these members or in Bank and Fund policy at that time.

The location of the Soviet-style members in the political arena affected Fund and Bank lending policies in the evaluation, negotiation, and final decision stages. Poland and Czechoslovakia were judged as poor investment risks in the evaluations of both the fact-finding mission and staff in Washington, D.C. because of their relationship with the Soviet Union. Negotiations with Czechoslovakia over obligations were defined and influenced by U.S. behavior. In all cases the final decisions were not to the advantage of the Communist members. These decisions not to lend to or to expel the Communist member were in all cases an attempt by the IMF and IBRD to punish these members for their failure to give any indication of less than complete loyalty to the Soviet Union. Refusals to lend may also have been a type of inducement to Poland and Czechoslovakia to change their foreign policies insofar as those refusals to lend were phrased in a manner which indicated that the possibility of Bank and Fund loans had not been completely eliminated, given certain Czech and Polish compromises.

In sum, foreign policy, an ascriptive variable in these cases, appears to be the predominant determinant of the arena into which a Soviet-style Communist member is placed. In these cases, a Soviet-based economic system and a pro-Soviet foreign policy created so many problems within the Bretton Woods system that withdrawal seemed to be the only alternative for Poland and Czechoslovakia. Any conclusions about the effect of a communist ideology and political system on relations with the IMF and the IBRD, however, must be postponed until an investigation of the remaining Soviet Bloc cases is completed in the following chapters.

Notes

1. *Proceedings and Documents of the United Nations Monetary and Financial Conference*, Department of State Publication 2866 (Washington, D.C.: U.S. GPO, 1948), pp. 593, 581, 1233. This publication is hereafter referred to as "Bretton Woods."

2. *New York Times* (NYT), 9/2/46.

3. *Articles of Agreement of the International Monetary Fund and International Bank for Reconstruction and Development* (Washington, D.C.: U.S. Treasury, 1944), Article II, Section 8(a).

4. Edward S. Mason and Robert E. Asher, *The World Bank Since Bretton Woods* (Washington, D.C.: The Brookings Institution, 1973), p. 170.

5. IBRD, *Annual Report, 1950* (Washington, D.C.: IBRD, 1950).

6. David A. Baldwin, "The International Bank in Political Perspective," *World Politics*, vol. 18 (October 1965), p. 69, and Teresa Hayter, *Aid As Imperalism* (Baltimore, MD: Penguin Books Ltd., 1971), p. 32.

7. Mason and Asher, p. 171. The Fund also defined creditworthiness rather broadly. See the IMF *Annual Report* for 1952 (Washington, D.C.: IMF).

8. Mason and Asher, p. 170. See also NYT 9/7/47, 7/22/47, and 6/11/47.

9. J. Keith Horsefield and Margaret G. deVries, *The International Monetary Fund, 1945–1965* (Washington, D.C.: IMF, 1969), vol. 1, p. 11.

10. Joseph Gold, *Membership and Nonmembership in the International Monetary Fund* (Washington, D.C.: IMF, 1974), p. 68.

11. See also Horsefield, p. 258; NYT 3/16/50; and Gold, *Membership*, p. 342.

12. NYT 5/31/53.

13. See the discussion about the Polish coal loan of this same period, above.

14. See the discussion of the Polish coal loan, above.

15. NYT 2/27/48. See also the discussion on Poland, above.

16. NYT 9/20/49. See also the IMF *Annual Report,* for 1949.

17. NYT 9/25/54.

18. There was a previous case of ineligibility in the Fund. France became *automatically* ineligible to use Fund resources in 1948 when it implemented an unauthorized change in the par value of the franc, a multiple exchange rate system and a number of discriminatory currency arrangements. See IMF *Annual Report* for 1955, p. 88, and Horsefield, pp. 200–204.

Ineligibility proceedings were commenced against Cuba in 1964, but Cuba withdrew before these proceedings were completed. The Fund has avoided the use of the ineligibility provision in the *Articles* due to the suggestion of expulsion which might be implied by such an action. See Gold, *Membership,* p. 481, and IMF, *Articles,* Article V, Section 5.

19. Gold, *Membership,* p. 359. See also NYT 5/31/53 for a discussion of the general reforms instituted in the Czech economy at this time.

20. IMF, *Articles,* p. 18; Horsefield, p. 363; and NYT 9/27/54.

21. GATT—General Agreement on Tariffs and Trade; ITO—International Trade Organization. Horsefield, p. 275.

22. Joseph Gold, *Voting.*

23. Horsefield, p. 362; NYT 9/29/54.

24. NYT 9/29/54. See Gold, *Membership,* p. 360, and Horsefield, p. 362, for more information on the U.S. role in the expulsion of Czechoslovakia.

25. NYT 9/29/54. India made a plea on behalf of Czechoslovakia which "urged the governors to adopt 'an attitude of sympathy and tolerance' as they had done in the past when other countries had failed to fulfill one or another of the articles of agreement" (NYT 9/29/54).

5

Yugoslavia: Market Socialism, the IMF, and the IBRD

Contrary to the predictions of critics of the Bank and Fund, one Soviet Bloc country, Yugoslavia, has maintained a close and cooperative relationship with the IBRD and the IMF during its years of membership. Yugoslavia, an original member of both organizations, received loans from the IBRD which totalled $3102 million in twenty-five years between 1950 and 1984, and received SDR 3262 million in eight SBA loans from the Fund during the same period. Compared to the records of Poland and Czechoslovakia in both organizations, Yugoslavia's relationships with the IMF and IBRD can be considered a "success;" as Chapter 2 has shown, the Yugoslav case also appears successful when compared to other members of the Bank and Fund.

At first glance, there appear to be several factors which might explain Yugoslavia's success in utilizing the resources of the IMF and IBRD. Yugoslavia is noted for its innovative practices in both politics and economics. Yugoslavia set a precedent in both foreign policy and socialist economic practice by first defying the Soviet Union and subsequently devising a unique economic structure combining elements of self-management, socialism and market forces. Its economic structure also incorporates significant elements of a market system and is often cited as an example of economic reform for other socialist states. The following analysis examines the relationship between economic reform (or the relative lack thereof) and Bank and Fund financial assistance to Yugoslavia. Special attention is paid to the timing of such assistance so as to assess whether leverage was employed and if so, what type.

Workers' Self-Management

Yugoslavia, because of its unique economic system of market socialism, is a particularly interesting case for the examination of IMF and IBRD aid leverage in Communist countries. Of all Communist states, Yugoslavia has diverged furthest from the Soviet model. This, coupled with the fact that Yugoslavia has received substantial amounts of aid from both the Bank and Fund, has led at least one analyst of the Fund to conclude that Bank and Fund aid leverage was a significant factor in the construction of Yugoslavia's unique "road to socialism."

There have been two distinct turning points in the evolution of market socialism in Yugoslavia. Worker's self-management was introduced by Tito on January 7, 1950, and reforms necessary to complete the transformation from an administratively-directed economy continued to be passed with increasing frequency until early in 1954.[1] The period 1949–1954 also roughly corresponds to a major shift in Yugoslav foreign policy. On June 28, 1948, the Cominform, led by the Soviet Union, officially ousted Yugoslavia from the Soviet Bloc. This move was soon complemented by a total economic blockade which effectively halted Yugoslavia's ambitious industrialization program. It was at this point, July, 1948, that Tito turned to Western sources, including the Bank and Fund, for aid. Bilateral and multilateral aid from the non-communist West was Yugoslavia's only source of economic (and military) aid until relations with the Soviet Union were repaired in 1954.

A second period of major reform in the Yugoslav economy occurred between 1960–1965.[2] The goals of the initial stage of reforms in the 1950s had been exceeded for the most part (Yugoslavia had one of the highest growth rates in the world in the 1950s), but several inconsistencies and problems also had appeared which exposed the deficiencies in the first set of reforms. The second period of reforms, therefore, was intended to refine the operation of workers' self-management to permit freer operation of market elements in the Yugoslav economy. The set of concepts introduced at this time eventually became known as market socialism and was a response to the successes of the Yugoslav regime in the economic, political, and foreign policy spheres. In addition to the impressive growth in the economy, Yugoslavia's major domestic problem, competition between ethnic and regional groups, seemed to be receding, and Tito's policy of non-alignment had brought Yugoslavia international prestige which was disproportionate to its size and geographical significance.

In the 1970s and 1980s, Yugoslavia further refined its market socialism system in response to both internal and external problems. Yugoslav authorities experimented with increased centralization and decentralization of the economy but did not abandon their commitment to workers' self-management and non-alignment.

The Formative Years, 1944-1950

Yugoslavia expressed an early and active interest in the proposals which later became the IMF and the IBRD. Both organizations represented a relatively rapid, inexpensive means of attaining recovery and development for Yugoslavia's ravaged, primarily agricultural economy. Yugoslavia participated in the United Nations Monetary and Financial Conference, therefore, for much the same reasons as its future Communist brethren, but Yugoslavia perhaps placed even more emphasis on the potential for development assistance inherent in the idea of the IBRD.

Yugoslavia was an active participant at the Bretton Woods meetings and served on the committee which was responsible for determining Fund subscriptions and quotas. The documents and proceedings for the Bretton Woods conference record only two reservations made by Yugoslav delegations; both were withdrawn prior to the end of the conference.[3] On December 27, 1945, Yugoslavia joined 27 other nations in signing the Final Agreements for the Fund and Bank and thus became an original member of both organizations.

Some of the concessions made to the Communist countries during the negotiations at Bretton Woods directly benefited Yugoslavia during the early years of Bank and Fund operations. Foremost among these was the war-damage clause (Fund, Article III, Section 3; Bank, Article II, Section 8) which was a product of the ad hoc committee to Commission I on "Special Problems of Liberated Countries" on which Yugoslavia served. This clause permitted Yugoslavia to delay the establishment of a par value for its currency with the IMF and to defer payment of the full two percent of its capital subscription to the Bank for five years due to the disarray in its economy, a direct result of World War II.[4] In part, Yugoslavia's decision to defer its capital payment to the IBRD was also due to the uncertain status of approximately $80 million in gold which had been frozen in Allied banks at the beginning of the war (NYT 8/31/46). The war damage provisions did provide Yugoslavia with extra time in which to reorder its economy while remaining a member in good standing in both the IMF and the IBRD.

In the controversy over U.N. agreements with the Fund and Bank, Yugoslavia's commitment to the new organizations was challenged. At the August 1947 meeting of ECOSOC in which the Soviet Union first attacked the "special privileges" contained in the proposed agreement between the U.N. and the Bank and Fund, Yugoslavia expressed its reservations, but ultimately Yugoslavia cast an assenting vote.[5] Yugoslavia did, however, introduce a resolution which proposed the creation of a subcommittee which would examine the Soviet allegations in detail

(NYT 10/19/47). In this manner, the Yugoslavs demonstrated their support of the Soviet Bloc in the U.N. without significantly damaging their commitment to the Bank and Fund. This careful, almost neutral stance characterized Yugoslav behavior in both organizations with respect to its interests as a Communist country until well into the 1950s.

Workers' Self-Management, 1950–1954

The concept of workers' self-management was formally introduced into the Yugoslav economy in June, 1950 after a year of self-examination and doctrinal redirection.[6] This major reform of the Yugoslav economy, which purported the return of control of the factory to the worker, was actually only one in a number of policy changes subsequent to the break with the Cominform and certainly was not the most desirable from the viewpoint of Western banking authorities who were skeptical about the authenticity of the break and the sincerity of these new reforms. IMF and IBRD assistance, therefore, was not overwhelming during this period.

Yugoslavia sought World Bank assistance almost immediately after the war, tentatively requesting $500 million in January of 1948,[7] and preliminary negotiations on that loan were in progress when the break with the Cominform occurred five months later. One year later, in June, 1949, the amount of the loan request had been revised to range from $50–$250 million. The Yugoslavs wanted the loan to replace the capital investments from the Soviet Bloc which had been withdrawn in the summer of 1948 (NYT 6/26/49), but Bank officials were apparently more interested in funding Yugoslavia as part of the timber project designed to supply Western Europe; the loan also included Poland. This scheme was considered feasible and "safe" by Bank officials on the basis that since the war Yugoslavia, "alone among the Iron-Curtain countries involved, [had] given evidence of its ability to complete the agreements with the Western European nations that [were] required to make the loan possible."[8]

Among the "evidence" mentioned above was certainly the dispute between Stalin and Tito, and Yugoslavia's subsequent turn to the West for assistance. In fact, Tito was actually soliciting U.S. support in the World Bank, a move that was branded as a betrayal of Communism by the Soviet Bloc.[9] Confidence in the Yugoslav shift was heightened when in July, 1949, Tito terminated his support of the Greek Communist Revolution by closing off the Yugoslav border. Though this was justified by Tito in terms of Yugoslav security interests, the action was favorably received in the West.[10] Yugoslavia's successful bid, with U.S. support, for a seat on the U.N. Security Council in October, 1949 (a seat also sought by Czechoslovakia) reinforced Western belief that Yugoslavia was now willing to conduct itself as a responsible member of the world community (NYT 10/11/49; Johnson, pp. 126–127).

Progress on the World Bank loan proceeded throughout the summer of 1949. A commission, led by A. S. G. Hoar, was dispatched to Yugoslavia by the Bank in August, prompting charges by the Soviet Union that Yugoslavia had become a "capitalist tool."[11] This charge was vigorously denied by Tito who maintained that although Yugoslavia was willing to shift the emphasis of its economic program toward export industries at the suggestion of the World Bank, Yugoslavia would remain a socialist state which would not tolerate any infringement on its sovereignty. The result of such cooperation, however, was the announcement in October, 1949 of both an impending $2.7 million World Bank loan for timber and a $3 million loan from the IMF. Since the amount of the projected World Bank loan was well below Yugoslav desires and had been preceded by only minor concessions (if they can be viewed even as concessions) in the foreign policy sphere, the Bank and Fund loans appear to be more of a reinforcement tactic than an attempt to induce or reward Yugoslav behavior.

In 1950, reform of the Yugoslav economy began in earnest. The new self-management system was designed to decentralize decision-making in the economic sphere by relying on enterprise workers to participate in enterprise decisions. The features of the old and new systems are detailed in Table 5.1. This reform was the culmination of 18 months of vigorous ideological debate and reevaluation initiated by the break with the Cominform.[12]

In foreign policy, however, some retrenchment was occurring in 1950, partially as a reaction to the total lack of support from other Communist states, which surprised Yugoslav leaders, and partially in response to an unexpected delay in the progress of the IBRD loan.[13] This foreign policy retrenchment took the form of renewed declarations of Yugoslav independence coupled with recognition of the new Communist regime in North Vietnam and support of the Czech motion to oust Nationalist China from both the Bank and Fund.[14]

Despite the delay encountered in the early part of 1950, the World Bank loan announced the previous year was officially concluded in October, 1950, with the original terms intact. In granting this loan to Yugoslavia, the IBRD was disregarding its own prohibition against lending to members that had defaulted on, or had not repaid to date, loans to private lenders made prior to World War II. Yugoslavia was one of seven members in this category.[15] Although this exception had not been made for Yugoslavia alone, the fact that a loan was made to Yugoslavia

TABLE 5.1: Yugoslav Economic Reform, 1950-1954

Features of Administered Economy - 1945-1950

      1. State ownership of the means of production
      2. Central planning
      3. Administrative allocation of goods
      4. Reliance on administrative rules
      5. Administratively fixed wages
      6. An all-embracing state budget
      7. De-emphasis on consumption
      8. Emphasis on collectivization in agriculture

Features of Workers' Self-Management Economy - 1950-1954

      1. Social ownership of the means of production
      2. Social planning
      3. Market determined allocation of goods
      4. Reliance on financial instruments
      5. Free disposition of enterprise/collectives income
      6. A budget for state administration, decentralized and separate
         from economic operations
      7. Consumption as an independent factor of development
      8. Agriculture organized as a business cooperative of peasants

---

Source: This table is derived from Branko Horvat, The Yugoslav Economic System (White Plains, NY: International Arts and Sciences Press, Inc., 1976).

and not to Poland or Czechoslovakia, which did not have any outstanding defaults, makes this exception particularly interesting.

In October, 1951, the World Bank announced its intention to extend a second loan to Yugoslavia in the following year. The loan was considerably larger than the first, $28 million, and appeared in the midst of an extensive period of economic and political reform which had been initiated in June, 1950. There also occurred in 1951 an interesting shift in Yugoslav foreign policy as Tito embarked on his policy of nonalignment which would ease the path of rapprochement with the Soviet Union in 1954.

Reform of the economy occurred at a rapid pace throughout 1951 in three basic areas of decentralization of decision-making: liberalization of foreign trade, reliance on market mechanisms, and liberalization of agricultural production. This reform was necessary, according to B. Kidrić, who was Tito's close advisor in economic matters, in order to redress certain problems and imbalances which were a product of the previous administered, centrally-planned economy. The most important of these problems were a decline in the balance of payments and an inability to obtain foreign credit.[16]

In the area of foreign trade, Yugoslav officials took the first of several steps to liberalize foreign trade and to integrate Yugoslavia into the world economy. They began to experiment with agricultural exports and permitted enterprises engaging in foreign trade to retain a portion of their foreign exchange earnings.[17] On December 30, 1951, as part of the Law on Planned Management of the National Economy, the dinar was devalued from 50 dinars per $1 U.S. to 300 dinars per $1 U.S. This was an attempt to bring Yugoslav prices into line with the world market prices.[18] At this time, what was essentially a multiple exchange rate system was introduced which used "price equalization coefficients" to regulate imports and exports through the process of assigning different coefficients to the value of various categories of goods (Horvat, "YEP," pp. 124–125; Dubey, p. 263). Finally, Yugoslav enterprises engaging in foreign trade were permitted to retain a portion of their foreign exchange earnings which they could use at their discretion.

Further decentralization in the domestic economy was pursued by the Yugoslavs in 1951, particularly in the areas of prices and planning. As Johnson states, during 1951 the Yugoslavs began in earnest to dismantle the command economy (*Transformation*, p. 144). In January, 1951, prices on a few selected products were made responsive to demand for these products (Johnson, p. 165), and by the end of the year prices of many industrial and mining products, as well as some foodstuffs, were determined by market forces. The purposes of this large-scale price reform were to bring Yugoslav prices in line with world market prices, to stimulate investment by increasing the prices of producer goods, and to generate savings through the increase in retail prices (NYT 12/11/ 51; Horvat, "YEP," p. 110).

This increased reliance on the market for price determination also required an adjustment in the reliance of the economy on a centrally-determined economic plan. The Law on Planned Management of the National Economy, promulgated in December, 1951, replaced detailed central planning with planning of "basic proportions" in which "the amount and broad allocations of investment" were centrally determined, "while the decisions regarding quantity and quality of output and its price were left to the enterprise" (Dubey, p. 31). As a result of both the change in planning and changes in the method of price formation, the relative efficiency of Yugoslav enterprises was now determined on the basis of cost accounting and profitability (Horvat, "YEP," pp. 180– 181).

Decentralization also extended to the agricultural sector which was under much strain as the result of a bad harvest and resulting famine in late 1950 and early 1951. In order to stimulate agricultural production, the Yugoslav government began to experiment with agricultural exports

(Horvat, "YEP," p. 124) and began to investigate alternatives to collectivism, including profit-sharing.

In terms of foreign policy, 1951 was a year in which Yugoslavia reaffirmed its political, ideological, and economic independence from the Soviet Bloc, and increasingly, from the West as well. In January, 1951 the Yugoslavs concluded a Mutual Defense Agreement with the United States (Johnson, p. 126). This prompted one observer to note that the U.S. was regarded by Yugoslavs "almost as an ally."[19] Tito, conscious of the continuing need for Western assistance, further cemented U.S.-Yugoslav relations during August in a speech in which he expressed Yugoslavia's desire for "the closest economic and other relations" with the West and stated that Western aid had been extended without requiring Yugoslav concessions (NYT 8/10/51).

By December, however, increasing problems with the flow of aid from the West led to a re-evaluation of Yugoslavia's international position. Boris Kidrić, in a speech to the Yugoslav Parliament, no longer expressed gratitude but spoke of Yugoslavia's "moral right" to Western aid because of its position as a buffer between East and West.[20] The Yugoslav regime also began to increase its contacts with African and Asian nations as the first step in what became the non-aligned movement (Johnson, p. 135).

The presence of the Bank and Fund in Yugoslavia was evident throughout 1951. Yugoslavia's application for a second World Bank loan provided the Bank with the opportunity to conduct a thorough examination of the newly-emerging self-management economy. In April, 1951, the Bank cited Yugoslavia's annual trade deficits as the "last important obstacle to the approval of a second Bank loan to Yugoslavia."[21] The Bank desired more evidence of Yugoslav actions to stabilize the economy before investing more Bank resources in that member. The IMF was also vitally concerned with the stability of the Yugoslav economy and dispatched a staff delegation to Belgrade for a six-week stay in September, 1951 to begin discussions on monetary reforms with Yugoslav officials. These discussions included exchange controls, inflation, and a reasonable exchange rate for the dinar.

Cheryl Payer claims that the economic reforms summarized above were a direct consequence of IMF pressure exerted by the IMF delegation (*Debt Trap*, p. 123). While Payer's assertions may be overstated, since many of the reforms occurred prior to the delegation's arrival in September, a number of reforms suggested by the Bank and Fund did occur shortly after the announcement on October 12 of a second Bank loan to Yugoslavia of $28 million in seven currencies, and it was speculated that Yugoslavia would seek yet another loan from the IBRD. As was also discussed above, the dinar was revalued in December, 1951 after "prolonged discussions" with the IMF, and the value of the coefficient was adjusted for several products. In addition, the annual rate of capital investments in Yugoslavia was cut by the regime from 28 percent to 20 percent of GNP as an explicit signal to Western aid agencies that Yugoslavia was willing to modify its industrialization program in order to ensure its feasibility.

Mason and Asher, in their history of the IBRD, note that the Bank loan to Yugoslavia, announced in October, 1951, and formally concluded a year later, served a purpose for the Bank as well as Yugoslavia.[22] Mason and Asher assert that Bank officials used the second Yugoslav loan to coax the Bank's Western European members into releasing the remaining 18 percent of their initial capital subscriptions. Bank officials claimed that an exclusively dollar loan to Yugoslavia might have had "adverse effects" on the New York market and that other hard currencies were necessary to offset these "effects;" in this endeavor the Bank's staff was successful.

The possibility of a third IBRD loan to Yugoslavia, hinted at in late October, 1951, dwindled in 1952 as the process of economic reform slowed and even reversed. In foreign policy as well, there were ambiguous signals emerging from Belgrade. Fund and Bank activity in Yugoslavia was minimal, and no new loans were announced.

The progress of economic reform in Yugoslavia slowed considerably in 1952 with the appearance of problems such as price gouging and cartels which had been previously associated only with market economies. The reimposition of controls in several sectors of the economy was designed to neutralize some of the negative effects of a quasi-market economy on a socialist society and to remind both Yugoslavs and the world that the goal of the regime was still communism.[23] However, decentralization of the economy continued in 1952, albeit at a reduced pace, and the Law on the Planned Direction of the Economy reinforced the devolution of economic decision-making to the Republics and local enterprises.[24] Ultimately the Federal Government was responsible only for producing laws and regulations on matters such as general economic planning and the national capital investment program.

Among the most notable of the few economic reforms which occurred in 1952 was the vesting of formal control in the Workers' Councils in all state enterprises (Dubey, p. 31). This signified the continued commitment of the regime to the infant self-management system. At the sixth Party Congress later that year, formal interest rates were introduced, a marked departure from a typical socialist economy, and declared to be a "characteristic of commodity production in general, not exclusively capitalism" (Johnson, pp. 165–166). Free market trading was established in agricultural products, foreign exchange, and some industrial raw materials. In foreign trade, the foreign exchange retention rate for enterprises was increased to 50 percent (Payer, p. 124).

Yugoslav foreign policy during 1952 continued the independent trend initiated in the closing months of 1951. A Yugoslav Communist Party warning to Yugoslavs and the world that the recent economic reforms were intended to create a more perfect socialist society, not a Western-style democracy, accompanied the imposition of restrictions on the scope of authority of Workers' Councils. Yet the Yugoslav position on Western European regional defense pacts had modified to such an extent that U.S. officials were giving consideration to the "possibility of requesting Belgrade to coordinate its foreign policy on certain issues with that of the West."[25]

One such issue was the conflicting post-war claims of Italy and Yugoslavia on the city of Trieste (Rijeka). At a speech at Dolenski Toplice in September, Tito temporized, claiming that Italy and Yugoslavia should first seek to improve relations between them through cooperation on other matters. He explicitly responded to the hints of U.S.-Yugoslav policy coordination, saying that 'tendencies' to extract concessions from Yugoslavia in return for economic assistance" were unacceptable insofar as Yugoslavia's continuing efforts to defend itself were also defending the West and therefore, should be considered sufficient repayment for any aid (NYT 9/15/52). Clearly Tito intended to maintain a non-aligned position between East and West whatever the cost to Yugoslavia in terms of Western aid.

The IBRD announced its decision to finance a third loan to Yugoslavia in February, 1953. This loan, at $30 million, was the largest IBRD loan to Yugoslavia to date and was earmarked for the completion of several industrial projects.[26] According to IBRD President Black, this loan was a consequence of the Bank-Yugoslav negotiations of the previous years in which the Yugoslavs' ambitious original investment program was "relaxed at the suggestion of the [World Bank] mission" (NYT 2/13/53).

Reports of a growing unemployment problem and rising prices accompanied the announcement of the third Bank loan. Despite these problems, however, the pace of the reform process, begun in 1950, quickened in 1953. In order to facilitate the new investment program, the Yugoslav government introduced plans to decentralize the operations of the National Bank, which acted as central bank for Yugoslavia. Credit would serve as the basic instrument of financing and would now be extended on the basis of performance rather than enterprise projections. As an intermediate step, a system of investment auctions was established in December, 1953 through which scarce investment resources were allocated to enterprises (Horvat, "YEP," p. 79; Dubey, p. 31). The introduction of interest rates and the creation of commercial banks were at once necessary to the decentralization effort and to the expansion of trade with the West.

Yugoslavia's desire to enhance and diversify its investment program was also evident in its decision to permit private foreign investment in Yugoslav projects on a very limited scale. Although the idea of permitting joint stock companies was debated, Yugoslav authorities were reluctant to authorize such a reform due to growing concern over Yugoslavia's rapidly increasing debt to the West.

In agriculture, where reforms had lagged behind other sectors of the economy, the principle of forced collectivization was abandoned in favor of a system which employed incentives and profits to increase production.[27] The Law on the Reorganization of Peasants' Work Cooperatives, promulgated in March 1953, gave the Yugoslav peasant the option of dissolving the production cooperatives and returning the land to the individual members of the cooperative. The law established the maximum size of an individual plot of land at 25 acres, however (Horvat, "YEP," pp. 78–79; Dubey, p. 32). As one observer noted, the World Bank had been consulted in reference to these reforms in the agricultural sector, which the Yugoslavs insisted were not an abandonment of socialism but merely a reflection of the futility and counterproductivity of the use of force (NYT 3/23/53).

Yugoslavia maintained its cautious but resolute foreign policy stance between East and West throughout 1953. The credibility of this position was hampered, however, by the relative absence of contacts between Yugoslavia and the Soviet Bloc. Acutely aware of this, Tito sought to repair the damage done to Soviet-Yugoslav relations in 1948, and Stalin's death in 1953 facilitated the reconciliation. The following year, 1954, was therefore a landmark for Yugoslav foreign policy, as the preceding four years had been for economic policy.

Josef Stalin's death in 1953 removed possibly the largest impediment to a Yugoslav-Soviet reconciliation. Accordingly, in early 1954 Tito began to indicate his desire for a "normalization of relations" between the two countries while emphasizing the unique and independent course which Yugoslavia had chosen after the Cominform break in 1948.[28] The first steps in the rapprochement with the U.S.S.R. were taken in the area of trade. The Cominform trade blockade had occasioned Yugoslavia's shift to the West for financial assistance in the summer of 1948; the blockade was terminated in September, 1954, with the conclusion of $10 million in trade contracts with Hungary, Czechoslovakia, and the GDR. Nearly one month later, Yugoslavia formally resumed trade relations with the Soviet Union in a short-term trade agreement for a $5 million barter exchange of nonstrategic materials. Although claims arising from the 1948 blockade hampered the progress of reconciliation, these trade agreements initiated a process which would culminate ten years later in observer status for Yugoslavia in the CMEA.[29] Evidence of Yugoslavia's increased solidarity with the Soviet Bloc nations also appeared in international forums; most notable of these was Yugoslavia's support for Czechoslovakia in the IMF and IBRD during the controversy which led to Czechoslovakia's ouster from both organizations in September, 1954.

Tito was careful, however, to maintain cordial ties with the West, particularly the United States. In October, 1954, Yugoslavia concluded a settlement with the U.S. on the claims of U.S. citizens for seized or nationalized property. This settlement served three purposes: first, it released $47 million in gold frozen in U.S. banks; second, Yugoslavia was no longer in violation of IBRD regulations governing nationalized property; and third, the settlement gave concrete evidence of Yugoslavia's desire for amiable and cooperative relations with the West. Further, in a speech in October, 1954, Tito applauded Western aid efforts in Yugoslavia and noted that such aid had not imposed "any conditions harmful to Yugoslav sovereignty and independence" (NYT 10/26/54).

The settlement of the Trieste issue, however, is perhaps the best evidence of Tito's desire to placate the West in the face of the growing cordiality with the Soviet Union. Throughout 1954, Tito stressed the importance of Trieste for Yugoslavia's military and economic relations with the U.S. and Great Britain. In October, negotiations on Trieste were concluded; although Tito was not satisfied with the outcome, he stated that the settlement was the "best Yugoslavia could achieve under the circumstances."[30]

In the economic sphere, the focus of the regime was on consolidation of previous gains. Decentralization of the banking system continued with the creation of communal banks to supplement the National and commercial banks (Dubey, p. 34). In foreign trade, the coefficient system was refined and enterprises were permitted to retain an increased share of their foreign exchange earnings.[31] The reorientation of foreign policy in 1954 seems to have coincided, therefore, with the end of the first year of economic reform.

It is interesting to note that no additional Fund or Bank assistance was extended to Yugoslavia during 1954, and indeed, Yugoslavia would not receive another World Bank loan until 1961. Similarly, a Fund Stand-by Arrangement was not negotiated until 1961. Yugoslavia's attempt to balance its relations with East and West coincides, then, not only with a period of consolidation in terms of the economic reform process within the country but with a pause in its growing interactions with the Fund and Bank as well. This pause can be viewed as evidence of Yugoslavia's desire to reinforce its non-aligned status by reducing its dependence on Western institutions and the West's cautious reaction to an obvious Yugoslav move to reconcile with its Communist brethren.

The first period of Yugoslav economic reform which instituted the workers' self-management system met with a positive, if skeptical at first, response from the Bank and Fund. The reforms enacted through the 1950-54 period were a direct consequence of the Cominform break in 1948 and would eventually extend throughout the entire society. Bank and Fund involvement in this reform process was not extensive in terms of frequency and size of loans. In fact, receipts from Yugoslavia's three loans from the World Bank totalled $60.7 million, less than the amount India received in 1950 alone. In 1950, the Bank loan to Yugoslavia was sixth of the nine loans extended by the IBRD in that year. Yugoslavia's loan ranked sixth out of 16 Bank loans made in 1952, and third out of nine loans in 1953. In relative terms, therefore, Yugoslavia did not fare poorly in terms of IBRD assistance, although Yugoslavia certainly lagged behind other developing nations' receipts for the entire period.

In a more intangible sense, both organizations did contribute to the reform process in Yugoslavia, at least minimally, through the regular procedures for consultation established in both organizations' charters. It appears, however, that Bank lending during the period coincided more closely with the perceived position of Yugoslavia with respect to the Soviet Bloc than to the magnitude and content of the reforms enacted in any given year and thus takes on the appearance of reinforcement until 1954, and perhaps punishment after. This is not unexpected, given the experiences of Poland and Czechoslovakia during the same period. Yugoslavia's association with the IMF and IBRD in the early 1950s, however, did demonstrate to both East and West that cooperation between both organizations and an Eastern European communist country was not inherently doomed to failure, but it would be another 18 years before that example would be trusted by another Eastern European country.

Market Socialism, 1960–1965

The second significant period of reform in Yugoslavia began with the "economic crisis" of 1960 and continued through 1965 with the introduction and implementation of a major set of market-oriented reform measures. The late 1950s had been a period of some retrenchment for Yugoslavia, both politically and economically,[32] and by 1960 the strains of the incomplete adaptation of market principles to a socialist economy had appeared. The rather incomplete nature of the reforms of the 1950s was particularly evident in the growing strains between the

Yugoslav and world economies, and this next set of reforms was intended to integrate the Yugoslav economy more efficiently into the international economic system (Crawford, p. 608). That such integration would also entail the inclusion of more market elements into the domestic economy soon became apparent.

In fact, the 1960–1965 period was actually one of refining and implementing theories introduced during the first stages of workers' self-management. The 1960s reforms, then, were almost a "fine-tuning" of the new self-management system (this is especially true of the 1961 reforms) which, by 1965, had led to an almost qualitatively different economic system called market socialism. The 1961 reforms, therefore, were merely a prelude to the almost complete acceptance of the market principle evinced by the 1965 reform which was ostensibly designed to bring Yugoslavia into a more advanced stage of development.[33]

It was during this time that Yugoslavia began to exploit fully the opportunities and resources offered by the IBRD and IMF, with the complete support of both organizations. Indeed, relations between Yugoslavia and these two agencies became so cordial that one observer noted in 1970, "[the] International Bank for Reconstruction and Development is [now] Yugoslavia's biggest foreign partner and creditor."[34] The initial hesitance to lend to a Communist country displayed by the Bank and Fund in the Fifties had completely disappeared by the end of this second period.

The first, preliminary set of reforms toward a market socialist system began in 1961, and the need for such changes was attributed by experts, both in Yugoslavia and the West, to four causes. Perhaps the most obvious impetus to the 1961 reform was the boom and bust cycle which afflicted the Yugoslav economy in 1960. The recession of late 1960 certainly highlighted the problems inherent in the early self-management system and contributed to the growing pressure for change within the government and the academic community (Horvat, *YES*, p. 197; Horvat, "YEP," pp. 82, 126; Crawford, p. 613). For the most part, the root of the recession, however, was identified as the inefficient integration of the Yugoslav economy into the world economy through the foreign trade coefficient system (see above). The coefficient system did not induce enterprises to produce more efficiently as expected but merely encouraged them to compete for assignment of lower coefficients (Horvat, "YEP," p. 125). As a result, the dinar was overvalued by 30 percent (Horvat, *YES*, p. 197). In addition, dependence on raw material and machinery imports had also contributed to a growing balance of payments deficit— Yugoslavia's trade deficit reached $341 million by 1961 (Crawford, p. 613).

Two domestic factors also contributed to the call for reform in 1960 and 1961. The banking reform of the mid-1950s had been an attempt to decentralize the provision of credit to the local communities which, it was presumed, were better aware of local needs and resources. Critics in 1960 claimed, however, that the decentralization of banks had led to the complete take-over of bank credit policies by local governments (Horvat, "YEP," p. 134). Government and/or political interference in the self-management process soon emerged as a dominant theme of the critics of the economy. Another area of concern to the critics was the relative lack of "business discipline" displayed by Yugoslav enterprises and economic decison-makers. Sources within Yugoslavia began to recommend adherence to standard economic laws (i.e., Keynesian theory) as a solution to problems in the Yugoslav economy.[35]

The recession of 1960, therefore, began what was the first *academic* discussion of economic issues in Yugoslavia (Horvat, "YEP," p. 83). This discussion soon evolved into a planning vs. market debate in which the entire Yugoslav economic community, but most particularly academic economists, participated. The "planning school" (as coined by Branko Horvat) argued that decentralization had reached its upper limits and that planning was now necessary along the lines of Soviet Five-Year Plans to ensure an optimal distribution of resources which would emphasize the interests of society over the narrow interests of individual enterprises and communities. According to the "planning school," economic development should be the first priority of the economy, and this could be achieved most rapidly only through centralization.[36] The "market school," on the other hand, argued that dependence on planning and centralization had brought about the current crisis and that even greater reliance on market mechanisms was needed to correct Yugoslavia's economic ills.[37]

The "market school" attributed inefficient planning and imperfect market mechanisms to the badly prepared and implemented reforms of the 1950s. These poorly constructed reforms, they argued, encouraged the financial irresponsibility of enterprises which resulted in inconsistent investment decisions and "wild" wage increases which were unrelated to increases in productivity. This caused Yugoslav prices to be inconsistent with world prices and consequently led, in conjunction with an awkward and inefficient foreign trade pricing system, to the current balance of payments deficit.

Tito accepted the market school's analysis and soon Yugoslav policy-makers were preparing another set of reforms for the economy. The bulk of the 1961 reforms attempted to correct the problems identified in the foreign trade sector. On January 1, 1961, the cumbersome coefficient system (which was, in effect, a multiple exchange rate system) was eliminated and replaced by a single rate for the dinar, 750 dinar to $1 U.S., which, although still considered too low by some experts (Horvat, "YEP," p. 197), was an effective devaluation of the dinar. Imports and exports would now be controlled through customs tariffs, quotas, export premiums, and tax rebates.[38] Enterprise imports were further controlled through the foreign exchange retention quota which, in 1961, required an enterprise to "sell" its foreign exchange to the National Bank which could, in turn, sell up to 7 percent of this foreign exchange back to the enterprise.[39] In addition, a full 1/5 of all imports were liberalized (Horvat, "YEP," p. 126). It was also at this time that Yugoslavia sought entry into the General Agreement on Tariffs and Trade (GATT), an organization devoted to the promotion of free trade; Cheryl Payer even goes so far as to claim that the 1961 reforms were the "price" of Yugoslav acceptance into GATT (*Debt Trap*, p. 118), although the long, arduous debate between the planning and market schools makes this contention appear unlikely.

A series of reforms were also introduced in the money and banking sector of the economy. Banking was further decentralized in order to expand credit opportunities to enterprises while minimizing administrative interference from political authorities.[40] Communal banks now became "basic and universal credit institutions" (Horvat, *YES*, p. 211) for enterprises. Reserve requirements of up to 35 percent of liquid deposits were used to control the expansion of credit and limits between 8 percent and 12 percent were placed on interest rates. Yugoslav authorities quite clearly felt that the solution to Yugoslavia's economic problems lay in control of the money supply and looked to credit policy as the means for manipulating money supply in a socialist economy (Horvat, "YEP," pp. 141–143).

In other areas, despite the criticism contained in the reports of the "market school," in 1961 "Workers' Councils became completely independent in determining wage rates and distributing income" (Horvat, "YEP," p. 115). This advance in the operation of the market was offset somewhat in 1961 by the rise of the number of administratively-controlled prices (Horvat, "YEP," p. 111).

Fund and Bank participation in the 1961 Yugoslav reforms took the form of advice and reinforcement. In 1961, Yugoslavia received its first Bank loan in seven years. At $30 million, it was seventh in terms of total receipts of the 20 loans made by the Bank in that year. Earlier in 1961, the Fund participated as part of a consortium of Western donors which provided "financial assistance to Yugoslavia, in order to facilitate a comprehensive reform of its exchange . . . system."[41] Drawings on this $45 million SBA were made conditional on the implementation of certain elements in Yugoslavia's reform program. The Yugoslav Stand-by did *not* contain the customary prior notice clause which permitted the Fund to suspend further use of stand-by funds as this was deemed to be "detrimental to Yugoslavia's interests" (Horsefield, pp. 486, 489).

Although Fund and Bank assistance did play a contributory role in the 1961 reforms, it would be difficult to attribute these measures *solely* to Bank and Fund actions as pressures for reform had been mounting within Yugoslavia for a long period during which there had been reduced interactions with both organizations. The form that the new measures took was the logical extension of the debate, again *within* Yugoslavia, between the planning and market schools, although IMF and IBRD advice was frequently an input into final decisions on reforms. Due to training and lack of relevant literature and experience from non-Keynesian sources, the market school economists also naturally reflected the monetarist perspective which also dominated the Bank and Fund at that time. As a result, Yugoslav interpretations of the nature of both the problem and solution during this second reform period were favorably received in the IMF and IBRD.

In the three years preceding the major reforms of 1965, the deficiencies of the 1961 reforms surfaced and evoked another round in the market versus planning debate. The boom/bust cycle which had produced the 1961 reforms continued in 1962. Once again, Yugoslav authorities placed the blame on a set of "poorly prepared, partly inconsistent, and badly implemented" reforms (Horvat, *YEP*, p. 21). In a more fundamental sense, however, the reforms were indeed responsible for the unpredictable behavior of the Yugoslav economy. One of the major goals of the 1961 reforms was to integrate the Yugoslav economy more closely with the world economy, but this integration also exposed the economy to fluctuations in the economies of its trading partners (Schrenk, p. 203), and thus control over the economy was not completely in Yugoslav hands. Consequently, the Yugoslav balance of payments suffered moderate deficits throughout the 1960s.

The Fund, in its efforts to reinforce the reforms, mitigated, in part, the 1962 deficit through the conclusion of a $30 million Stand-by Arrangement with Yugoslavia. As is customary with Stand-by Arrangements, the gesture had the effect of demonstrating the Fund's confidence in and support of the reforms passed by the Yugoslav government in 1961.

In 1963, the boom cycle continued, and a newly-promulgated constitution further enhanced optimism both at home and abroad. The 1963 Constitution introduced few new reforms but merely made formal the progress in workers' self-management which had occurred during the previous decade. The new constitution did extend self-management to business and non-profit organizations.[42]

Beside the constitution, the most significant arena of reform was in credit policy. Refinements were made in credit policy which would permit monetary authorities to regulate the demand for credit as well as the supply (Horvat, *YES,* p. 213). Among the new measures were regulations which stipulated that credit would be extended to enterprises only *after* evidence that a commodity transaction had taken place and that credit would not be extended for sales to final buyers (Horvat, "YEP," p. 135). The formative stages of a money market in Yugoslavia also appeared during 1963 with the introduction of negotiable government bonds (Horvat, *YES,* p. 223).

The coincidence of even more market-oriented reforms with the fluctuations in economic performance initiated a demand for the reintroduction of central planning from a growing sector of the Party. At a January meeting in Zagreb, the Association of Economists and the Federal Planning Bureau criticized the new reforms, claiming that the market destroyed socialist principles by placing the needs of the individual over the needs of the community (Horvat, *YES,* pp. 84–85). This dispute would reach dangerous proportions for the Party by 1965.

In foreign policy, Tito continued to strive for cordial relations with both East and West. He attempted to play a moderating role in the growing Sino-Soviet split but was rebuffed by the Chinese who perceived Tito as partial to the Soviets. In the second half of 1963, Yugoslavia also opened negotiations with the Soviet Bloc in order to obtain observer status in the CMEA. It was reported that the Soviet Union requested Yugoslavia to join as a full member, but Tito, citing his desire to maintain good trade relations with the West, remained firm, and Yugoslavia joined the organization as an observer in early 1964. Tito tempered his growing involvement with the Soviet Union, however, in response to a 1962 U.S. Congress action which prohibited the extension of Most-Favored Nation treatment to Communist nations. This would have seriously damaged Yugoslav exports, and consequently, Tito spent much of 1963 trying to convince U.S. officials of Yugoslavia's friendship and intention to remain non-aligned.[43]

Meanwhile, as part of the Fund and Bank's discussion with Yugoslavia prior to the 1961 reforms, the Bank had agreed to a third loan. This loan was formally concluded in 1963 for $65 million. The loan was designed, in part, to improve Yugoslavia's railways. It was the second largest loan concluded by the Bank in that year and was the largest IBRD loan to Yugoslavia to date.

The economic upswing of 1963 continued into early 1964, but recession set in by the end of the year. Inflation increased dramatically, with consumer prices rising 4 percent in just ten weeks, and wage strikes were reported as Yugoslav officials attempted to control the tendency of self-management to lead to spiraling wage increases which only added to the inflation problem (NYT 3/18/64; Horvat, "YEP," p. 83). In addition to, and partially as a consequence of, these problems, the balance of payments deficit grew steadily. As the economy steadily declined, recognition of the need for yet another set of reforms grew.[44]

Yugoslav officials endeavored to stem rising inflation in 1964 in three related areas. Tito identified the cause of the growing inflation as over-investment in industrial capacity which had resulted in the under-utilization of plant capacity in several areas (NYT 3/18/83). In an effort to resolve this problem, the central Investment Funds were abolished in 1964 and those monies transferred to the corresponding banks in local communities.[45] This had the effect of allowing most investment resources to respond to market forces. An additional attempt to control inflation was made through efforts to control the money supply. By mid-1964 Yugoslav officials had begun to restrict credit to both enterprises and consumers. The reserve requirement to banks was increased to the legal limit of 35 percent, a move which quickly curtailed new investment. By the close of 1964, the money supply had grown by only 28 percent and this continued to decrease until it reached a low of 4 percent in the first half of 1966.[46] In a final effort to tackle the inflation problem, Yugoslav officials increased price controls and instituted a partial price freeze (Lang, p. 233).

In the foreign trade sector, a decline in exports and a sharp rise in imports in 1964 led Yugoslav authorities to impose additional restrictions on imports and to increase the tariff by 3 percent to 23 percent (OECD, 1966, p. 25; Horvat, "YES," p. 126). Foreign exchange was now allocated conditional on export sales, and the system of export premiums and tax reductions for exporting enterprises was expanded, thus encouraging exports. While these measures did have the effect of reducing the balance of payments deficit, they also amounted to the reappearance of a multiple exchange rate system (Horvat, "YES," p. 126), a circumstance counter to the goals of the IMF (*Articles of Agreement*, Article VIII, Section 3).

The debate between the planning and market schools continued into 1964 but took on increasingly political overtones as the Party hierarchy split into the two camps. Criticisms of the "Stalinist methods of command" (NYT 3/16/64) promoted by elements of the planning school surfaced at the very highest levels of the League of Communists (NYT 3/16/64, 9/22/64). Yet the general tone of the 8th Party Congress of the League, held in December, 1964, prompted some observers to speculate on Yugoslavia's "step eastward" (NYT 12/10/64). This domestic controversy, which would be resolved in 1966 with the ouster of Aleksander Ranković, who led the planning school within the Party,[47] was reflected in Yugoslav foreign relations which simultaneously sought closer trade ties with the East while looking to Western economic theory for solutions to domestic economic problems.[48]

The Bank and Fund continued to reinforce the direction of Yugoslav economic policy, both foreign and domestic, throughout 1964. The IMF opened negotiations for another Stand-by Arrangement which would ease the payments deficit, and the IBRD concluded a sixth loan to Yugoslavia. The $35 million loan was ninth in total value of 28 Bank loans in 1964 and was extended to support various projects related to Yugoslavia's industrialization program. So, despite growing economic problems and increasing support for a command economy within Yugoslavia, the Bank and Fund continued to demonstrate their support, in part because the direction of reform continued to reflect a market orientation.

A third period of intensive economic reform began in early 1965. The pressure for reform (the nature of which was by no means agreed upon) had been mounting since 1962, and this pressure had been supplemented by increasing difficulties in the economy. In fact, pressing economic problems were the impetus behind the decision to proceed with another set of reforms so soon after the reforms of 1961. As was discussed above, the 1964 recession occasioned some serious discussion within Yugoslavia about the nature and direction of the economy. The rate of inflation was climbing; the cost of living rose 24 percent in the first half of 1965, with prices and wages increasing by over 20 percent.[49] Experts considered productivity to be below the level necessary to sustain Yugoslavia at a high rate of development.[50] The growing balance of payments deficit ($205.4 million in 1964) worried financial officials both in Yugoslavia and abroad (Dubey, p. 38; Lang, p. 228; Horvat, "YES," p. 127).

Clearly, the 1961 reforms had not had their intended corrective effects. The 1965 reforms, thus, were not only designed to remedy persistent economic problems but were intended to correct imperfections in the system which were due to over-experimentation throughout the 1950s and early 1960s.[51] Experts recognized the preliminary and almost haphazard nature of previous reforms, and therefore, the 1965 reforms were designed, in the opinion of Branko Horvat, as a "more radical and more consistent, edition of the 1961 reform" ("YEP," p. 83). That the new reforms were to follow the same general direction of 1961 was an indication that the ongoing "political battle" (Bičanić, p. 634) between the planning and market schools had once again been decided in favor of the "young economists" (NYT 10/20/65) of the market school. "The Reform" of 1965, as it came to be called, therefore, was a response to economic *and* political pressures.

On July 23 and 24, 1965, 25 laws, two decisions and two recommendations were promulgated by the Yugoslav government (Vukmanović, p. 5). These laws constituted the beginning of a three-year period of reform which established market socialism in Yugoslavia. The reform was explicitly intended to adjust the Yugoslav economy to the new, "higher" stage of economic development which it had attained largely as a result of war-time reconstruction and the self-management system (Mačešić, p. 41; Lang, p. 228). Despite the successes of the 1950s, the recent dislocations in the economy were attributed to the fact that the institutions and procedures employed in economic decision-making were more suitable to an earlier stage of economic development. As noted Yugoslav economist Branko Horvat comments,

> "Almost overnight a backward Balkan country reached an European standard of economic development, and an administrative economy was transformed into a market economy. At the same time responsible authorities often lacked the necessary understanding of how a modern market economy operated ("YEP," p. 87).

The Yugoslav conception of a "developed" model of the Yugoslav economy, which represents the ideal to which the 1965 Reform aspired, is presented in Table 5.2. The Reform, therefore, was intended to move from the "extensive" pattern of industrial development typified by other Soviet bloc economies to a more "intensive" pattern of development which assigned a greater role to consumption and which would more efficiently utilize Yugoslav resources and productive capacity.[52]

There were four themes employed by the regime to promote the Reforms: decentralization, de-étatization, de-politicization, and democratization (Bičanić, p. 643). In effect this slogan reflected the secondary goal of the Reform, which was to achieve intensive development through reliance on the market and stabilization of the economy.[53] In the opinion of the market school, of course, these two intermediate goals were linked: stabilization could only be achieved on a lasting basis through reliance on market mechanisms (a view shared by the IMF and IBRD).

Although many elements of a market economy were incorporated into the Yugoslav economy during the self-management period, market mechanisms were by no means the dominant factor in economic decision-making prior to 1965. The 1965 Reforms were intended to remedy this situation by extending the role that market mechanisms played in the economy. Yugoslav economic authorities believed that allowing the operation of more competitive market conditions would enhance the efficiency of Yugoslav enterprises, both domestically and abroad (Mačešić, p. 42; Horvat, *YES*, p. 21; Lang, p. 230, Hawlowitsch, p. 125).

TABLE 5.2: Models of the Yugoslav Economy, 1953-1965

Model of the Undeveloped Economy	Model of the Developed Economy
1. Maximized growth at any cost	Growth constrained by profit-ability
2. Centrally-planned investment	Induced investment, decisions made by enterprises
3. Priority given to production	Priority given to consumption
4. Planned, administered prices	Market prices
5. Monoply central planning	Polycentric planning
6. Income redistribution by the state	Income redistribution by producers
7. Administrative decision of flows of goods, labor, capital	Goods, labor, capital flows decided by economic factors
8. Foreign trade autarky	Integrated into the world market
9. Inflationary tendency	Deflationary tendency

Source: This table is derived from Rudolf Bićanić, "Economics of Socialism in a Developed Country," *Foreign Affairs*, vol. 44, no. 4 (July 1966), pp. 645-646.

In practice this meant reducing, and eventually eliminating, government (or administrative) interference and control in areas such as prices and disposition of enterprise income (Mačešić, p. 42; Lang, p. 230; Horvat, "YEP," p. 85). This was the meaning of de-étatization. Also, prior to 1965, many decisions had been made by government authorities with reference to local political necessities rather than according to economic criteria. By relying on "objective" market mechanisms it was hoped that economic decision-making would become apolitical, or de-politicized (Bićanić, p. 636; Horvat, "YEP," p. 85).

Domestically, the Reform focused on price formation, enterprise decision-making, planning, and banking institutions and investment. As was the intention of the reforms passed in July, 1965, prices would henceforth "be formed economically, and (would) depend on relations between supply and demand, not only on the home market but also on the international market" (Vukmanović, p. 12). Accordingly, beginning that same month a "radical" restructuring of the entire pricing system was conducted with the new domestic prices of most goods based on prevailing world market prices.[54] Price subsidies to enterprises and to consumers, in the form of lower than market rates on rents, public transportation and electricity among others, were drastically reduced or eliminated.[55]

Administrative interference in price formation was not completely eliminated, however. The central government still determined the prices of selected "essential goods" such as raw materials and some semi-finished goods (Schrenk, p. 121; Vukmanović, p. 9). Price ceilings were imposed on goods such as meat, electric power and communal services within ten days of the announcement of the Reform in July (NYT 10/20/65; Mačešić, p. 46). The price freeze of March, 1965 was replaced by a new freeze in July, when prices on 90 percent of all goods were increased and then frozen (OECD, 1966, p. 8; Lang, p. 234; Horvat, "YEP," pp. 111–112). This was done to prevent any drastic and uncontrolled jump in prices which might have occurred as a result of the announcement of the Reform, but it also demonstrates that unqualified commitment to the market ideal was not yet a reality.

Reform of the banking system served two purposes: to streamline an increasingly cumbersome and inefficient institutional framework and to harmonize the system for distributing credit and investment with the newly proclaimed market principles. Prior to 1965, the institutional structure in Yugoslavia appeared as follows:

National Bank
3 Specialized banks for investment, agriculture, and foreign trade
6 Republic Banks
200+ Local banks (OECD, 1966, p. 10).

These banks were characterized by the essentially political or administrative character of their decision-making. The vast majority of these banks operated only in the territory of the government which had established them (Mačešić, p. 51), and therefore were easily "captured" by local political interests.

In two reforms (March and August, 1965), the number and types of banks were reduced to the following:

National Bank
8 Investment banks
61 Commercial banks
39 "Mixed" banks, performing a variety of functions (OECD, 1966, p. 10; Mačešić, p. 53).

In order to reduce the amount of political control exerted on these banks by local political units, no one "founder" of a bank was permitted to hold more than 10 percent of the total number of votes on the bank's mortgaging board (Mačešić, p. 10).

One of the primary concerns of the Reform was the allocation of scarce investment resources. Once again, the goal was to minimize administrative and political interference in investment decisions.[56] Control of investment funds was not vested in enterprises and banks, the latter being conceived of as autonomous economic organizations, "which collect the free resources of the economic organizations . . . and allocated such resources where they will produce the best economic results" (Vukmanović, p. 30). In keeping with the shift in priorities toward consumption envisioned by the Reform, opening investment to market forces was also intended to decrease the level of investment, and investment declined by 5 percent by October, 1965 (Bičanić, p. 633; Dubey, p. 38; NYT 10/20/65) after the availability of credit sharply declined.

In keeping with the market orientation of the 1965 Reform, the primary goal of the Reform in the foreign trade sector was to integrate the Yugoslav economy into the international economy (Horvat, *YES*, p. 21; "YEP," p. 83; Dubey, p. 18). Yugoslav authorities believed that abandoning the relatively autarkic policy emphasis of previous years was a crucial step in eliminating the balance of payments deficit which had recently appeared (Bičanić, p. 643; Lang, p. 230; Horvat, *YES*, p. 127). The first step in this integration process was to make Yugoslav goods competitive by bringing the price of Yugoslav goods into line with world market prices and then permitting prices to fluctuate according to the pressures of the world market (Bičanić, pp. 638, 642; OECD, 1966, p. 8). As was mentioned above, this task was accomplished in July as part of the reform of the internal price system.

Three adjustments in the value of the dinar formed an integral part of the reforms in the foreign trade sector. Accompanying the proclamation of the Reform was an announcement of a currency reform in which 100 "old" dinars would be equal to one "new" dinar (NYT 7/25/65; OECD, 1966, p. 8). At the same time, the system of export premiums and tax subsidies, which effectively constituted a multiple exchange rate system, was abolished in favor of a single, unified exchange rate.[57] The new exchange rate also represented a devaluation from the old rate of 750 dinars per $1 U.S. to 1250 dinars per $1 U.S.[58] These currency adjustments were a necessary first step in attaining full convertibility of the dinar by 1970, a stated goal of the Reform (NYT 10/20/65; Horvat, "YEP," p. 127).

Another crucial step in the integration of the Yugoslav and world economies was the reduction of foreign trade protectionism. Quantitative restrictions were removed on 25 percent of all imports, particularly raw material imports, and the customs tariff rate was decreased from 23 percent to 11 percent.[59] These measures were designed to expose Yugoslav enterprises to increased competition from abroad which, it was hoped, would have the effect of increasing enterprise efficiency.

Decreased administrative control over economic decision-making at all levels had important implications for the behavior of enterprises and the role of planning in the Yugoslav economy. One of the main consequences of the Reform, and also one of its goals, was to increase the decision-making autonomy of the enterprise, particularly with respect to the distribution of enterprise income (Horvat, p. 223; Mačešić, p. 42; Schrenk, p. 26). Enterprises were now permitted to disburse freely between investment and wages a full 70 percent of their income; the remaining 30 percent was designated for the use of the social community (Bičanić, p. 638; Vukmanović, p. 28). As a result, not only were prices freely formed, but wages and investment were also made responsive to market forces. The need for and effectiveness of central planning was almost completely eliminated. Planning would now be "multicentric" with inputs from all levels and sectors of the economy, rather than a monopoly of the central government (Horvat, "YES," p. 83) and would be indicative, not compulsive.

This package of "laissez-faire inspired" reforms (Horvat, *YES*, p. 27) was favorably received by the Bank and Fund. A $70 million loan was made by the IBRD to Yugoslavia for transportation projects. For the most part, IBRD monies were designated for projects which were intended to facilitate the delivery of exports to major Yugoslav ports (such as the Belgrade-Bar Railway Project). This was consistent with the foreign trade emphasis of the Reform. The IMF also contributed to the reform process through the conclusion of an $80 million Stand-by Arrangement with Yugoslavia. This agreement demonstrated the Fund's confidence in the new reforms to potential leaders worldwide and to Yugoslavia's creditors. Funds from this Stand-by Arrangement benefited Yugoslavia in addition to the confidence it inspired in international financial circles. The IMF loan was used to bolster Yugoslav foreign exchange reserves against any unexpected drains which might have resulted from the reforms (Horvat, *YES*, p. 127; OECD, 1966, p. 4).

The Fund's support of the 1965 Reform went beyond financial assistance, however. IMF officials had been consulted about the details of the Reform beginning in 1964. This has led one analyst, Cheryl Payer, to conclude that the Fund played more than an advisory role in the Reform and had actually orchestrated a large part of it (*Debt Trap*, p. 132) as a condition of extending monetary aid. This conclusion is misleading, however. Yugoslav economic thought since the Cominform break had been distinctly monetarist, an orientation which was also prevalent in the Fund. Economic experimentation in Yugoslavia had always emphasized monetary policy, primarily because fiscal policy was almost non-existent in Yugoslavia until well into the 1970s.[60] Since the Yugoslavs' conception of the causes of their economic problems was couched in monetarist terms, it is hardly surprising that the solutions devised, such as restriction of bank credit and emphasis on controlling the money supply, reflected that perspective.[61]

That the Yugoslav and IMF perspectives coincided was not a matter of coercion but of coincidence based in part on circumstance and in part on cooperation. Once the Yugoslavs had rejected the Soviet model, which occurred *prior* to Bank and Fund involvement in Yugoslavia, the Keynesian model used by the Bank and Fund was one of the alternative examples on which Tito and his party could rely for relevant economic theory in constructing a new Yugoslav economic order. In addition, the Soviet Bloc's embargo forced Tito to seek development aid from the West and therefore ensured that he would at least consider the advantages the Keynesian model had to offer Yugoslav economic thought. Furthermore, the multinational character of Yugoslav society and the need for popular support in the face of a Soviet "threat" gave additional weight to the consideration of any alternative which could possibly aid in defusing the potentially dangerous "nationality" issue; the impersonal forces of the market and decentralization were two such alternatives.

It can be concluded, therefore, that the 1965 economic reform in Yugoslavia was not enacted solely in return for aid. Historical circumstance and coincidence played key roles in the direction of Yugoslav economic reform. The need for economic assistance due to the embargo and the political need for decentralization ensured that the IMF's perspective and advice would be given serious consideration by Yugoslavs in search of new structures, but it did not *guarantee* that the market alternative would be chosen (Albania is an example of another possible alternative). The fact that market socialism was selected was due to a deliberate decision of the Yugoslavs which was made in accordance with local conditions and needs, of which reconstruction and development aid were only a part.

Adjustment of Market Socialism, 1971–1975

Beginning in 1972, Yugoslav authorities implemented a third set of adjustments to the economic system. These new policies and structures were a response to both external and internal conditions, and represent a "fine tuning" of the system for the most part. The need for additional reforms derived from the inherent contradictions in the 1965 Reform and the disappointing economic performance which resulted and from the need to codify a number of incremental changes in the system which had accrued since 1966.[62]

A nascent political crisis also gave impetus to the need for reform. The decentralization of economic control had contributed to the underlying ethnic conflicts in Yugoslav society by indirectly increasing income disparities among the republics and provinces. Revived nationalism in Croatia in particular threatened the very survival of the political and economic systems and prompted intervention by the LCY and Federal authorities.[63] Within fourteen months, the Government and the Party had reasserted central control, but the underlying issues were only slowly resolved in the following two years and culminated in the 1974 Constitution.

The political crisis was directly linked to the operation of the new market socialist system. Croatia, one of the more economically developed regions of the country, demanded more control over foreign exchange earned by enterprises within its borders and more autonomy from federal control in both domestic and foreign trade operations. In particular, Croatian dissidents resented the diversion of investment capital, through instruments of the Federal Government, to the lesser developed regions of the country (NYT 2/5/71, 2/10/71). Economic decentralization had exacerbated the already intense pressures within the system for political decentralization. The 1974 Constitution incorporated these factors and established new political structures which devolved most of the Federal Government's powers onto the republican governments. The new political structures therefore mirrored the decentralization which had been institutionalized in the economy in 1965.

Economic Performance and Reform

Yugoslavia's economic policies in the 1970s corresponded to those pursued by other members of the Soviet Bloc during that period, as well as by many other developing nations. Until the late 1970s, Yugoslavia continued its policies which emphasized domestic economic growth as its first priority. Revival of domestic demand and rapidly expanding employment accounted for much of this growth, however, and was slow to slacken after the onset of the first oil price increase in late 1973 (OECD, 1975:5, 7, 8, 15; 1973:5; 1974:5; 1976:20). These policies were successful, culminating in a 6 percent increase in GDP in 1976 alone. Yet there were signs of impending problems which could not be ignored.

This emphasis on growth contributed to an "investment boom" between 1973 and 1975 in which fixed assets increased at a rate of 9–10 percent per year (OECD, 1976:6; 1975:13–14). Investment in Yugoslavia had a political component, however, which hampered the efficiency of investment in that country and eventually led to the "illiquidity problem." Many new enterprises were formulated using strictly political criteria, such as republic location; these were the so-called "political factories." These enterprises consistently operated at a loss which the Federal and Republican governments were required to subsidize because these enterprises were not created using efficiency and profitability criteria, and the Federal and Republican authorities were unwilling to risk the political costs of bankruptcy within their competencies (OECD, 1972:9, 13; 1973:13; 1978:25).

This consistently high demand for credit contributed to a continual problem with inflation in Yugoslavia which became more severe as the decade closed. Both industrial and consumer prices increased sharply during this period; the cost of living index jumped 23 percent between 1972 and 1974 alone (OECD, 1975:21). Yugoslavia's inflation rate remained one of the highest in the OECD, in which it had observer status, throughout the 1970s (OECD, 1975:21; 1974:18). Inflation received highest priority in Yugoslav economic policy until the late 1970s (OECD, 1973:44).

Yugoslav inflation corresponded to a broader world inflationary trend, but it was also a consequence of Yugoslavia's distinctive economic system (Schrenk, p. 111). The extreme decentralization of the system, which was enhanced after the 1970s reforms, fragmented economic authority and made it difficult to impose financial discipline on illiquid enterprises (Dubey, p. 17). The worker self-management system also contributed to cost-push inflationary pressures within Yugoslavia during the early 1970s as workers' councils consistently awarded themselves wage increases disproportionate to productivity and profit margins (Crawford, p. 631; OECD, 1972:20).

The Yugoslav Government actively intervened in the economy in order to stem the precipitous increases in inflation in the 1970s. To a certain extent, this reflected the incomplete nature of the 1965 Reform. Although the ideal was freely determined market prices, reality included several categories of price formation on a continuum from direct control to market determination (Schrenk, p. 121; OECD, 1974:18). Yugoslav economic authorities intervened to direct prices, and thus control inflation, in a number of ways, including price freezes, direct price controls, and restrictions on illiquid enterprises (OECD, 1973:44; Schrenk, p. 119). Consequently, a price freeze was in effect from November 1971 through April 1972,[64] and a wage freeze was imposed for six months in 1972 and 1973 (OECD, 1973:19). Numerous forms of inflation-induced government intervention continued throughout the period (OECD, 1976:27).

Monetary policy, the primary instrument of demand management in Yugoslavia during the 1970s (Dubey, p. 17; OECD, 1973:21), was at best ineffectual at containing inflation, and at worst, contributed to the climb in prices. Policies of restraint adopted as early as 1971 were unevenly applied, were often incomplete, and were implemented after long delays (OECD, 1972:17–19). The money supply actually grew at record rates in 1972 and 1973, at 42.3 percent and 36.8 percent, respectively, at the very time the authorities professed a policy of restraint (OECD, 1975:8, 30; 1973, 21; Schrenk, p. 129). This apparent contradiction can be explained by the relative inefficiency of monetary policy in Yugoslavia at that time and the Government's continued commitment to economic expansion (OECD, 1976:20).

The external sector received high priority in the development and stabilization plans of the Yugoslav Government in the early 1970s. Imports were substantially liberalized by 1971, and foreign exchange became more available to enterprises to use at their discretion (Dubey, p. 265; Schrenk, p. 227). Particular emphasis was placed on production for export markets and exports grew steadily as a result, from $2.2 billion in 1972 to $4 billion in 1975 (OECD, 1978:64). Imports also increased during this time as a result of Yugoslavia's import substitution strategy which required raw material and energy imports, the prices of which had risen sharply after 1973. Imports in 1972 registered $3.2 billion and $7.6 billion in 1975; thus Yugoslavia's trade balance was in deficit for the entire period. The trade deficit ranged from $992 million in 1972 to $3.6 billion in 1975 (OECD, 1978:64). The steady increase in the gap between imports and exports led to the imposition of import controls in August 1974 (OECD, 1976:25) and four devaluations of the dinar before 1975 (Schrenk, p. 225; Dubey, p.265; OECD, 1976:25).

The direction of Yugoslavia's trade also shifted during the period preceding the third set of reforms. In 1972, 65 percent of Yugoslavia's imports originated in the developed industrialized states; by 1975, this figure had declined to 60 percent. Imports from the CMEA countries were relatively stable at 24.7 percent. In contrast Yugoslavia's exports displayed a distinct shift toward the CMEA countries during the 1972–1975 period. Exports to the OECD states declined from 56.8 percent in 1972 to 36 percent in 1975, while exports to the CMEA states increased from 35.6 percent in 1972 to 47.2 percent in 1975. This trend mirrored the effects of the 1973 oil price increase on the world economy, sharply restricting the demand for Yugoslav exports of raw materials products to the industrialized West. In order to compensate for this decline in exports, Yugoslavia increased its exports to the CMEA which sought manufactured products. During this time, the Soviet Union emerged as Yugoslavia's largest trading partner.[65]

The balance of payments improved just prior to the reforms after several years of slight deficit and as a result of the government's efforts to restrict domestic demand. In 1972 and 1973, the current account registered a surplus of over $400 million, but by 1975 a large deficit, $1 billion, had again appeared.[66] Increased borrowing supplied the necessary capital to finance this growing debt (NYT 12/28/72) and by 1976 Yugoslavia's net external debt reached $1 billion (Woodward, p. 528). While in the mid-1970s Yugoslavia's debt was within manageable proportions, continued borrowing to finance a growth strategy which was quickly becoming obsolete soon brought the country into crisis (Woodward, p. 528; Schrenk, pp. 209, 222; Dubey, p. 6).

Reform or Adjustment?

The combination of political unrest and dissatisfaction with the increasing problems in the economy led to pressure for further economic reform in the early 1970s. The Croatian crisis demonstrated the power of the Yugoslav Republics and the need to accommodate their political interests within the new economic framework. The solution was an interesting combination of political and economic decentralization with elements of recentralization in those same spheres of policy.

The policy changes instituted between 1971 and 1974 were less "reforms" than adjustments to the market-socialist system which was established in the 1960s. The Yugoslavs did not alter the fundamental nature of the system, but merely "fine-tuned" certain aspects of that system to accommodate new interests and problems. Direct political bargaining was wedded to market imperatives in an effort to gain some control of the direction and speed of the development process (Horvat, p. 38) This was accomplished by devolving most authority over economic decision-making onto the Republics and Provinces while recentralizing political control within those units of goverment (Tyson, *YES*, pp. 4–5; Linden, p. 218). Policy was now made through a series of agreements or compacts between economic, social, and political groups. Recentralization occurred under the guise of decentralization; central political control was now indirect and located in the Republics and Provinces (Horvat, p. 40; OECD, 1976:33).

The 1974 Constitution institutionalized the "guiding" role of the LCY and the Party quickly reasserted itself in economic policy. Again, however, this guidance was indirect and exercised through established political and economic organs (Linden, pp. 217–218; Comisso, pp. 198–200). In theory, political guidance would guard against the monopolistic tendencies inherent in market socialism (Comisso, p. 197). The 1970s adjustments, therefore, strengthened the intervention capabilities of the party and the state.

This heightened concern for control appeared in the revival of the view of the central plan as more than just an indicator of desired economic trends and performance. Convergent planning emerged as a means of supplementing the market by ensuring that societal goals were met in the most efficient manner possible (Tajnikar, pp. 91–94). Thus, the plan would compensate for the deficiencies in the market mechanism which derived from Yugoslavia's particular political and economic arrangements and level of development (Schrenk, p. 71). There was concern within Yugoslavia that complete dependence on the market would hamper the achievement of important social goals and that the new arrangement include mechanisms which would assure that societal goals would be protected (Tyson and Eichler, p. 141). Convergent planning thus represented a compromise between the positions of the market and planning schools of the decade before.

This new type of plan was be formulated through self-management agreements and social compacts. In a series of laws between 1971 and 1976, including the 1974 Constitution, the authorities established a system of economic policy-making which relied on agreements at every level of production; this system is still in place in the mid-1980s. Workers are organized into sub-firm units known as Basic Organizations of Associated Labor (BOALs) and are given direct authority over the management of the enterprise and the distribution of its profits. BOALs in different enterprises formulate legally binding agreements contracting for supplies and services; these are Self-Management Agreements. These agreements comprise part of a larger system of Social Compacts which are concluded between the Federal and Republican Governments, government organizations, economic organizations, and BOALs. These compacts are statements of policy objectives in several sectors and serve as guidance for the formulation of the plan. Social compacts are not legally binding, but the government can wield significant political and moral pressure to assure compliance with these documents.[67]

The adjustments made to the 1965 Reform, therefore, combined elements of further decentralization and recentralization. The Republics and enterprises gained authority over economic decision-making within their boundaries which theoretically would encourage the operation of market forces. Simultaneously, the political authorities regained authority through the system of agreements, compacts, and convergent planning. What resulted was an interesting "multilateral and polycentric bargaining process" (Comisso, p. 192) in which the basic elements of the 1965 Reform remained the same; Workers' Self-Management and the market now coexisted with increased LCY intervention and planning (Tyson, p. 1). Yugoslavia's economy is consciously neither capitalism nor central-planning (Crawford, p. 633).

Several adjustments were made in the foreign trade and payments sector in the mid-1970s. The Republics assumed responsibility for the administration of the balance of payments, with each unit negotiating its "share" through a social agreement (Woodward, p. 530). A series of laws significantly liberalized imports and exports, with a "free list" of over 1600 products (Crawford, pp. 617–618; Woodward, p. 531). In 1973 a limited foreign exchange market was introduced to coincide with the "floating" of the dinar (Dubey, p. 267; Schrenk, p. 225). The new policy adjustments permitted enterprises more latitude over retention and use of their foreign exchange earnings (Schrenk, p. 227). Finally, the Yugoslav Government confirmed its commitment to joint ventures with non-Yugoslav firms and foreign investment.[68]

Recentralization and the World Bank and the IMF

As in previous reform periods, the IMF and the World Bank were not obvious actors in the reform process. Yugoslavia received only two Standby Arrangements during the entire decade of the 1970s; those occurred in 1971 ($56.18 million) and 1972 ($90.65 million), before the impetus for the adjustments became apparent. Both of these SBAs were in support of a stabilization program which the Yugoslav Government had negotiated with the IMF, and the more stringent monetary and investment policies which followed the SBAs can be attributed, in part, to IMF influence.[69] As the previous discussion demonstrates, however, these policies were not consistently and effectively enforced, and the Yugoslav economy began to exhibit signs of strain. The reforms which followed the outbreak of dissent in the early 1970s did partially approximate standard Fund prescriptions, but again, it would be inaccurate to attribute the policy adjustments which followed solely to IMF pressure. As in the 1950s and 1960s, the 1970s adjustments were primarily a consequence of Yugoslavia's internal dynamics.

Yugoslavia's relations with the World Bank during the 1970s are an interesting example of the interaction of the Bank's organizational philosophy with Yugoslavia's ability to influence Bank operations. As Table 5.3 demonstrates, Yugoslavia received a steady flow of IBRD assistance throughout the 1970s, totalling $2463.8 billion from 1971–1979. This was not an unusually large amount of funds relative to other countries which received loans during this period. In this case, the growth in the number and size of Bank loans to Yugoslavia can be explained largely by changes in the lending philosophy under Bank President McNamara which posited a greater role for the Bank in development financing.

Bank loans to Yugoslavia in the 1970s are unusual in the sense that if the supposed "threshold" of Bank lending had been rigorously enforced at that time, Yugoslavia would not have been *eligible* to receive any loans from the Bank at all.[70] That the Bank continued to lend to Yugoslavia

TABLE 5.3: World Bank Loans to Yugoslavia, 1950-1985 (in millions of U.S. dollars)

Year	Total Amount	No. of Loans	Lesser Developed Region Project
1950	2.7	1	*
1952	28.0	1	*
1953	30.0	1	*
1961	30.0	1	*
1964	35.0	1	1 of 1
1965	70.0	1	*
1966	260.7	8	*
1967	270.7	9	*
1968	60.5	2	*
1969	16.0	1	*
1970	98.5	2	*
1971	90.0	3	*
1972	75.0	1	*
1973	90.4	2	1 of 2
1974	128.0	5	1 of 5
1975	263.0	5	1 of 5
1976	242.0	6	4 of 6
1977	216.0	4	2 of 4
1978	328.0	4	2 of 4
1979	385.0	5	4 of 5
1980	347.0	6	4 of 6
1981	321.0	4	4 of 4
1982	256.6	5	4 of 5
1983	520.0	4	2 of 4
1984	451.0	5	2 of 5
1985	292.5	4	4 of 4

*---denotes not determined

Source: The data from which this table is derived are contained in IBRD, Annual Reports (Washington, D.C.: IBRD).

is evidence that non-economic criteria enter into Bank decisions with respect to Yugoslavia. The nature of the 1970s loans is a clue to why and how these political criteria operated.

During the 1970s, the Bank adopted a "basic human needs" philosophy to guide its lending policies. This approach stressed lending to the poorer segments of society in order to reduce social and economic inequality while raising productivity. Yugoslavia's republics were in essence a miniature of the international dichotomy of developed and developing regions; the average per capita incomes of Slovenia and Croatia were more than double those in Macedonia or Kosovo. By lending to the lesser developed regions of Yugoslavia the Bank could justify continuation of its lending to Yugoslavia without violation of its internal norms. Simultaneously, the Yugoslavs employed Bank loans to redress the imbalance between the economic development of its regions without significant cost to itself. Bank loans provided supplemental investment funds at a time when the authorities were dismantling the administered investment funds which had previously supported projects in the lesser developed regions of the country.

IBRD lending to Yugoslavia's lesser developed Republics provided an ideal solution for a number of problems for the Bank and Yugoslavia and is clearly a case of mutual influence and benefit. In the Bank's own words, "By 1974, Bank lending worldwide was aimed at making the poorest members of society more productive, and in Yugoslavia it was trying to channel the greater part of its resources to the less developed republics."[71] What is not noted here is that the Bank did so with the full cooperation of the Yugoslavs.

Crisis and the Market

By 1980, the Yugoslav economy was once again in near crisis. The second round of oil price increases made it obvious that Yugoslavia could no longer pursue its rapid growth strategy by borrowing abroad. Contrary to the 1970s, terms on additional financial assistance were much harsher, requiring short maturities and floating interest rates. Internal events, such as the 1979 earthquake, had worked to increase Yugoslavia's needs at the very time that private and governmental lending agencies began to question the creditworthiness of many of the Eastern European nations, including Yugoslavia. While most of the creditors' concerns arose as a result of the Soviet invasion of Afghanistan and the political and economic problems in Poland (WSJ 10/8/80; Woodward, p. 535), Yugoslavia's precarious economic situation did not inspire confidence.

The trade balance reached a record deficit in 1979 at $7.2 billion. This was due in large part to the second oil price increases which boosted Yugoslavia's oil bill by 59 percent, or $2.2 billion.[72] Yugoslavia's trade with the industrialized countries increased and its trade with the CMEA decreased during this time (IMF, *Survey* 5/21/80:128). By 1983, however, the total value of Yugoslav trade had dropped, and this situation reversed. In 1983, trade with the CMEA states had grown from 25.4 percent to 36.9 percent of total trade, while trade with the OECD states fell from 60.8 percent to 46 percent of total trade. Because most trade with the CMEA was not conducted in convertible currency, this shift in Yugoslavia's direction of trade was clearly reflected in the balance of payments.

Yugoslavia registered a record current account deficit in 1979. The persistent payments deficits, from the late 1970s until 1983, were financed by borrowing abroad; consequently, Yugoslavia's external debt soared from $6.6 billion in 1976 to $20 billion in 1982.[73] For example, Yugoslavia's external debt grew 400 percent in the decade from 1972 to 1982 and nearly 89 percent of domestic investment funds to fuel the rapid growth strategy derived from loans (Cichock, p. 27); this drove inflation rates from 37 percent in 1980 to nearly 80 percent in 1985 (IMF, *Survey* 2/ 9/81:No. 3; WSJ 2/4/86). The $3.6 billion deficit was arrested and reversed by 1983 through a severe restriction of domestic demand, implemented as part of an austerity program. In 1983, Yugoslavia's balance of payments showed a small surplus of $274 million, and this position was maintained in 1984.[74]

Policy Changes

The magnitude of the debt problem propelled Yugoslavia into further intervention in the market. Yugoslav authorities vowed to avoid any significant increase in debt and to "considerably reduce" existing debt by 1983 (IMF, *Survey* 3/8/82:75; WSJ 11/21/81). The Yugoslav Government inaugurated the first of several austerity and stabilization measures early in 1980 in an effort to fulfill its promise, and the IMF approved these programs with three Stand-by Arrangements in four years (IMF, *Survey* 7/7/80:186, 4/23/84; WSJ 12/29/80). The stabilization programs contained standard measures advocated by the Fund for drastic reductions in domestic demand.

Prices were alternately raised, frozen, and freed throughout the five year period covered by the stabilization programs (OECD, 1980–1985). Interest rates were increased to 1 percent above inflation, and the supply of bank credit was sharply curtailed in an effort to stem the demand for investment (IMF, *Survey* 3/8/82:73; OECD, 1982; Klemenčič, p. 5). In the external sector, the dinar depreciated in 1980 and almost continuously through 1981 (IMF, *Survey* 3/8/82:75; OECD, 1982:23). The National Bank reasserted its control over foreign exchange in 1983 in order to channel scarce convertible currency into the effort to repay the debt.[75] Complementing these policies was a renewed emphasis on import substitution as a means for decreasing costly imports (Cichock, pp. 212, 233; Woodward, pp. 509–510).

The Yugoslav Government actively sought to reschedule its loans which were scheduled to come due in the early 1980s. In 1983 Yugoslavia arranged a rescheduling agreement with its creditors which eventually involved over $5 billion (Linden, p. 223; Cichock, p. 222; NYT 3/26/ 83). Yugoslavia adopted a stringent austerity plan in part to reassure its creditors that it was serious about meeting its debts and as a result was able to negotiate another refinancing package for 1985–1988 (Klemenčič, p. 6; Klarič, p. 25).

Like the 1960s and 1970s, the burgeoning economic crisis provoked increasing criticism from almost every sector of Yugoslav society, including the LCY and members of both the planning and market schools (Woodward, p. 542; Linden, p. 224). This discussion identified the policy adjustments of the 1970s as the primary source of Yugoslavia's internal problems. The extreme decentralization instituted by the 1970s measures had fragmented the system, causing an increase in bureaucratic regulation and the duplication of facilities. The need to obtain each Republic's approval for economic policy in many areas lengthened the response time of the Federal Government and rendered Yugoslavia unable to accommodate the rapid changes which were occurring in the international economy.[76]

In 1980–1981, the Yugoslav Government formed a commission to investigate the current problems and to suggest solutions. The Commission for Problems of Economic Stabilization (Kraigher Commission) returned with a stinging criticism of the manner in which the 1970s adjustments had been implemented and a call for a return to market mechanisms (Woodward, pp. 536–538). This renewed reliance on the market was to occur *within* the 1970s structure of associated labor, however (Cichock, pp. 222, 226). The Commission merely recommended increasing central coordination of economic policy by the Federal Government and the enforcement of fiscal responsibility. To date, these recommendations have not culminated in new structures but have merely reiterated many of the intentions of the 1965 Reform, such as the renewed emphasis on the possibility of enterprise bankruptcies.

Yugoslavia, Crisis, and Bank and Fund Lending

The World Bank was one of the few creditors from which Yugoslavia was willing to borrow after its decision to curtail its debt and in fact, Yugoslav authorities assigned high priority to acquiring new Bank credits (Klemenčič, p. 7; Cichock, p. 223). The IBRD extended loans to Yugoslavia in all five years examined in this section (see Table 5.3) for a total of $2.18 billion. The loans were designated for a wide variety of projects, with the most frequent projects appearing in the transportation and energy sectors. What is most interesting about Bank lending to Yugoslavia during this time is that it continued the trend toward lending to the lesser developed regions which was established in the 1970s. Of the twenty-eight projects in Yugoslavia approved for Bank loans between 1980 and 1985, 20 of them were either located in a lesser developed region of the country or at least one portion of the project was designed to benefit those areas (IBRD, *Annual Reports, 1980–1985*). Again, this was a deliberate policy of both the Bank and Yugoslavia (Cichock, p. 219). There was no sign of increasing tension between Yugoslavia and the World Bank into the mid-1980s. Yugoslavia hosted the Bank and Fund Annual Meeting in 1979 and was one of the first countries to receive a Structural Adjustment loan from the Bank, in 1983.

Relations with the IMF were not as cordial, however, and serious criticism of the Fund emerged from Yugoslavia, perhaps for the first time. The Fund lent over $2.1 billion to Yugoslavia in three SBAs between 1980 and 1984. The 1981 SBA for $1.6 billion was at that time the largest single SBA ever negotiated by the Fund. Each of the SBAs was in support of the austerity and stabilization measures planned by Yugoslavia and the policy package strongly resembled other such agreements negotiated by the Fund at that time.[77] The SBA negotiated for 1985–1986 even contained slightly relaxed performance criteria (Klemenčič, p. 8).

To a large extent, Yugoslavia could not avoid recourse to the Fund. Its creditors, wary of further lending to an East European borrower, demanded the Fund's participation in any negotiations on the Yugoslav debt as a type of guarantee that Yugoslavia would adhere to its course of austerity (NYT 11/27/84, 3/26/83). Yugoslavia was reluctant to incur additional debt with the Fund and formulated a unique arrangement in 1986 whereby Yugoslavia would permit "greater IMF supervision" of its monetary policies without necessarily drawing on an SBA (WSJ 2/4/86). The Yugoslavs hoped that this would be sufficient to satisfy its creditors.

The extent of IMF influence over Yugoslav economic policy in the 1980s is again problematical. It is obvious that Yugoslav policies closely approximated those usually prescribed by the Fund, but a cursory examination of the policies of many other states at this time, both market and non-market, reveals that those policies were widely adopted in response to the debt crisis. It is almost impossible to distinguish, therefore, where IMF leverage began and ended. Complicating this situation is the influence of private and governmental creditors who relied on the Fund to supervise debt management in their borrowers. The ultimate question is, then, did Yugoslavia adopt a market-based solution to its economic problems because it believed that such an approach would solve its problems, because it was compelled to do so by the IMF, or because of a combination of these two factors forced upon it by the need to reschedule its debts with private and government lenders?

Evidence from Yugoslavia itself suggests that the IMF has played a greater role in policy choice than ever before. Sharp criticism of the

Fund has appeared in Yugoslavia which parallels criticisms of the Fund endorsed by the political critique (see Jovović).Charges that "[p]olitical stands play an important role in . . . pushing otherwise primary economic criteria into the background" and the unusual arrrangement with the Fund in 1986 to avoid another SBA hint that perhaps Yugoslavia's relationship with the Fund has deteriorated. Reports of intense political conflict within Yugoslavia over the adoption of specific forms of IMF austerity support this speculation (Woodward, p. 541). Fundamentally, however, it is not the Fund which has coerced Yugoslavia into this situation but a combination of internal and external factors, including its international creditors.

Conclusion

The strong support of the Bank and Fund for the course of Yugoslav economic development since 1950 took the form of reinforcement rather than inducement or reward. The pattern of Yugoslavia's relationship with both organizations tended to be one in which Yugoslav officials sought technical advice and financial support from the Bank and Fund for reforms which had been previously debated and tentatively accepted. Periods of major reforms were preceded by at least two years of intense debate within Yugoslavia. Bank and Fund assistance in the 1950s and 1960s was of a frequency and level which does not suggest that the Yugoslavs were unusually well-rewarded if they had indeed adopted reforms in conformance with IMF demands. It was only after the Bank and Fund were convinced that the break with the Cominform was genuine that they agreed to lend, and even then, the first Bank loan to Yugoslavia was for a project which was designed to aid Western European recovery.

These loans were reinforcing in nature; both the 1953 and 1965 reforms had been vigorously debated for at least 12 months before support was sought from the Bank and Fund, although in 1965 both organizations did provide assistance in formulating the details of the new policies. In both cases, however, the resulting policies were a logical extension of previous developments within Yugoslavia.

This conclusion is further confirmed when one notes that the period during which Yugoslavia received a steady, high flow of aid, 1970-1980, was a period of relatively little major reform. Between 1970 and 1980, the World Bank lent Yugoslavia $2306.9 million, whereas Yugoslavia received only $270.7 million during the period 1948-1970. Yugoslavia's Stand-By Arrangements to 1965 totalled $110 million but came to $135.25 million between 1970 and 1980. Yet during the 1970-1980 period, Yugoslav authorities actually retreated slightly from the market orientation of the

1960s and adopted a "convergent planning approach" which purported to guard against the "anti-social" effects of a market system.[78] Convergent planning did not result in a marked turn toward a more typical form of central planning, however, and the basic elements of market socialism remain intact. Given these facts, one can conclude that Bank and Fund loans to Yugoslavia in the 1970s were intended to reinforce what appeared to be a desirable, or at least familiar, course of events.

Problems with debt management, one of the potential costs of active participation in the international economy, became increasingly evident in Yugoslavia in the 1980s. Yugoslavia's public external debt amounted to $1.8 billion in 1967 and $2.4 billion in 1973, but by 1980 that figure had risen to $18 billion. In addition, the balance of payments deficit rose to $2.1 billion in 1980. This sharp increase in indebtedness in Yugoslavia paralleled the trend in the Third World and can be largely attributed to the coincidence of sharply increased oil prices and the onset of recession in the U.S. and the EEC (WSJ 10/20/81). To date, Yugoslavia has been able to withstand the uncertainty and debt caused by increased interaction in the international economy because of the domestic popularity of its regime, which allows it to institute often unpopular austerity measures. This support is waning as the austerity period persists, however. In any event, membership in the "capitalist" Bank and Fund has not yet become a focus of debate in Yugoslavia as government officials struggle to revive their flagging economy.

The factor of time and experience cannot be excluded when reviewing the reasons for Yugoslav success in the Bank and Fund. By 1960, the Bank and the Fund had clarified their roles and established procedural precedents. Both organizations were more secure and confident in their roles as international lending agencies and were more willing to take chances and to tolerate unusual circumstances. Also, the massive influx of newly independent states in the membership of the IMF and IBRD forced these institutions to adapt to a wide variety of economic structures and problems. Yugoslavia provided the Bank and the Fund with valuable experience upon which both institutions are likely to rely in the future.

Yugoslavia's relationship with the Bank and the Fund has benefited from that nation's non-aligned foreign policy stance. Long the "maverick" of the Soviet Bloc, Yugoslavia provided the Bank and Fund with an opportunity to demonstrate tolerance toward centrally-planned econo-mies without significant costs to any of the parties concerned. Since the early 1950s, Yugoslavia has received consistent and strong support for its nonaligned position from the United States and Western Europe, and this has been reflected in the Bank and Fund. Yugoslavia's non-alignment serves political, economic, and strategic purposes for the West, and its experimentation with market socialism only reinforces the desire of the Western industrialized nations, and the organizations in which they predominate, to preserve this maverick's independence.

Notes

1. See Branko Horvat, *The Yugoslav Economic System* (YES), (White Plains, NY: International Arts and Sciences Press, Inc., 1976); and Rudolph Bićanić, "Economics of Socialism in a Developed Country," *Foreign Affairs*, vol. 44, no. 4 (July 1966), pp. 633–661.

2. See Branko Horvat, "Yugoslav Economic Policy in the Post-War Period: Problems, Ideas, Institutional Developments" ("YEP"), *The American Economic Review*, vol. 61, no. 3, pt. 2 (June 1971), pp. 69–169.

3. *Proceedings and Documents of the United Nations Monetary and Financial Conference*, Department of State Publication 2866 (Washington, D.C.: U.S. GPO, 1948), pp. 653, 707, 1045, 1199.

4. *New York Times* (NYT) 8/31/46, 9/2/46.

5. Edward S. Mason and Robert E. Asher, *The World Bank Since Bretton Woods* (Washington, D.C.: The Brookings Institution, 1973), p. 54.

6. A. Ross Johnson, *The Transformation of Communist Ideology: The Yugoslav Case, 1945–1953* (Cambridge, MA: The MIT Press, 1972), p. 103, and the entire Johnson argument. See Horvat, YES, and J. T. Crawford, "Yugoslavia's New Economic Strategy: A Progress Report," in *Economic Developments in Countries of Eastern Europe* (Washington, D.C.: U.S. Congress, Joint Economic Committee, 1970), for discussion of Yugoslavia's early relations with the PRC.

7. The following account is taken from articles in the *New York Times* unless otherwise noted.

8. NYT 7/16/49.

9. NYT 5/5/49. According to this account, Yugoslavia "has asked the United States through its representative on the bank to take a friendly attitude" toward Yugoslavia's application for a loan. See also NYT 5/23/49.

10. NYT 7/11/49; Johnson, p. 126.

11. The following is taken from the NYT 7/29–10/11/49.

12. For a full discussion of the reforms see Horvat, YES, and "YEP"; Rikard Lang, "Yugoslavia," Chapter 8 in Hans-Hermann Hohmann, Michael Kaser, and Karl C. Thalheim (eds.), *The New Economic Systems of Eastern Europe* (Berkeley: University of California Press, 1975), pp. 223–250; Bićanić, "Economics of Socialism;" Johnson, *Transformation*; Laura D'Andrea Tyson, *The Yugoslav Economic System and Its Performance in the 1970s*, Research Series No. 44 (Berkeley: Institute of International Studies, 1980); Maks Tajnikar, "The Coexistence of Market and Plan in the Development of Yugoslav Economic Thought," *Eastern European Economics*, vol. 16, no. 1 (Fall 1977), pp. 74–101; Vinod Dubey, *Yugoslavia: Development with Decentralization* (Baltimore, MD: The Johns Hopkins University Press, 1975); Martin Schrenk, Cyrus Ardalan and Nawal A. El Tatawy, *Yugoslavia: Self-Management Socialism and the Challenges of Development* (Baltimore, MD: The Johns Hopkins University Press, 1979); NYT 1/7/50 and 2/8/50.

13. See Johnson, p. 124 for discussion of the PRC. NYT 2/9/50, 9/15/50, 9/17/50.

14. NYT 2/19/50, 2/20/50; J. Keith Horsefield and Margaret G. deVries, *The International Monetary Fund, 1945–1964*, vol. 1 (Washington, D.C.: IMF, 1969), p. 258.

15. Mason and Asher, p. 157; Johnson, p. 30; NYT 10/10/54. The remaining six states were Greece, Brazil, Peru, Bolivia, Ecuador, and Costa Rica. Brazil received two World Bank loans totalling $31 million in 1949 and 1950.

16. NYT 4/7/51; Horvat, *YES* and "YEP."

17. NYT 4/27/51; Horvat, "YEP," p. 124. For the following discussion, see articles in the NYT 4/7–12/29/51, unless otherwise noted.

18. NYT 12/29/51; Horvat, "YEP," pp. 78, 124; Dubey, p. 263.

19. C. L. Sulzberger, NYT 4/7/51.

20. NYT 12/30/51, 1/13/51.

21. See NYT articles for 4–12/51.

22. Mason and Asher, p. 112.

23. NYT 2/12/52, 3/16/51. Unless otherwise noted, the following discussion relies on articles from the NYT; see Note 21.

24. Johnson, p. 144; Johann Hawlowitsch, "Yugoslavia: The Pioneer Still Leads," in L. A. D. Dellin and Hermann Gross (eds.), *Reforms in the Soviet and Eastern European Economies* (Lexington, MA: D. C. Heath and Co., 1972), p. 124.

25. NYT 1–3/52.

26. NYT 2/13–7/8/53.

27. NYT 3/23/53; Bićanić, pp. 636–637; Johnson, p. 144; also the discussion earlier in this chapter.

28. NYT 2/1/54, 9/7/54; Johnson, p. 139. It is interesting to note that this renewed interest occurred soon after the ejection of Milovan Djilas from the Party provoked Party leaders into emphasizing the socialist nature of Yugoslav society.

29. See also Dubey, p. 19; Horvat, "YEP," p. 121.

30. NYT 4/9–10/7/54. Yugoslavia, which claimed the entire city of Trieste, received 10 square miles of Zone A and all of Zone B in the settlement.

31. Horvat, "YEP," p. 125; NYT 1/5/54; 2/9/54.

32. Crawford, p. 612.

33. Lang, pp. 223, 228.

34. Radio Free Europe, "World Bank Aids Yugoslavia's Economic Development," *Radio Free Europe Research: Communist Area*, no. 0761 (October 16, 1970).

35. See Horvat, *YES*, especially pp. 22–23, and "YEP," especially pp. 143, 83.

36. Tajnikar, pp. 78–81.

37. This and the following discussion of the market school are derived from Horvat, "YEP," p. 84, and *YES* p. 23; Pedro Ramet, *Nationalism and Federalism in Yugoslavia: 1963– 1971*, chapter 6: "The Reform Crisis " (Bloomington: Indiana University Press, 1984); Dennison Rusinow, *The Yugoslav Experiment* (Berkeley: University of California Press, 1977), especially chapters 2,4, and 5.

38. See Horvat, *YES*, p. 20, and "YEP," p. 82; Payer, p. 129; Dubey, p. 264; Schrenk, p. 225.

39. Horvat, "YEP," p. 126 and *YES*, p. 198, Hawlowitsch, p. 124.

40. See Hawlowitsch, p. 125, and Horvat, "YEP," pp. 134, 137, and *YES*, p. 211, for further discussion of monetary reforms.

41. IMF, *Annual Report of the Executive Board, 1961*, p. 29; Payer, p. 129.

42. See also Horvat, "YEP," p. 143 and *YES*, p. 20; Bićanić, p. 634; Schrenk, p. 18.

43. See NYT 4/12–6/9/64, and Horvat, *YES*, p. 191, and "YEP," p. 83 for discussion of these issues.

44. Branko Horvat attributes the cause of the 1965 reforms directly to the 1964 recession. See *YES*, p. 198, and "YEP," p. 83.

45. OECD, *Economic Surveys: SFRY* (Paris: OECD, 1966), p. 11.

46. See Horvat, "YEP," p. 228, and *YES*, p. 144, and OECD, 1966, pp. 23–24, for details on the preceding discussion.

47. See NYT 1/10–7/22/66.

48. See NYT 5/15/64 and 12/27/64 for examples.

49. NYT 7/15/65; 10/20/65; Bićanić, p. 634; Horvat, "YEP," p. 85; Dubey, p. 38.

50. Svetozar Vukmanović, *Economic Reform in Yugoslavia* (Belgrade: Confederation of Trade Unions of Yugoslavia, 1966), p. 7.

51. George Mačešić and Dimitrije Dimitrijević, *Money and Finance in Contemporary Yugoslavia* (New York: Praeger Publishers, 1973), p. 41.

52. See also Bićanić, p. 640; Dubey, p. 38.

53. On the market goal, see Mačešić, p. 42; NYT 10/20/65; Horvat, *YES*, p. 21 and "YEP," p. 83; Schrenk, pp. 119–121. On the stabilization goal, see NYT 7/25/65; Hawlowitsch, p. 131; Bićanić, p. 634; Lang, p. 230; Horvat, "YEP," pp. 85–86; Dubey, p. 38.

54. See Dubey, pp. 39, 18; Horvat, *YES*, p. 198; Bićanić, p. 638; OECD, 1966, p. 5.

55. After the 1965 reforms, rents in Yugoslavia increased by an average of 100 percent, while the prices for public transportation and electricity increased 45 percent and 50 percent, respectively. See NYT 10/20/65; Mačešić, p. 44.

56. NYT 10/20/65; Horvat, *YES*, p. 223; Laura D'Andrea Tyson and Gabriel Eichler, "Continuity and Change in the Yugoslav Economy in the 1970s and 1980s," in *East European Economic Assessement, Part 1—Country Studies, 1980* (Washington, D.C.: U.S. Congress, Joint Economic Committee, 1981), p. 145.

57. Dubey, p. 18; OECD, 1966, p. 8; Schrenk, p. 26; Bićanić, p. 642; NYT 7/25/65; Lang, p. 235; Mačešić, p. 49; Vukmanović, p. 12.

58. NYT 7/25/65; Cheryl Payer, *The Debt Trap: The International Monetary Fund and the Third World* (New York: Monthly Review Press, 1975), p. 132; Horvat, "YEP," p. 126; Dubey, p. 264; OECD, 1966, p. 8; Bićanić, p. 642.

59. Lang, p. 235; Dubey, p. 18; Horvat, *YES*, pp. 198–199; Payer, p. 132; OECD, 1966, p. 8; Bićanić, p. 643.

60. Horvat, "YEP," p. 130. See also Mačešić; Dubey; Horvat, *YES*; Bićanić.

61. See Lang, pp. 235–237; Bićanić, p. 641; and Dubey, p. 17, for discussion of specific policies stemming from the Reform.

62. See Schrenk, et al., *Yugoslavia: Self-Management Socialism*; OECD, *Economic Surveys: SFRY* (Paris: OECD, 1972, 1973); Tyson, *YES*, p. 3; Ellen Comisso, "Yugoslavia in the 1970's: Self-Management," *Journal of Comparative Economics*, vol. 4, no. 2 (1980), p. 193; Susan Woodward, "Orthodoxy and Solidarity: Competing Claims and International Adjustment in Yugoslavia," *International Organization*, vol. 40, no. 2 (1986), p. 527.

63. Horvat, *YES*, p. 38; Tyson, *YES*, pp. 3–4; Woodward, p. 527; NYT—see issues in February, April, July and December, 1971 and in January, 1972.

64. OECD, 1973:20; 1972:20–22; J.J. Hauvonen, "Money and Banking in Yugoslavia: Since 1965," *Finance and Development*, vol. 9, no. 1 (1972), p. 47.

65. OECD, 1979:62; Schrenk, pp. 206–207; Dubey, pp. 19–20, 268; Ronald H. Linden, "The Impact of Interdependence: Yugoslavia and International Change," *Comparative Politics*, vol. 18, no. 2, p. 213.

66. OECD, 1978:64, discussions in 1973–1976 volumes; Schrenk, pp. 203, 209; Dubey, pp. 4, 35.

67. For reference, see Schrenk, p. 41; Linden, pp. 217–218; Horvat, pp. 39–40; Tyson and Eichler, "Continuity;" Tyson, *YES*, p. 5; Dubey, pp. 2, 42.

68. Woodward, p. 530; Horvat, *YES*, p. 205; Crawford, p. 618; NYT 1/1/72.

69. Margaret Garritsen deVries, *The International Monetary Fund, 1966–1971: The System Under Stress*, vol. 1, (Washington, D.C.: IMF), pp. 310, 320; Dubey, pp. 20, 4; Schrenk, p. 224.

70. See Chapter 1.

71. IBRD, *Yugoslavia and the World Bank* (Washington, D.C.: IBRD, 1979), p. 34.

72. OECD, 1984:78; Woodward, p. 534; IMF, *Survey* 5/21/80:127; M. Klarič, "Yugoslavia and the International Monetary Fund," *Review of International Affairs* vol. 35 (Apr. 5, 1984), p. 26.

73. Mark A. Cichock, "Reevaluating a Development Strategy: Policy Implications for Yugoslavia," *Comparative Politics*, vol. 17, no. 2, p. 211.

74. OECD, 1984:78; Woodward, p. 542; IMF, *Survey* 3/8/1982:72–73; Vladimir Klemenčič, "Yugoslavia and Its External Debt," *Review of International Affairs* vol. 36 (1984), p. 5.

75. Milan Jovanović, "Changes in Yugoslavia's Economic System," *Review of International Affairs* vol. 35 (Mar. 5, 1984), p. 26; Woodward, p. 537.

76. See Tyson and Eichler for a complete discussion of the problems stemming from the 1970s economic adjustments. Also see OECD, 1982; Woodward, pp. 516, 533; Cichock, pp. 216–217; WSJ 7/22/80; NYT 2/20/80, 10/29/84; Jovanović, "Changes in Yugoslavia's Economic System."

77. IMF, *Survey* 2/9/81:37, 4/23/84:125; NYT 1/22/83; Dejan Jovović, "Yugoslavia and the International Monetary Fund," *Review of International Affairs* vol. 36 (June 20, 1985), p. 25.

78. See the following for analyses of convergent planning: Tyson, *Yugoslav Economic System*; Tajnikar; Tyson, "Continuity;" Dubey; Schrenk; and OECD, *Economic Surveys: SFRY, 1972–1975*.

6

Romania:
Central Planning and the IMF

Romania became the fifth avowedly Communist state to join the IMF and the IBRD, but at the time of Romania's entrance into both organizations in 1972, only one other Communist state, Yugoslavia, remained. Like Yugoslavia, Romania's relationship with the Bank and Fund has been cordial, but unlike Yugoslavia, the minimal amount of economic reform which has occurred in Romania since 1972 has been in the direction of recentralization with an expanded role for political intervention in economic decision-making.

Romania's economic structure and policies are excellent examples in many ways of a typical socialist economy found in a Communist country. The Romanian economy has been described as "one of the most tightly controlled and centrally directed economies in Eastern Europe."[1] A system of comprehensive central planning is expedited by the state, which in turn, is directed by the Romanian Communist Party. The political and economic aspects of economic decision-making are almost completely fused in Romania, and this principle is actually enforced by law.[2] Economic development has been the primary economic goal of the Ceauşescu regime which assumed power in 1965, and the state has been designated by Ceauşescu as the "agent and executor of development policies and programs."[3] This has led to a growing "bureaucratization" in the economy which in recent years has been identified by the regime as a hindrance to further development (Graham, p. 82).

In terms of development strategy, Romania, like other members of the Soviet bloc, chose a strategy of extensive development. In this strategy, emphasis is placed on the industrial sector of the economy and saving at the expense of consumption. An extensive pattern of development also relies on a substantial shift of labor from the agricultural sector of the economy to industrial jobs. During this period, the economy is also relatively autarkic, relying on domestic production as much as possible to conserve scarce foreign exchange.[4]

Romania's development program exhibited all of these characteristics into the late 1970s. The economy was characterized by high levels of investment in new industrial facilities (Jackson, "Perspectives," p. 273; Ioţa, p. 105). Although the agricultural sector was secondary in terms of Romanian economic priorities, modernization of agriculture was attempted through the familiar method of collectivization and investment in farm machinery.[5] Autarky, or as the Romanians express it, economic independence, was an integral part of Romania's push for development, and the Romanian government consistently attempted to minimize the foreign trade sector until the mid-1960s (Gamarnikow, p. 182; Jackson, "Perspectives," p. 299, and "Industry," pp. 888–889, 940). In addition, central planning was explicitly identified by Romanian authorities as an integral part of that independence (Ioţa, p. 103).

Romania's economic independence was accompanied by an ever-increasing political independence. In the 1960s, Ceauşescu slowly moved Romania from a position of reliance on the CMEA and Warsaw Pact, the economic and political arms of the Soviet Bloc, and began to seek contacts with non-aligned states, and to a lesser degree, Western, capitalist states.[6] This posture of political independence assisted Romania's development effort in that it engendered popular support for Ceauşescu. This was necessary in order for the regime to endure in spite of the pressures created by the economic sacrifices required of the population by an extensive growth strategy.[7]

Despite the appearance of invariability, the Romanian economy can be analyzed in three periods: two periods of "reform," at least by Romanian standards, and one of crisis. Soon after his accession to power, Ceauşescu instituted a re-examination of the Romanian economy. There ensued a discussion which concluded that the Romanian economy had progressed to a stage where an intensive development strategy would be more productive. The preliminary stages of this reform had barely been implemented, however, when a second set of reforms was effected which negated the effects of the first, for the most part. It was during this second period that Romania joined the Bank and the Fund and theoretically, became vulnerable to their "capitalistic" influences. In the final period under examination, 1978–1984, economic crisis propelled Romania into an even closer relationship with both organizations and a more subtle consideration of market-oriented policies.

In the following section, a brief description of the aborted 1967 reform is provided as a background for evaluating Romanian reform actions in the 1970s. The 1967 reforms indicate the direction of Romanian economic thought *prior* to any contact with the IMF or IBRD. In particular, an understanding of the 1967 reforms will place in perspective the influence of the IMF and IBRD on the 1978 reforms.

Aborted Reform, 1967–1972

By the mid-1960s, Ceauşescu and other members at the top of the Romanian Communist Party hierarchy concluded that Romania had reached the limits of the extensive development strategy and would have to shift to an intensive pattern if the successes of the previous two decades were to continue.[8] By 1966, this recognition of the need to streamline the administration of the economy was coupled with an increasing awareness that comprehensive development of the Romanian economy would require the most modern technology and equipment, and this meant increased participation in the international economy, particularly with the West.[9] This increased interaction with capitalist and non-aligned states in economic matters was consistent with Romania's independent foreign policy position and therefore, reinforced Romanian independence.

Ceauşescu identified excessive centralization and bureaucratization as the main obstacles to further economic development. Thus, the original thrust of the 1967 Reform contained a familiar element of decentralization. Public discussion of the reforms focused on the need to strengthen the decision-making authority of both local administrative organs and enterprises themselves.[10] This seeming trend toward self-management was deceptive, however. What was actually intended by the reform was to make planning and control more efficient and effective through a diminution of bureaucratic "red tape" which appeared to hinder effective decision-making, particulary with respect to foreign trade. The actual goal of the 1967 Reform was de-bureaucratization, not decentralization (Rohleder, pp. 119–121).

It was at the 9th Party Congress of the RCP in July, 1965 that the need for some type of economic reform was officially recognized (Rohleder, p. 116). The issue was quietly debated by the Party hierarchy until the Central Committee meeting of October, 1967, at which the outline of the Reform was introduced (Gamarnikow, p. 183). The "Directives of the Central Committee of the Romanian Communist Party on the Perfecting of Management and Planning the National Economy," the actual blueprint for the Reform, was formally approved by the party in December, 1967, and initiated a reform period which endured until 1972.[11]

Decentralization in the context of the 1967 Directives did not mean the devolution of final decision-making authority to the enterprise, as in the Yugoslav case, but merely bringing management closer to production. Prior to 1967, ministry officials had assumed an active role in the daily management of enterprises, and the inevitable delays and inefficiency frequently associated with this practice resulted (Smith, p.

38; Gamarnikow, p. 213). The Directives assigned strictly supervisory roles to the ministries, such as the drafting of plans, and placed responsibility for routine daily decisions with the enterprises (Kaser, p. 177). For the first time, the enterprise was permitted to retain up to 10 percent of its profits to dispose of freely (Kaser, p. 189), and enterprises and local authorities were now to participate in the planning process, albeit in a very minor capacity (Smith, p. 36; Ioţa, p. 102).

Within the enterprise, the Directives hinted at a rudimentary form of workers' self-management. The Directives advocated replacing one-man management of enterprises in all sectors with a form of collective management (Smith, p. 38). The manner in which "collective management" was defined approximated an early stage of self-management as practiced by Yugoslavia between 1950 and 1953. In April, 1968, Boards of Management were introduced, which were composed of 5–21 members, of whom 1–5 were elected by enterprise employees. In October, 1971, these numbers were revised so that the Boards now consisted of 9–25 members with 3–11 elected members. These boards only possessed minimal advisory powers, however, and were often dominated by political appointees (Kaser, p. 184; Rohleder, p. 117; Gamarnikow, p. 209).

Creation of industrial and agricultural centrals was the most notable innovation of the Directives. Centrals were administrative units which were intended to operate like branch holding companies at a level between the ministries and enterprises (Rohleder, p. 118; Gamarnikow, p. 208). According to Alan H. Smith:

> "The Central would, in consultation with the ministry and their economic bodies, estimate targets for its output and assortment plan, the volume of deliveries to the market and other centrals, exports, indices for cost reduction, imports, inputs of materials, and its financial plan" (*Romanian Economic Reforms*, p. 38).

The central linked enterprises which produced similar outputs or which were at different stages of production of the same good (Rohleder, p. 118). Ceauşescu emphasized that centrals were production bodies intended to unify and concentrate production into larger units, not merely another type of administrative, coordinating body (Smith, p. 40). The creation of centrals did coincide with a reduction in the number of industrial and agricultural units in Romania, a phenomenon not frequently associated with decentralization (Kaser, pp. 177, 186).

The Directives assigned a marginally increased role to price and credit levels, although this new role in no way approximated a free market. Bank credits were introduced to aid investment financing, and the pricing system was revised (Smith, pp. 38–39; Gamarnikow, p. 213; Rohleder,

p. 119). In addition, the minuscule private sector of the Romanian economy benefited from some relaxation of control which permitted private businesses to hire labor at a fixed minimum wage (Kaser, pp. 190–191). It must be emphasized again, however, that these measures were *not* intended to initiate a market economy in Romania.

Finally, the Directives called for substantial revisions in the foreign trade system. In September, 1969, the Ministry of Foreign Trade was reorganized to perform coordinating functions only, and by 1970 only three foreign trade enterprises remained under the Ministry's control; the others had been absorbed by the relevant industrial ministries. A new foreign trade bank was also created to handle foreign currency and foreign investment transactions. This was accompanied by a revised foreign trade pricing system and an export premium of 4-6 percent.[12]

The geographical distribution of Romania's trade was shifted towards capitalist and Third World countries in order to obtain the equipment and technology needed to support the new, intensive phase of Romanian development and to increase Romania's independence from the CMEA (Montias, pp. 871–872; Brada, p. 1264). The Romanian government also sought short- and medium-term credits from commercial and private lenders in the West to increase its investment supply (Montias, p. 872; Smith, p. 37; Jackson, "Industry," pp. 893, 912). Marvin R. Jackson estimates that Romanian foreign debt had increased by $1 billion between 1965 and 1970, the peak year of Romanian borrowing from Western sources (Jackson, "Industry," pp. 893, 889). It was also during this period that Romania began to experiment with joint ventures, the first Soviet bloc country to do so. The Foreign Trade Law of 1971 permitted foreign firms to invest in jointly-owned ventures with Romanian enterprises. Foreign firms were limited to a 49 percent share of investment, but repatriation of profits and equity was sanctioned.[13]

The Directives originally set December 31, 1969, as the deadline for implementation of the reforms. This deadline was subsequently delayed three times to December, 1972, when the reforms were abandoned (Garmarnikow, p. 209). This delay is directly attributable to the political struggle which the reforms had initiated within the Party and between Party members and the State bureaucracy. The Directives represented a compromise between those forces which desired a reduction in the number of centrally-determined indices, greater use of incentives and levers, and the use of profits as a measure of success, and members of the state apparatus who wanted even more centralization (Smith, p. 37). Consequently, the compromise represented by the Directives was inconsistent; the reform contained elements of both centralization and decentralization. Enterprises were given more decision-making authority without the instruments to implement it (Smith, p. 39; Garmarnikow, pp. 184, 207). The Party/State apparatus debate continued even after the Directives were issued, and the bureaucratic opposition which resulted effectively delayed, then destroyed, the entire reform process (Smith, p. 40; Garmarnikow, p. 183).

As the preceding analysis indicates, early attempts at economic reform in Romania made only marginal adjustments in economic structure and policy. The economic reform of 1967 was never intended to be comprehensive. What was desired by Ceauşescu was merely an "improvement" in economic efficiency, not a complete overhaul of the structure of the economy (Kaser, p. 173). The fact that the retention of central planning was never in doubt and mandatory indicators continued to be imposed on enterprises attests to the incremental nature of the Directives (Rohleder, p. 117; Gamarnikow, pp. 208–209). Thus, when the reform stalled and finally yielded to a renewed centralization effort, there were very few changes to be made.

Membership and Recentralization, 1972–1977

Romania's economic structure when it joined the IMF and IBRD in December, 1972, (NYT 12/6/72) differed very little from its economic structure in the 1960s. Beginning in 1973, Ceauşescu embarked on a course to bring the Romanian economy to a level comparable to that which prevailed in Western Europe. As had been recognized but not acted upon in the Directives, a strategy of intensive development was vital to the achievement of this goal.[14] "Multilateral development," which was the term given to the intensive development of all sectors of the economy, was explicitly linked to the acquisition of the most modern scientific and technological techniques and equipment.[15] This goal would require hard currency, however, and earnings of that commodity had not reached desired levels in the previous years (Smith, p. 37). Ceauşescu concluded that remobilization of the Romanian economy was necessary (Jackson, "Industry," p. 890; Tyson, *Economic Adjustment*, p. 74); consequently, the reforms of 1967, already delayed, were deemed too costly and were abandoned in favor of recentralization.

In part, recentralization was an attempt by the RCP hierarchy to reassert control over the state bureaucratic apparatus, which was also a goal of the 1967 Directives. Toward this goal, management of the economy was consolidated by merging Party and State administrative positions (Smith, p. 41; Ioţa, p. 102; Linden, p. 349), and the economy was directed according to a unified national plan, a partial reversal of the intention of the Directives (Ioţa, pp. 102–103; Smith, p. 41). As a result, the number of compulsory indicators was increased, centrally allocated products increased from 180 in 1973 to 720 in 1974, and investment allocation was recentralized (Smith, p. 43; Jackson, "Industry," p. 891).

Institutionally, the power of the centrals to direct enterprise activities was enhanced at the expense of the ministries. While this may appear to be a movement toward decentralization, it was actually an attempt by Party officials to bypass recalcitrant state bureaucrats to bring production closer to the technical staff (Smith, pp. 42–43). Although the amount of earnings retained by enterprises was raised to 40 percent in 1973, many of the other administrative rights which had been extended to enterprises by the Directives were rescinded.[16] The number of enterprises and centrals was reduced; only 102 of the 207 centrals which existed in 1972 remained active in 1973.[17]

Centralization also occurred in the foreign trade sector. Ceauşescu realized that multilateral development could only progress through participation in the international economy, but he desired to minimize the effects of that participation (Ioţa, p. 109; Montias, p. 878). This could only be accomplished, in the Party's view, by restoring control over foreign trade enterprises to the Ministry of Foreign Trade and reducing the number of enterprises engaged in foreign trade activities. By 1975, all but four foreign trade organizations were placed under the Ministry's control, and the number of foreign trade enterprises was reduced from 56 in 1972 to 40 in 1975.[18]

Romania's foreign trade continued to shift away from the CMEA countries between 1973 and 1977. The largest portion of this geographical shift in trade went to Third World states to which Romania was able to export its manufactured goods and thus maintain a trade surplus.[19] Increased economic interactions with the Third World at the expense of both the West and the Soviet Bloc also lent credence to Romania's quest for independence. However, trade with the developed capitalist countries also expanded such that, according to one estimate, imports from and exports to those countries accounted for 47.3 percent of total Romanian trade in 1973 (Montias, p. 872). This growth in trade with the convertible currency countries was primarily in imports and, therefore, led to an increase in Romania's trade deficit. Romania financed this deficit through credits from Western financial sources so that Romania's foreign debt grew by $900 million during the 1970-1975 period (Montias, p. 873; Jackson, "Industry," p. 912; Crowther, p. 564).

Romania's foreign policy also reflected a shift toward the West and the Third World. During this period, Romania applied for membership in the Group of 77 but was granted only observer status because of its membership in the Warsaw Pact.[20] At the same time, Romania expanded its contacts with the West. For example, Romania served as an intermediary between the U.S. and North Vietnam during the peace negotiations and assisted in the arrangements for Henry Kissinger's trip to China (NYT 12/5/73, 7/25/71). In the year prior to its entrance into the IMF and IBRD, Romania was granted Most-Favored-Nation status by the United States, a sign of the growing cordiality between the two states (NYT 7/25/71).

Nationalism and independence from the Soviet Union were the primary motives underlying Romania's decision to join the Bank and the Fund. These decisions were the culmination of at least a decade of concentrated effort to distinguish Romanian interests and foreign policy from those of the Soviet Union.[21] In part, this desire to separate itself from Soviet influence resembled Yugoslavia's split with the Soviets in that both countries resisted and resented the Soviets' attempt to subordinate their economies through the CMEA (Crowther, p. 555). Romania's increasing need for oil also reinforced its shift toward trading with the West.[22]

Romania also desired access to the development resources of the World Bank to enhance and support its strategy of extensive growth, since the Bank favored large, investment intensive infrastructure projects similar to those the Romanians preferred. Membership in the Bank was contingent upon membership in the Fund, however. Thus, although Romania did not actually need the financial resources of the Fund at that time, there were other factors which made IMF membership attractive (Pissulla, p.66).

Romania joined the IMF and the IBRD at the onset of the recentralization period and since that time has been referred to as the "spoiled child" of these two organizations (Jackson, "Perspectives," p. 261). Romania's application for membership was facilitated by its earlier negotiations to join the GATT in 1971 (NYT 7/25/71) and its achievement of eligibility for help from the U.S. Export-Import Bank and the U.S. Overseas Private Investment Corporation (WSJ 9/22/72). Romania's efforts to participate in these facilities was clear evidence of its desire to cooperate with all states in the international economy. Consequently, the membership of the IMF and the IBRD approved Romania's entrance by an "overwhelming margin" in December, 1972,[23] and in the next five years Romania received $626.2 million in 13 IBRD loans and an IMF Stand-by of $95 million.[24] Clearly, the decision to recentralize did *not* hamper Romania's relations with both organizations, although the "liberalizing" nature of the 1967 reforms may have induced the Bank and Fund to believe that this most recent reversal of policy was temporary.

Romania's membership did require some adjustments on the part of the Bank and Fund, however. According to the *Articles of Agreement* of the Fund (Article VIII, Section 5), provision of information regarding key economic indicators and the balance of payments was a condition of membership, as was regular consultation with the Fund's staff (Article

VIII). It was assumed that Romania had agreed to these conditions when it accepted membership (NYT 12/6/72). Yet information on export and import flows was (and is) considered a state secret in Romania (Brada, p. 1269), and Romania had refrained from releasing any information on its balance of payments and other financial transactions until 1980 (Jackson, "Industry," pp. 889, 892, 906).

The Fund respected Romania's desire for discretion with respect to its financial affairs and did not divulge any of the information provided by Romania in pursuance of its membership requirements. In addition, like Yugoslavia, Romania received its first World Bank loan without settling outstanding debts to foreign citizens from World War II, a violation of the *Articles*. This issue was "permanently" settled in 1975 when Romania compensated such bondholders at 40 percent of the face value of the bonds (NYT 6/26/75). Apparently, such problems were not considered serious enough to hamper Romania's loan applications in the Bank and Fund.

Renewed Reform

In March 1978, the Romanian government announced a set of economic reforms which were scheduled for implementation beginning in 1979 (Smith, p. 35). This new set of reforms resembled in many respects the 1967 Directives (Smith, p. 52) and thus appeared to be a minor departure from the recentralization trend of the previous five years. A decline in industrial performance beginning in 1976, coupled with a devasting earthquake in 1977, provoked Party and State economic authorities to examine once again the direction of the Romanian economy (Smith, p. 54; Jackson, "Perspectives," pp. 263, 301).

Despite the rhetoric favoring a shift toward intensive development which had prevailed among Romanian economic authorities since 1967, economic policy had actually reflected an extensive strategy of development.[25] Yet objective conditions clearly indicated that an extensive development program was no longer productive in the Romanian context. The rate of investment was declining, a labor shortage began to emerge as available labor resources in agriculture dwindled, and popular pressure for increased consumer goods mounted (Jackson, "Perspectives", pp. 274–275, 286–288; Smith, p. 54; Crowther, p. 363; Tyson, *Economic Adjustment*, pp. 73–74). Increasing trade deficits and growing difficulties in attracting credit also contributed to the realization within the RCP that implementation of an intensive development strategy had now become a necessity (Smith, p. 54; Crowther, p. 559).

Workers' self-management, briefly mentioned in the 1967 Directives, was one of the major themes of the 1978 reforms. Workers were once again able "to participate in the profits of enterprises and to improve the functioning of the economic system through greater use of self-management techniques" (IBRD, p. xxxiii). The 1978 measures were intended to give the workers' committees instruments, such as financial levers, which would enable them to carry out their responsibilities. These responsibilities were still limited to the "supervision of centrally determined objectives," and to a lesser degree, to provide the regime with feedback from the lower levels of the economy. Ceauşescu did not intend to institute workers' self-management as practiced in Yugoslavia, but rather to increase the amount of information available to the regime, increase productivity, and enhance the power of the Party apparatus, much as the 1967 Directives had intended.[26]

Increasing productivity, a necessary part of intensive development, was a second major goal of the 1978 economic adjustments. Incentives were identified as a major tool in accomplishing this goal. In 1978, net output and profits replaced gross output as the primary indicator in determining the level of incentives (Jackson, "Perspectives," p. 295; Smith p. 47). Monetary incentives were thus directly linked to productivity, especially reduced costs (Smith, p. 50). Another type of incentive, personal gardens, was also quietly expanded (Jackson, "Perspectives," pp. 295–297). These changes in the incentive system were designed to link workers more directly to production in order to raise the output per worker.

Augmenting worker self-management and the changes in the incentive system were changes in the banking system. Banks were now empowered to finance centrally determined investments, and credit levers were partially to replace budgetary financing from the central government (Smith, pp. 47–49). Together, these three sets of reforms: self-management, incentives, and credit levers, gave the appearance of a significant decentralization of the economy. This was not the case, however.

As was true in 1967, the 1978 reforms were actually only a minor adjustment in the structure of economic decision-making in Romania. The single, national plan remained the predominant instrument of economic policy, although the 1978 reforms called for more lower level input into the plan (Smith, pp. 41, 43, 50, 51). Indicators, which determined enterprise profitability, also continued to be centrally determined, as were investment priorities and decisions (Smith, pp. 35, 43, 52).

Foreign trade received a high priority in the 1978 reforms, as it had since 1967. In the 1970s, the Ceauşescu regime targeted chemicals and metallurgical products, rather than agricultural goods, as industries for development as exports (IBRD, p. 2; Jackson, "Perspectives," p. 298). Romania's export performance in these areas had been steady, and chemicals and metallurgy promised to assist Romania's drive for multilateral development. Romanian economic authorities continued to encourage in a limited way joint venture agreements with Western corporations. Nevertheless, "foreign competition in internal Romanian markets [was not] considered important for improving the efficiency of Romanian firms" (Jackson, "Perspectives," pp. 298, 300), and the magnitude of the joint venture experiment was restricted. This increased participation in the international economy, the 1977 earthquake, and the decline in productivity led to a rapid increase in Romania's foreign debt after 1975, and large trade deficits were registered in 1978 and 1979 (Jackson, "Perspectives," p. 175).

Thus, once again, Romania's economic reforms were superficial and actually worked to increase the power of the state. The ensuing economic crisis quickly eclipsed the "reform" movement, and it quietly expired.

Fund and Bank support of the Romanian development effort continued throughout this period. The IMF concluded a Stand-by Arrangement with Romania in 1977 (WSJ 9/13/77) and the $64.13 million loan was made available to Romania in 1978 in support of its "stabilization" program, which in fact strongly resembled previous policies. This loan, therefore, was actually intended by the Fund to reinforce the general direction of the 1978 reforms. Romania also received $876.5 million in 14 loans from the IBRD between 1978 and 1980 to finance projects in the tire, pork, fruit, and hydroelectric industries.[27] It is interesting to note that these projects support agricultural exports; obviously, the IBRD felt that Romania's export strength still resided in its agricultural products and until 1980, at least, the Bank was hesitant to invest in the new export target areas. The Bank loans, then, were an inducement to the Romanian government to refrain from neglecting the agricultural sector.

As the preceding analysis indicates, reform in Romania in the 1970s was incremental, never significantly deviating from the basic model of central planning. Despite Romania's steadfast adherence to a non-capitalist model, the Bank and Fund lent Romania $1502.8 million and $159.13 million, respectively, in just eight years. It would be a mistake, however, to conclude that the two organizations supported or approved Romanian economic policy during this period (Pissulla, p. 66). Bank and Fund lending in this case was actually an example of a variation in reverse influence. Since both institutions aspire to the organizational goal of universal membership, the relative absence of Soviet Bloc countries from their memberships has been a persistent concern. Romania was the first central planning member of the Soviet Bloc to seek membership in the IMF and IBRD since Czechoslovakia's withdrawal in 1954 and consequently served as a crucial example, or test case, of the two organization's ability to accommodate orthodox centrally-planned members. The Bank and Fund were more willing, therefore, to adapt their procedures to Romania's special needs and conditions at that time.[28]

One example of the cooperative attitude of the Bank and Fund toward Romania occurred in 1979. Critics contended that the World Bank's analysis of the Romanian economy, published in 1979, looked as if "it was written by the Romanian government . . ." and that the Bank "placed politics ahead of credibility" (WSJ 8/10/79). Sources reported that the Bank's professional staff were "chagrined" by such "imaginative fiction" (WSJ 8/10/79); the report was based on official Romanian statistics which experts agreed were notoriously unreliable (Jackson, "Perspective," p. 261).

Economic Crisis, 1978–1984

By 1978 the weaknesses of Romania's extensive development strategy were apparent. Contrary to its strong performance after the first round of oil price shocks in 1973, Romanian economic performance began to deteriorate *prior* to the second oil price shocks in 1978 due to internal economic pressures and rigidities.[29] The highly centralized and administrative nature of Romania's economic structure and its determination to pursue an extensive development strategy emphasizing investment had resulted in increasing supply bottlenecks and pent-up domestic demand at a time when world economic conditions were deteriorating (Tyson, *Economic Adjustment*, p. vii, 85). Yet Romania failed to adjust to these rapidly changing conditions, in part due to the fact that the impressive successes of the 1960s and 1970s had convinced Ceauşescu of the rectitude of the extensive model.[30]

Adjustment was inevitable, however, as the Romanian balance of trade, particularly with the West and the oil-exporting nations, declined and Romania was forced to borrow abroad to compensate for raw material and other industrial shortfalls (Tyson, *Economic Adjustment*, pp. 85, 86; Linden, p. 362). According to Tyson, Romania's policy of import substitution, which aided in avoiding an economic crisis in the 1973–1977 period, now exacerbated Romania's problems (*Economic Adjustment*, p. 75) because in pursuing such a strategy, Romania had become dependent on energy and other industrial raw material imports in order to export manufactured and agricultural goods to the West. These imports were now steadily increasing in price while simultaneously, Romania's hard currency exports were declining in both volume and value. Consequently, Romania's terms of trade declined, also forcing Romania to seek financing abroad to finance the deficit. By 1979, Romania's hard currency debt reached $6.7 billion.[31]

This combination of adverse internal and external conditions was soon reflected in a deceleration of the growth rate which had maintained a healthy 5–7 percent in the 1976–1980 period.[32] Despite the rhetoric of 1978, Romania had yet to implement adjustment policies, the trade balance also declined; between 1979 and 1980 Romania registered a balance of trade deficit of between $3.1 and $3.5 billion (Tyson, *Economic Adjustment*, p. 89; IMF, *Survey* 4/19/82:118). In an attempt to rectify this problem, Romania quietly began to redirect its trade toward the CMEA countries, especially in raw materials and energy, but for several reasons, it was not sufficient (Linden, pp. 366–367; Crowther, p. 569). The current account of the balance of payments mirrored Romania's increasing economic difficulties, registering a $2.4 billion deficit which was approximately 4.2 percent of Romania's GNP for 1980 (IMF, *Survey* 9/7/81:262, 6/22:194; Crowther, p. 565).

To finance these deficits, Romania resorted to borrowing in Western commercial and government financial markets. In 1980, Romania's external debt had ballooned to $10.3 billion, of which $9.1 originated in the Western advanced industrial nations (Tyson, *Economic Adjustment*, p. 89; IMF, *Survey* 4/19/82:119). The terms of lending in the 1978–1980 period were much more stringent than in the 1973–1977 period when Romania had carefully restricted its borrowing. By 1980, lenders globally were demanding much higher interest rates than in the previous period; these rates were pegged to LIBOR (London Interbank Offered Rate) and thus were also sensitive to international trends. This trend, combined with the increasingly shortened repayment periods, sharply increased the costs of borrowing for Romania and other oil-importing nations (and would culminate in the debt crisis of the early 1980s). Romania's external debt nearly doubled from the previous planning period (Tyson, *Economic Adjustment*, p. 89).

Romania's creditors began to be concerned about the adverse trends in Romania's economy and its apparent reluctance to implement policies designed to adjust to its changing economic conditions.[33] By 1980, Romania did begin to respond to its increasing difficulties by incorporating growth targets into the plan for the next, 1981–1985, plan period which were lower than the growth rate actually recorded for the previous plan period (IMF, *Survey* 4/19/82:119). As Tyson notes,

"Concern among international lenders about the ability or willingness of the Romanians to fashion a workable adjustment strategy was heightened by temporary payments arrears and by Romania's failure to provide lenders with timely, reliable information on its external financial situation" (*External Adjustment*, p. 110).

No longer were Romania's creditors willing to overlook its reluctance to provide "sensitive" information and its steadfast refusal to reform its central planning system. The economic environment had changed, the risks to lenders had multiplied, and Romania was not successfully adapting.

In mid-1980, Romania attempted to allay its creditors' concerns about the lack of reliable information about its financial operations by permitting the IMF to publish such information in its *International Financial Statistics* (IMF, *Survey* 6/3/80:167). This marked an important milestone in Romanian-Fund relations and can be interpreted either as evidence of Romania's increased trust in the organization or as documentation of the Fund's leverage over Romania. The fact that provision of information was also a critical issue with Romania's creditors in the private capital markets lends credence to the former explanation.

Increased Romanian interaction with the Fund was also evident in June, 1980 when the Fund announced that it had concluded a $1.4 billion Stand-by Arrangement with Romania (to be implemented in 1981) in support of its "economic reform and stabilization efforts" and to offset declining export revenues (WSJ 6/16/80). Approximately $468.7 million of the total SBA was part of the Fund's ordinary resources and the remaining $937.4 million was to be drawn from the Fund's Enlarged Access Policy (IMF, *Survey* 6/22/81:194). The latter required repurchase in three years rather than the customary one.

According to the IMF, Romania had agreed to reduce its planned growth rates for investment and consumption, depreciate its exchange rate on trade transactions, and increase its exports and import substitutes. Romania also agreed to reform its system of multiple exchange rates and to bring prices into closer alignment with world prices (IMF, *Survey* 9/7/81). In essence this stabilization program was quite typical of other Fund supported programs of the period and reflected the recognition that it was imperative that Romania move toward a more intensive development strategy. Many of the policy changes (they were not extensive enough to be termed a "reform") included in the Fund version of the stabilization program were already part of the 1981–1985 Plan (Linden, pp. 365–366; Crowther, p. 567) and thus, it is difficult to assess the influence of the Fund's leverage on Romanian policy at that time.

Romania continued in 1980 to take advantage of the project assistance offered by the World Bank. The World Bank approved four loans to Romania in 1980: $50 million to enhance fruit production; $100 million to aid in the construction of a canal which would travel through one of Romania's poorest regions; $90 million for a project which would enhance Romania's irrigation and drainage capabilities; and $85 million for a livestock project (IBRD, *Annual Report, 1980*; WSJ 6/24/80). Romania ranked eighth of a total of nineteen countries which received loans from the IBRD that year. Romania's economic difficulties obviously did not overly concern the Bank.

In 1981, Romania's growth rate continued to decline, reflecting in part deliberate government decisions and adverse external conditions including poor agricultural harvests (IMF, *Survey* 4/19/82:118–120). Traditional IMF analysis attributed the mounting debt and trade problems of the Eastern European nations, as well as developing nations, to inadequate macroeconomic policies, excessive borrowing on unfavorable terms, and adverse exogenous events. In Romania, all of these conditions were present (Pissulla, *The IMF*, p. 66; Tyson, *Economic Adjustment*).

Romania's policies of the late 1970s and 1980 did result in a reversal of the negative trend in the balance of trade and by the end of 1981, Romania's trade balance showed a $300 million *surplus* (NYT 12/26/ 83; Linden, p. 366). This success in the foreign trade sector was primarily attributable to an improved balance of trade with the Western indus- trialized states (a surplus of $210 million) in which imports from those countries declined by 17 percent in 1981 (Tyson, *Economic Adjustment*, p. 91; Crowther, p. 566).

Romania's indebtedness predictably increased in 1981 as Romania sought to counter declining growth and investment rates by borrowing abroad. Gross debt in 1981 rose to $10.5 billion, with $9.6 billion of that sum owed to developed market economies.[34]

Access to additional credit rapidly declined and ultimately disappeared in 1981, however, as "uneasiness" about the creditworthiness of the Soviet Bloc increased (WSJ 5/19/81, 9/26/81). Prior to 1981, international financial lenders had lent almost freely to members of the Soviet Bloc, including Romania, on the assumption that the Soviet Union and the CMEA would cover any potential delay or default in repayments—the "umbrella" theory (WSJ 5/19/81). By 1981, Romania was approaching the point where it could not meet some of the payments on its short term debt (Crowther, p. 566; Pissulla, p. 66). Doubts about Romania's ability to repay, Romania's refusal to provide its creditors with adequate information about its economic situation, and the severe economic and political crisis in Poland combined to frighten creditors into witholding any new credit to Romania (Tyson, *Economic Adjustment*, p. 90; WSJ 5/19/81). Unable to meet its payments with new credits, Romania was forced to request a delay in making its payments and to request rescheduling negotiations (Tyson, *Economic Adjustment*, p. 111; NYT 11/ 4/81).

The austerity/stabilization program agreed upon with the Fund in the previous year was implemented in 1981. In the program, Romania was compelled to confront the limitations of its extensive growth strategy which was partially responsible for its current situation (Tyson, *Economic*

Adjustment, p. 10). The program required Romania to reduce its imports, particularly of raw materials and consumer goods, and to increase its exports.[35] Ceauşescu announced a plan to retire at least 25 percent of Romania's debt by 1985 and to liquidate it by 1988 (NYT 12/26/83). In conjunction with these targets, both the growth rate and the rate of investment were lowered.[36]Simultaneously, the Romanians instituted a price reform which raised the cost of several consumer and industrial goods and brought prices closer to their world market equivalents.[37]

The consequent effect of this austerity program on domestic consumption was severe and almost immediate and prompted civil unrest, a rare occurence under Ceauşescu. Strikes, work stoppages, and demonstrations erupted throughout Romania to protest the declining standard of living (Crowther, pp. 567–568). The Ceauşescu government responded at first in a conciliatory manner but within months proceeded to repress any further outbreaks of unrest, punctuating the entire episode with a purge of the Romanian Communist Party (Crowther, p. 568). These events in Romania testify to one of the relative strengths of Soviet Bloc nations from the perspective of the IMF; they can implement austerity programs with relatively little or no concern for their effects on legitimacy or electoral advantage.

The policy changes enumerated above did not constitute economic reform. The basic characteristics of the central planning system, such as administratively determined prices and planning by material balances, remained intact. What occurred more closely resembled "tinkering" than meaningful reform (Tyson, *Economic Adjustment*, p. 91; Majda, p. 92). No reform occurred in the political sphere as well.

A slight shift occurred in Romania's foreign policy as a result of its economic problems. As an alternative to incurring further debts in Western financial markets, Romania looked to the Soviet Union and the CMEA market as a means of supplementing its trade balance. This strategy did not yield the expected results as the Soviets declined to assist Romania in this crisis and the other members of the CMEA were either reluctant to help or experiencing financial difficulties of their own. Soviet assistance has traditionally been tied to the strength of a state's "military, political, and ideological allegiance," and Romania's questionable record in all three areas explains the Soviets' reluctance to come to Romania's aid (Tyson, *Economic Adjustment*, pp. 111, viii). Since the political price of complying with the Soviet Union's conditions was unacceptable, Romania was forced to purchase Soviet oil with hard currency and at world market prices and eventually incurred large ruble trade deficits (WSJ 5/19/81; Crowther, pp. 569–570; Tyson, *Economic Adjustment*, p. 111).

Romania's relations with the West also deteriorated throughout 1981. It was natural for Romania to identify the Western capitalist system as the cause of its economic problems, as it was its growing trade and financial deficit with that area which precipitated the crisis, at least superficially. Romania began to criticize vociferously the "unjustifiably high interest rates" charged by Western banks and the credit terms those nations offered (Crowther, pp. 570–571). As Linden so aptly observes, "Ceauşescu began to see the Romanian economy becoming hostage to the very economic forces that had helped it develop" ("Socialist Patrimonialism," p. 375), and he resented that position, perhaps in part due to his own role in the process.

Even as Romanian relations with the West crumbled, Romania's interactions with the IMF increased as a result of its economic crisis and the consequent effect this crisis had on Romania's balance of payments. In 1981, Romania took advantage of its right to draw on the Compensatory Financing Facility (SDR 169.5 million) and received funds as part of the Trust Fund facility (IMF, *Survey* 6/22/81:194, 4/6/81:107). During that same period the Ceauşescu government also concluded a Stand-by Arrangement.

As noted above, Romania's creditors were concerned about Romania's reluctance to implement necessary policy changes and worried that they were "being asked to reschedule a nation's debts without any assurances that steps [would] be taken to correct basic economic problems" (WSJ 5/19/81). The conditionality associated with IMF Stand-by Arrangements was an ideal solution to this problem; therefore, Romania's creditors pressured Romania to conclude an SBA with the Fund almost as a precondition to future rescheduling negotiations (Tyson, *Economic Adjustment*, p. 111). For the first time, the IMF became an active participant in rescheduling negotiations between Western banks and one of its members, and together both the Fund and the banks convinced Romania of the necessity for an austerity program (NYT 3/8/82).

A $1.4 billion SBA was a product of the combined efforts of the Fund and Romania's creditor banks, with the associated austerity program described above. Romania's needs were so great at this time that it accepted elements of the austerity program which previously would have been unacceptable to the Ceauşescu government (Majda, p. 92). Linden notes, however, that this was merely a "temporary acceptance [by Romania] of the Fund's conditions regarding economic reform" ("Socialist Patrimonialism," p. 369), although Romania's willingness and desire to resolve its problems was genuine (Pissulla, p. 67). The extent to which the IMF conditions coincided with the Romanians' own analysis of the situation is, therefore, difficult to assess.

The World Bank continued its lending to Romania despite the country's obvious financial problems. Romania received four loans during 1981 for a wide range of projects. The Bank approved a $125 million project for thermal and hydroelectric power development, two irrigation loans totalling $150 million, and $80 million for another dairy project. Given its past performance and potential, Romania obviously remained a good, long-term investment for the Bank.

The 1981 austerity program demonstrated results as early as 1982 when Romania posted a $1.4–1.6 billion surplus on its trade balance as imports from the West declined by 45 percent (Tyson, *Economic Adjustment*, p. vii; NYT 12/26/83; Crowther, p. 566). To encourage these trends, the leu was devalued in 1983 and a single commercial exchange rate established for transactions in convertible currencies (IMF, *Survey* 7/25/83:224). Developments in Romania's foreign policy threatened further advances in this area in 1983 when the United States objected to changes in Romania's policies regarding emigration, but these were resolved when the U.S. renewed Romania's Most-Favored Nation status (Crowther, p. 571).

Although Romania's debt had not significantly increased, it was still compelled to request rescheduling of its existing debt in 1982 and 1983 and threatened to suspend payments if the banks did not comply (Linden, pp. 355, 376; NYT 1/22/83, 3/8/82). The IMF took an active part in these negotiations with Romania's creditors and suspended new installments on Romania's SBA pending their outcome (NYT 3/8/82). By July 1982, however, agreement was reached on Romania's debts, both commercial and official, and the Fund resumed payments to Romania, renewing the SBA for the second year (NYT 7/5/82).

The austerity program implemented in 1981 began to deteriorate by 1983. According to Pissulla, Romania had made

"great efforts to implement the adjustment measures required of it primarily in the field of demand management by means of price, exchange rate and incomes policy measures to the detriment of the already low standard of living, but they [were] clearly more than it [could] manage" (p. 67).

When the Fund requested further adjustments in the program designed to restore Romania's compliance with the agreement, Romania balked (Pissulla, p. 67). At this point Romania had violated the terms of its SBA agreement, and in accordance with Fund rules, the IMF suspended the remainder of the loan, approximately $298.38 million (Pissulla, p. 67; Linden, p. 376). Another SBA was negotiated in 1984 which explicitly recognized Romania's concerns, but Romania declined to draw from it, possibly to avoid the imposition of Fund conditions (Linden, p. 376). Relations between Romania and the Fund had deteriorated.

Romania's interactions with the World Bank have also decreased since 1982. In 1982, Romania incurred three loans with the Bank for $321 million. These loans were to support projects in agriculture and energy related projects. Romania ranked 11th out of the 43 countries which received Bank loans in 1982. Between 1982 and 1985, Romania refrained from increasing its debt to the Bank.

This is consistent with Romania's avowed strategy to eliminate its foreign debt by 1988. Between 1980 and 1984, Romania's foreign debt declined from approximately $10 billion to $7.5 billion (Linden, p. 376). Admittedly, Ceaușescu has imposed severe hardship on the Romanian population in his pursuit of political and economic independence in the 1980s. While the strategy seems to be working with respect to Romania's relations with the West, economic necessity has forced Ceaușescu to moderate his stance with the Soviet Union and the CMEA and relations between the two groups appears to be closer than at any time during Ceaușescu's tenure in Romania. This does not mean that Romania has chosen to renounce its non-aligned preferences, however, and Romania continues to work toward expanding its relations with the developing countries. It is highly likely that the "thaw" in Soviet–Romanian relations is merely temporary and born out of expediency.

Conclusion

Until 1978, the IMF and IBRD were acutely aware of the somewhat public nature of Romania's experiences in both organizations. In the early years of Romanian membership in the Bank and Fund, the organizations were prepared, therefore, to focus on the strengths of Romania's economic system[38] and to minimize its weaknesses and the fact that it contradicted the prevailing organizational ideology in both institutions. As one member of the IMF staff described it, Romania's membership in the IMF had been a "learning experience" for both parties and one from which, in 1980, the Fund felt it had the most to learn.[39] Bank and Fund lending in the 1972–1977 years was thus an attempt to retain Romania's membership—an example of reverse influence with aspects of inducement.

Romania's relations with the World Bank in the 1978–1985 period did not alter. Romania's borrowing pattern remained constant until 1983 when Ceaușescu's desire to eliminate Romania's foreign debt led him to avoid all creditors, including the Bank. It is also possible that the increased concern within the Bank for sound economic policies, which took a decided turn toward market definitions in the 1980s, also influenced

Ceauşescu's decision to refrain from borrowing from the Bank. From the Bank's perspective, Romania's fundamental economic propects hadn't changed. Romania was merely undergoing a temporary setback.

In contrast, in the post-1978 years Romania's relationship with the Fund changed dramatically. Ceauşescu publically blamed the West, and the IMF as its instrument, for Romania's economic problems, although privately there were signs that he recognized the internal sources of those problems (NYT 12/26/83). His apparent "obsession" with reducing Romania's foreign debt (WSJ 1/27/86) is evidence of the priority Ceauşescu places on restoring Romania's financial and political independence, even if this must be accomplished at the expense of economic growth and popular consumption. Romania had abided by the rules of the international monetary system in the 1960s and 1970s (Crowther, p. 573) as part of the cost of maintaining that independence, but in the 1980s that cost had begun to threaten maintainance of that same independence.

As a result of the 1980s economic crisis in Romania, the Fund's leverage in that country increased markedly. Because Romania's dependence on a steady influx of new loans depended on the IMF, the IMF was in a position to insist that Romania conform to the same market-oriented conditions imposed on its other members.The Fund's insistence on the implementation of genuine policy change in Romania contained a strong element of inducement and threat of punishment since Romania's failure to satisfy the Fund would have resulted in a credit embargo by its major creditors and the global financial community. Romania's special status within the Fund had ended. Since Romania's other alternative, dependence on the Soviet Union, was equally as threatening to the cherished Romanian goals and values, Ceauşescu turned to his final choice, increased autarky. While this policy might satisfy Ceauşescu's goal of independence, it does not enhance Romania's short-term economic prospects.

There are several explanations for the changes in Romanian and Fund attitudes brought about by the economic crisis. As noted above, Romania's position within the Fund had changed; Romania now *needed* the Fund's assistance and could no longer choose to remain aloof from the Fund's resources and conditionality. From the Fund's perspective, Romania also was no longer needed to set an example for the rest of the Soviet Bloc since Hungary and Poland had applied for membership in 1981. Romania's moderate rapprochement with the Soviet Union further underscored the declining value of Romania to the Fund since part of Romania's attraction for the Fund was its independent, and almost hostile, stance toward the Soviet Union.

The Fund's role in the international financial system had also changed. The Fund became a vital intermediary and regulator for the major lenders and no longer needed to "court" members to assure itself of continued relevance. In addition, the distinct trend within the Fund after 1978 toward more classical market interpretations of economic problems and their solutions[40] prompted the Fund to interpret more narrowly its traditional conditionality. It is entirely comprehensible that Romania would find these trends disturbing and seek to extract itself from their influence. Inducement and punishment, therefore, did not result in Romanian compliance; rather, they compelled Romania to reject the organization (although it did not withdraw) and to seek other means of resolving its problems whenever possible.

Notes

1. Patrick J. Nichols, "Western Investment in Eastern Europe: The Yugoslav Example," in *Reorientation and Commercial Relations of the Economies of Eastern Europe*, pp. 725–743 (Washington, D.C.: U.S. Congress, Joint Economic Committee, 1974), p. 740; Michael Gamarnikow, "Balance Sheet on Economic Reforms," in *Reorientation and Commercial Relations of the Economies of Eastern Europe*, pp. 164–213 (Washington, D.C.: U.S. Congress, Joint Economic Committee, 1974), p. 182; Marvin R. Jackson, "Industrialization, Trade, and Mobilization in Romania's Drive for Economic Independence," in *East European Economies Post-Helsinki*, pp. 886–940 (Washington, D.C.: U.S. Congress, Joint Economic Committee, 1977), p. 891.

2. See V. Iota, "Main Bases of Romania's Domestic and Foreign Economic Policy," translated by Leon Mindlia, *East European Economics*, vol. 15, no. 4 (Summer 1977), p. 103.

3. Lawrence S. Graham, *Romania: A Developing Socialist State* (Boulder, CO: Westview Press, 1982), p. 81.

4. See also Jackson, "Industrialization," pp. 887, 938; Marvin R. Jackson, "Perspectives on Romania's Economic Development in the 1980s," in Daniel N. Nelson (ed.), *Romania in the 1980s* (Boulder, CO: Westview Press, 1981), p. 300; Andreas C. Tsantis and Roy Pepper, *Romania: The Industrialization of an Agrarian Economy Under Socialist Planning* (Washington, D.C.: IBRD, 1979), p. 2–5.

Ceausescu claims an extensive strategy was necessary for rapid development and justifies this by referring to the high growth rate of the Romanian economy since 1950 (Iota, p. 104).

5. Tsantis, p. 3.

6. See Stephen Fischer-Galati, *Twentieth Century Romania* (New York: University Press, 1970); Jackson, "Industrialization," p. 889.

7. Jackson, "Perspectives," p. 301 and "Industry," p. 888.

8. Claus D. Rohleder, "Rumania: The Laggard," in L.A. D. Dellin and Hermann Gross (eds.), *Reforms in the Soviet and Eastern European Economies* (Lexington, MA: D.C. Heath and Co., 1972), p. 115; Jackson, "Industrialization," p. 894.

9. Gamarnikow, pp. 182, 184; Jackson, "Industrialization," p. 893; John Michael Montias, "Romania's Foreign Trade: An Overview," in *East European Economies Post-Helsinki*, pp. 865–885 (Washington, D.C.: U.S. Congress, Joint Economic Committee, 1977), p. 871.

10. Josef C. Brada and Marvin R. Jackson, "Strategy and Structure in the Organization of Romanian Foreign Trade Activities, 1967– 75," in *East European Economies Post-Helsinki*, pp. 1260–1276 (Washington, D.C.: U.S. Congress, Joint Economic Committee, 1977), p. 1264; Rohleder, p. 117; Michael Kaser, "Romania," in Hans-Hermann Hohmann, Michael Kaser and Karl C. Thalheim (eds.) *The New Economic Systems of Eastern Europe* (Berkeley: University of California Press, 1975), p. 174.

11. Alan H. Smith, "Romanian Economic Reforms," in *Economic Reforms in Eastern Europe and Prospects for the 1980s*, Nato Colloquium, April 16–18, 1980, Brussels, Belgium (New York: Pergamon Press, 1980), pp. 37, 40.

12. The preceding discussion is taken from Brada, pp. 1265–1266.

13. Rohleder, p 119; Kaser, p. 182; Smith, p. 37; Brada, p. 1264. Nichols, pp. 740–741, lists the regulations governing Romanian joint ventures as follows: 1. 51 percent Romanian participation is required. 2. Joint ventures may be concluded with centrals only. 3. The joint venture contract is reviewed by the State Planning Committee, the Ministry of Finance, the Ministry of Foreign Trade, the Ministry of Labor, the Foreign Trade Bank, and approved by the Council of Ministers. 4. Foreign partners must prepare one and five year plans. 5. A premium is placed on joint ventures in export and high technology industries. 6. A reserve fund of 25 percent of invested capital is created. 7. A 30 percent tax is levied on profits with a rebate on reinvested profits. 8. Profits and equity can be repatriated.

14. Ioţa, p. 105; Laura D'Andrea Tyson, *Economic Adjustment in Eastern Europe*, R-3146-AF, Prepared for the U.S. Air Force (Santa Monica: The Rand Corporation, 1984), pp. 73–74; Ronald H. Linden, "Socialist Patrimonialism and the Global Economy: The Case of Romania," *International Organization* 40(2):353, 1986.

15. Ioţa, pp. 100–109; Graham, p. 81.

16. Elizabeth M. Clayton, "Economic Reforms in Bulgaria and Romania: Prospects for the 1980s," in *Economic Reforms in Eastern Europe and Prospects for the 1980s*, NATO Colloquium, April 16–18, 1980, Brussels, Belgium (New York: Pergamon Press, 1980), p. 142; Kaser, p. 189.

17. Kaser, p. 177; Clayton, p. 142; Smith, pp. 42, 46; Jackson, "Industrialization," p. 891.

18. Brada, pp. 1269–70; Jackson, "Industrialization," p. 891. Brada cites a U.N. analysis which suggests that perhaps Romania possessed more foreign trade organizations than was profitable for its volume of trade so that centralization was actually a productive decision ("Strategy," p. 1271).

19. Montias, p. 874; Jackson, "Industrialization," p. 912; William Crowther, "Romanian Politics and the International Economy," *Orbis* 28(3):563, 1984.

20. Robert R. King, "Romania and the Third World," *Orbis*, vol. 21, no. 4 (Winter 1978), pp. 875–892.

21. Petra Pissulla, "The IMF and the Countries of Eastern Europe," *Intereconomics* 19(2):66, 1984; Crowther, p. 553.

22. Crowther, p. 555; Klaus Schröder, "The IMF and the Countries of the Council for Mutual Economic Assistance," *Intereconomics* 17(2):87, March–April 1982.

23. *Wall Street Journal* (WSJ) 12/6/72).

24. Romania's IBRD loans ranked as follows (out of the total number of loans extended by the IBRD in that year): 1974, 15th/48; 1976, 11th/52; 1975, 6th/52; 1977, 13th/54

Romania's ranking on its Fund Stand-by Arrangements in 1976 was 2nd out of 19. See IMF, *Annual Report* (Washington, D.C.: IMF) and IBRD, *Annual Report* (Washington, D.C.: IBRD) for the years in question.

25. Emphasis remained on increasing inputs rather than increasing productivity, and manufacturing industries were still heavily favored over consumer industries. See discussion in Jackson, "Industrialization," p. 938, and Iota, p. 105.

26. The preceding discussion is derived from Smith, pp. 35, 51.

27. Romania's standings with respect to total IBRD loans for each year were: 1978, 9th/46; 1979, 11th/44; 1980, 9th/48. See WSJ 3/28/78, 3/23/79, 6/24/80, 12/26/80.

28. Interviews at the IMF, 9/5/80 and 11/24/80.

29. Tyson, *Economic Adjustment*, pp. vii, 85–86.

30. Tyson, *Economic Adjustment*; Linden, p. 372.

31. Crowther, p. 563.

32. IMF, *Survey* 9/7/81:262, 4/19/82:119; Linden, p. 355; Pissulla, p.66.

33. WSJ 5/19/81; Tyson, *Economic Adjustment*, p. 90.

34. Linden, p. 367; Crowther, p. 566; Pissulla, p. 66; IMF, *Survey* 4/19/82:119; *New York Times* (NYT) 12/26/83.

35. NYT 12/26/83; IMF, *Survey* 9/7/81:262–263; *Survey* 6/22/81:263.

36. IMF, *Survey* 9/7/81:262–263, 6/22/81:194, 4/19/82:119; Linden, p. 369; Tyson, p. vii; Schröder, p. 88.

37. IMF, *Survey* 9/7/81:263, 6/22/81:194, 4/19/82:119; Linden, p. 369; Pawel Majda, "L'importance du Fonds Monetaire International pour la Pologne et les autres pays d'Europe Orientale," *Revue d'études comparatives est-ouest* 13(4):92, 1982; Schröder, p. 88.

38. For example, in its 1979 report, the World Bank remarks that state control of productive resources had given Romania relatively greater ability to mobilize its resources for reconstruction and development (Tsantis, p. 5). A similar comment was made by an IMF official in an interview conducted on 11/24/80.

39. Interview at the IMF, 11/24/80.

40. See Valerie J. Assetto and Ronnie J. Phillips, "Reagan, the IMF, and Eastern Europe," paper presented at the annual meetings of the Allied Social Sciences Association, December 28–29, 1985.

7

The CMEA in the IMF and the IBRD: Hungary and Poland

While the presence of Yugoslavia and Romania greatly enhanced the IMF and IBRD's claim to universality, both organizations had yet to include a member in good standing of the CMEA on their membership rosters. Until the second oil price shock of 1978, the prospects for increased Soviet Bloc participation did not appear likely. Neither of the amendments to the IMF *Articles* (in 1969 and 1978) had removed the features which had proved objectionable to the Soviets at Bretton Woods. In fact, the replacement of gold as the primary international reserve unit, implied by the floating exchange rate system accepted in the second Amendment of *Articles*, served to alienate the Soviet Bloc even further.[1]

By 1980, however, several factors had altered which made Fund and Bank membership more attractive to at least two members of the Soviet Bloc; Hungary and Poland. Both countries noted the apparent success of Romania in securing Bank and Fund loans without unwelcomed political and economic concessions.[2] Romania's experience proved that the Bank and the Fund could accommodate widely divergent political and economic systems; thus, membership in the Bretton Woods organization at least appeared relatively "safer" than was previously believed. Like Romania, both Hungary and Poland were confronting rapid and serious changes in the international economic system as the second oil price shock combined with changes in the availability and terms of credit to make their previous adjustment strategies obsolete. This impending economic crisis was enhanced by increasing difficulties in the CMEA and the announcement of reduced subsidies from the Soviet Union. Both countries' need for the resources of the Fund and Bank increased, and the Fund's new role as credit mediator added to the benefits of membership. By 1982 Poland and Hungary's international creditors were literally insisting on Fund supervision as the condition for the extension of new credits.

In Hungary's case, Fund membership did not pose as large as threat to its internal arrangements as it did to Romania and Poland. In 1968 and again in 1980 Hungary had implemented significant market-oriented reforms which became known as the "New Economic Mechanism." Hungary had thus adopted many of the economic policies which the Fund was likely to request. Poland also had considered reforms before the imposition of martial law in 1981 as a means of resolving its deepening economic crisis, though these reforms were not as far-reaching as those in Hungary. Both countries, then, were not as antithetical to the Fund's standard policy prescriptions as they might have been in the previous decade.

Hungary: Reform and Participation

The Hungarian economy has undergone two periods of significant reform, in 1968 and 1980, and a brief period of recentralization. Like Romania, any analysis of the operation of Bank and Fund leverage in Hungary must begin with a brief description of the economic structure which Hungary possessed upon entrance into the two organizations. What follows establishes the basis for the subsequent analysis of Hungary's experiences in the Bank and Fund.

Hungary has experienced two substantially different types of economic systems since 1948. Until 1968, the Hungarian economy closely resembled the type of centrally-planned economy found in the U.S.S.R., characterized by central, bureaucratic allocation and control of resources. The 1968 reforms which initiated the New Economic Mechanism altered the planning and allocation mechanisms to permit more enterprise autonomy in planning, investment, and wage decisions. By 1973, growing economic difficulties led to a short period of recentralization in which the central authorities increased their intervention in the economic system in an effort to insulate Hungarian enterprises and consumers from the more negative effects of the first oil price shocks. This recentralization merely led to even greater economic problems in the late 1970s, and a return to the principles of the New Economic Mechanism (NEM) followed in 1980. What resulted is an interesting blend of both a central planning and market system in which the government continues to intervene in an economic system which exhibits a market orientation and which is gradually integrating into the world economy.[3]

The 1968 Reforms: The New Economic Mechanism

On January 1, 1968, Hungary implemented a set of economic reforms which "completely abolished in one stroke" the traditional central planning model (Kornai, p. 1693) and replaced it with a market-oriented system which sought to diminish central bureaucratic control in favor of allocation of resources based on market imperatives.[4] What ensued was actually a "guided market" system which retained a significant component of government direction and intervention in the economy.[5] In the industrial sector, the traditional One-Year Plan was abandoned in favor of autonomous enterprise decisions on short-term production and allocation, and the Five-Year Plan no longer dictated long-term decision-making but rather served as a "guide" to macroeconomic policy (Tyson, *Economic Adjustment*, pp. 32–33; Comisso and Marer, p. 425). Enterprise decisions now were formulated with reference to market incentives (which were still manipulated by the central authorities), and profits became the primary indicator of enterprise success or failure (Tyson, *Economic Adjustment*, p. 33).

Some of the most substantial reforms occurred in the agricultural sector. Many of the price distortions customarily associated with centrally-planned agricultural production were reduced, and compulsory deliveries of agricultural production were eliminated (Kornai, p. 1702). Like their enterprise counterparts, cooperatives gained more control over the disposition of their profits and began to diversify into non-agricultural activities (Kornai, p. 1702). Private plots and private ownership of farm machinery and livestock were legalized, although the size of such plots remained small (Kornai, p. 1702; Tyson, *Economic Adjustment*, p. 32). Hungarian authorities had recognized the benefits of agricultural surplus in promoting economic growth and increasing exports (Tyson, *Economic Adjustment*, p. 32; IMF, *Survey* 1/24/83:24), and CMEA policy at that time also encouraged this strategy.

A major price reform designed to reinforce the NEM accompanied these changes in industrial and agricultural structure. Producer prices were brought into closer alignment with corresponding world market prices, and many prices were deregulated and allowed to fluctuate according to market demands (Tyson, *Economic Adjustment*, p. 33; Kornai, p. 1695). The central authorities did not relinquish control over most prices, however, particularly consumer prices, and central control was retained over national macroeconomic policy (Tyson, *Economic Adjustment*, p. 33). In the foreign trade sector the reform was supported by a reduction in the number of its exchange rates to two; a commercial and non-commercial rate (IMF, *Survey* 1/24/83:24).

The NEM had a demonstrable impact on several of Hungary's key economic indicators. Between 1968 and 1973, Hungary registered a 6.2 percent annual growth rate of Net Material Product and a 5.4 percent annual increase in consumption; agricultural production increased approximately 3 percent, while industrial production grew by nearly 7 percent per year (IMF, *Survey* 1/24/83:23; Tyson, *Economic Adjustment,* p. 35). Hungary increased its exports in convertible currencies by 20 percent during this time which kept the balance of payments in relative equilibrium until 1974 (IMF, *Survey* 1/24/83:23-24). Thus, at the onset of the first oil price shock of 1973, Hungary was in a strong economic position to weather the crisis.

Recentralization, 1974-1978

The 1968 NEM was not intended to establish a genuine market system in Hungary. The actual goals of the reforms were to increase efficiency, intiative, and ultimately performance without sacrificing the prerogatives of the central authorities (Comisso and Marer, p. 444; Tyson, *Economic Adjustment,* p. 34). There remained significant latitude for government intervention in the economy, in part to preserve the ability to insulate the domestic economy from cycles and shocks in the international economy and to assure that salient political goals, such as relative income equality, were retained. The net effect of these interventions, however, often impeded the operation of market elements in the Hungarian economy (Comisso and Marer, p. 446) and resulted in lower levels of economic performance than was expected after the reforms.

Several characteristics of the former central planning system persisted after 1968. Despite the efforts of the reforms, Hungarian industry and agriculture remained highly concentrated and actual competition between enterprises was discouraged (Kornai, p. 1699; Comisso and Marer, p. 426). These large firms generally had better access to resouces which were still centrally controlled, such as investment, and were often shielded from adverse market effects by the central authorities. This had related effects on firm autonomy and investment as enterprise autonomy was limited by government regulations on the amount of profits a firm could retain and invest (Comisso and Marer, p. 425; Tyson, *Economic Adjustment,* p. 34). The Hungarian government preserved its authority over investment policy and allocation after 1968 and the consequent emphasis on growth through increased investment led to excess demand for investment in Hungarian firms which closely resembled that in other members of the Soviet Bloc (Comisso and Marer, p. 438; Kornai, p. 1716) This excess demand ultimately resulted in increased imports and foreign borrowing and established the roots of the 1980s economic crisis.

Reaction to the NEM appeared beginning in 1972 and intensified after the oil price shocks of 1973. The contradictions contained within the NEM became evident in growing disparities in income distribution and declining economic performance and caused many to reevaluate the reforms. Much of the government's legitimacy stemmed from the successes of its economic policies, and the emerging problems posed a threat to continued support of the Communist Party's policies (Tyson, *Economic Adjustment,* p. 72). There was also a great deal of residual opposition to the NEM from local bureaucrats who had never fully accepted the new system (Comisso and Marer, p. 444). Declining economic conditions merely revealed problems and conflicts which had been masked by prosperity.

Declining economic conditions provided the overt rationale for gradual recentralization between 1973 and 1978. Although Hungary's Net Material Product increased beyond planned growth, at 9.8 percent for the 1971–1975 plan period, this was due to a sharp increase in investment and consumption which threatened to drive imports beyond manageable levels (IMF, *Survey* 4/19/82:119; Tyson, *Economic Adjustment,* pp. 35–36). Exports, however, had also noticeably increased; between 1967 and 1973, exports to the West constituted 44 percent of Hungary's total exports, greater than any other member of the Soviet Bloc (Tyson, *Economic Adjustment,* p. 35). The strength of these statistics was misleading; such strong upward trends in investment, consumption, and imports were portents of future problems.

The first oil price shock, in 1973, only exacerbated existing trends in the NEM. Oil and raw material prices rose precipitously and Hungary's terms of trade and balance of payments deteriorated in response (IMF, *Survey* 1/24/83:22). These developments in internal and external conditions supported those opposed to the NEM, and consequently, Hungary sought to protect its economy from the adverse effects of the sudden increase in world market prices through government intervention in the economy (Comisso and Marer, p. 447; Kornai, p. 1722). Confident that such intervention was sufficient to eliminate any potential problems stemming from external sources, Hungary continued its strategy of extensive growth and took advantage of easy credit terms in the international credit market to finance this policy (Kornai, p. 1721).

Internally, Hungary responded to these external shocks by increasing government control of prices, wages, and investment. Many prices were fixed and subsidies to firms grew to compensate for losses due to rising import prices (Tyson, *Economic Adjustment,* p. 37; Comisso and Marer, p. 427). Supply of credit and investment resources was sharply curtailed in an effort to restrain domestic demand, particularly for imports (Kornai, p. 1719; IMF, *Survey* 1/24/83:22). Hungary's recentralization in effect encouraged policy makers to behave in a manner similar to other Soviet Bloc members; increased growth rather than adjustment was chosen as the reaction to the first external shock, and inward-oriented strategies were selected as the primary means of avoiding externally-generated problems. Like many developing countries which also pursued such policies, Hungarian actions aggravated the conditions which led to the subsequent economic crisis.

Crisis and Reform, 1978–1981

As both Kornai and Tyson observe, Hungary's policy of increased borrowing abroad, while rational in 1974, reflected a similar reluctance of the Soviet Bloc to adjust their economic policies to changing external conditions and ultimately resulted in serious economic crisis after 1978.[6] The consequences in Hungary appeared as early as 1978 when Hungary's terms of trade worsened. Changes in international financial markets meant that the resulting trade deficit could no longer be financed on favorable terms. By 1979 Hungarian officials realized that Hungary would soon be unable to service its mounting debt if significant policy reform were not enacted to adjust to changing external conditions (Comisso and Marer, p. 429; Tyson, *Economic Adjustment*, p. 105).

Growing concern about the level of international debt prompted a return to the original principles of the NEM and led to government recognition of the inherent contradictions in the system which had developed since 1973. This recognition of the inability of the central planning model to adjust in a timely fashion to alterations in external conditions brought renewed commitment from Hungarian officials to further market-oriented reforms (Tyson, *Economic Adjustment*, p. 64; Comisso and Marer, p. 432).

The new reforms, or perhaps the *return* to the NEM, were initiated in January 1980. Once again, the explicit goals of these reforms were to promote enterprise autonomy and profitability (IMF, *Survey* 1/24/ 83:22; Comisso and Marer, p. 421). As in 1968, the market was intended to determine enterprise decisions regarding prices, wages, and investment and by 1982, it appeared that the government was slowly relinquishing control in these areas (IMF, *Survey* 1/24/83:23–25). Enterprise investment decisions were still dependent on credit, which was still highly centralized despite the intentions of the reform to the contrary. The government still controlled the demand for credit through its control over its supply rather than through interest rates as in a market system (Kornai, pp. 1696, 1713).

Government price subsidies and subsidies to unprofitable enterprises declined as a result of the reform.[7] Hungarian authorities instituted a major price reform in July 1979 in an attempt to "rationalize" prices by bringing them into closer alignment with world market prices. These changes in prices were "guided by changes in convertible-currency prices and in the commercial exchange rate"; domestic prices were linked to production costs and world market prices (Tyson, *Economic Adjustment*, p. 64). Consequently, prices increased rapidly; food prices rose 20 percent and energy prices climbed 34 percent, accomplishing the goal of the price reform (Tyson, *Economic Adjustment*, p. 63). The price reform excluded the agricultural sector for the most part, although the degree of distortion in agricultural prices was reduced (IMF, *Survey* 1/24/83:22; Kornai, p. 1702). The reform was not complete, however, and several categories of prices were either determined directly by the government or required government approval prior to any alteration (Kornai, p. 1695).

Changes were made in the foreign trade sector to reinforce and complement the reform. In order to increase enterprise productivity, the Hungarian government approved changes in the exchange rate which would subject Hungarian firms to increased foreign competition. One of the most important decisions in this sector established a unified exchange rate (IMF, *Survey* 1/24/83:22; Comisso and Marer, p. 452). This was a direct attempt to remove government subsidies, transferred through favorable exchange rates, from enterprises which engaged in production for the export market and to force them to produce goods which would be competitive in Hungary's major export markets, particularly the developed countries. As part of this outward-oriented strategy, investment funds were also targeted to promote goods for export (Schröder, p. 88). These policies in the foreign trade sector reflected a shift in Hungarian planning from an emphasis on growth using inward-oriented policies to a preoccupation with external balance (IMF, *Survey* 1/24/83:22, 25).

The 1980 reforms also exhibited a concern to heighten the level of competition between enterprises, again in order to increase efficiency and productivity. The new regulations disbanded many near monopolies, reduced the size of others, and altered legal regulations to permit the formation of new firms (IMF, *Survey* 1/24/83:23; Schröder, p. 88). Formerly illegal activities judged by the government to be socially "useful" were legalized, and enforcement of the law in "ambiguous cases" was relaxed (Kornai, p. 1708; Tyson, *Economic Adjustment*, p. 67).

This was perhaps the "boldest break with orthodoxy"[8] in that these regulations virtually legitimized a wide range of private activities and firms. Individuals could now enter into separate agreements with state enterprises or cooperatives, and private firms could operate in areas formerly restricted to the state sector (Tyson, *Economic Adjustment*, p. 67). Only small firms employing a maximum of seven non-family members were legalized, however (Kornai, p. 1704). Large scale competition with the socialist sector was still prohibited.

In agriculture authorities adopted a "liberal" policy toward private plots, although their size was still restricted, and consequently the number of such plots increased rapidly (IMF, *Survey* 1/24/83:25; Kornai, p. 1702; Tyson, *Economic Adjustment*, p. 68). Individual producers could now own animals and farm machinery, and there were no restrictions on the sale of the output produced by private plots; agricultural prices were to be determined by the free market (Kornai, p. 1702). Authorities declared private plots a "permanent component of agriculture under socialism" (Kornai, p. 1702).

This tolerance for private production and the emphasis on competition was somewhat misleading, however. The socialist sector remained the primary concern of the central administration and by 1982, 98 percent of GDP still originated in the socialist sector (IMF, *Survey* 1/24/83:24). There were only approximately 164 thousand officially licensed private firms in 1984 and these "rarely" received government credit (Kornai, p. 1705).

An austerity program accompanied the new reforms. Hungary's steadily increasing debt with its unfavorable terms after 1978 was no longer a viable means of financing the trade deficit. The austerity program was designed to eliminate the need for further financing by reducing the trade deficit with convertible currency countries and curtailing domestic demand (Comisso and Marer, p. 79; Tyson, *Economic Adjustment*, pp. 79, 105; IMF, *Survey* 1/24/83:23). Unlike the 1973 period, adjustment occurred through a planned decrease in the growth rate[9] and renewed emphasis on exports to the West.

The 1980 reforms were an integral part of this program, especially the increases in the price level and the efforts to encourage competitiveness in the export market. Thus, as Comisso and Marer note, "reform of the economic structure [was] a distinctive element of Hungary's foreign economic strategy" in the early 1980s (p. 421). That this shift in priorities occurred simultaneously with economic reform was unusual given the strong impetus toward centralization during crisis which is characteristic of centrally planned economies (Tyson, *Economic Adjustment*, p. 106).

The combined austerity and reform program had almost immediate effects on the growth rate of Net Material Product which slipped to only 2 percent in 1981 (IMF, *Survey* 1/24/83:23). The trade deficit responded to the reduction in imports which accompanied the declining growth rate. By 1981, the $1.1 billion trade deficit with the West had been reduced to $788 million and achieved a surplus of $461 million in 1982; however, the 1982 surplus was largely due to Hungary's increased trade surplus with the CMEA countries (Tyson, *Economic Adjustment*, p. 62). The balance of payments also improved temporarily, with a deficit of only $510 million in 1980, but the current account deficit rose again in 1981 to $931 million (IMF, *Survey* 1/24/83:24). Hungary's debt continued to increase, from $7.3 billion in 1979 to nearly $9 billion in 1981; Hungary's per capita debt was the highest in the Soviet Bloc in 1981, and its debt service ratio ranked second only to Poland.[10]

Membership and Austerity

In November 1981, Hungary "unexpectedly" applied for membership in the International Monetary Fund.[11] Fund and Bank membership had several advantages for Hungary in the 1980s and relatively fewer costs than at any time since Bretton Woods. Hungary, like all members of the Soviet Bloc in 1980, was suffering from a liquidity crisis resulting largely from the reluctance of international creditors to lend to the Bloc in the wake of the Polish political and economic crisis (Pissulla, p. 67; Schröder, p. 89); thus, the Fund represented an additional source of financing (Comisso and Marer, p. 430). Fund membership could provide the continued financing which was crucial for the success of Hungary's renewed reform process and would also reinforce the reform's goal of further integration of the Hungarian economy into the international economic system (Comisso and Marer, p. 431; Pissulla, p. 67; Schröder, p. 88). Hungary's application to the IMF, then, represented a continuation of trends in Hungary which began in 1968 and intensified in 1980.

Problems within the CMEA also contributed to Hungary's decision to join the IMF, and later the IBRD. The Hungarian economy had suffered from interruptions in raw materials supplies from Poland (Tyson, *Economic Adjustment*, p. 62) and the Soviet Union was no longer willing to subsidize the Bloc's entire debt and energy burdens, which had eased Soviet Bloc adjustment in the 1970s, forcing Hungary to look outside the Bloc for its needs. The Soviet Union had also informed Hungary that it must reduce its ruble deficit with the U.S.S.R (Majda, p. 80; Tyson, *Economic Adjustment*, p. 62; Schröder, p. 87). In 1981 Hungary maintained a large dollar surplus with the socialist countries which partially offset its dollar deficit with the industrialized market economies (Tyson, *Economic Adjustment*, p. 62). Reportedly, Hungary did not formally request the Soviets' permission to enter the IMF (Schröder, p. 87), but it is not unreasonable to assume that the Soviet Union tacitly approved of Hungary's actions.

Hungary's application for IMF membership was approved by an overwhelming margin in the Board of Governors, including the United States.[12] Hungary's quota was established at $413.66 million which in 1982 enabled Hungary to borrow a maximum of $1.4 billion over a three year period.[13] The IBRD approved Hungary's membership a few months later, and despite speculation that Hungary's per capita income had exceeded the Bank's lending threshold, the Bank classified its new member as a developing state and declared it eligible for Bank loans.[14]

By 1982, Hungary's economy had acquired many of the characteristics which appealed to the IMF's market orientation. Hungary's austerity program, formulated *before* its application to the Fund, bore a striking resemblance to the program which Romania and other developing countries had designed in cooperation with the Fund (Pissulla, p. 68; Tyson, *Economic Adjustment*, p. 106). The information problem was not a factor since Hungary already published most of the required information (IMF, *Survey* 7/5/82:202). Hungary's membership in the GATT demonstrated that country's willingness to abide by the rules of the international economic system and its interest in assuming full responsibilities in that system (IMF, *Survey* 1/24/83:23). It is fair to say that in 1982, "Hungary [was] probably closer to the principles and goals of the IMF than many other countries" (Schröder, p. 89).

Between 1982 and 1985 Hungary received two Stand-by Arrangement loans. In December 1982, the Fund announced that it had approved a $497.3 million SBA for Hungary in support of the "Government's economic program" (IMF, *Survey* 12/13/82:399). The loan required repayment in thirteen months. This loan was approximately 126.7 percent of Hungary's quota at that time and well within its borrowing limits. The SBA supported Hungary's attempts to reduce its foreign trade deficit and resolve its lingering liquidity crisis, and the Fund was careful to praise Hungary's efforts to adjust its policies (IMF, *Survey* 12/13/82:399; Pissulla, p. 68). The IMF extended a second, $416.58 million SBA to Hungary for the same purposes, noting that while Hungary's austerity program had made "considerable progress," its problems persisted (IMF, *Annual Report 1984*; IMF, *Survey* 1/23/84:30). A *New York Times* evaluation of the Fund's largest borrowers from 1980 to 1983 revealed that Hungary already ranked tenth (NYT 1/9/83).

Hungary's experiences with the IBRD have been even more profitable. Since it joined the institution in 1982, Hungary has received ten Bank loans. In 1983, Hungary borrowed $239.4 million from the Bank to assist in grain storage and energy projects. Hungary ranked 14th of the 44 countries which received Bank loans in that year. The following year, 1984, Hungary received $238.8 million to support agricultural, energy, and industrial projects and again ranked 14th among 42 borrowers. In 1985 the Bank lent Hungary $324.7 million in support of projects in agriculture, energy, industry and transport. Of the 44 countries which received Bank loans in 1985, Hungary placed 10th. Industrial and energy projects were again the focus of Bank loans to Hungary in 1986; the total amount of Bank lending to Hungary dropped to only $189 million in that year and Hungary's relative rank dropped to 17th out of 44.[15]

The stabilization programs which Hungary pursued during this time were not significantly different from those which it had instituted prior to its membership in the Fund. Consumption, investment, and credit remained tightly controlled by the central authorities in an effort to improve Hungary's foreign trade and balance of payments position (IMF, *Survey* 1/23/84:30, 2/6/84:45). Hungary's current account position in 1983 achieved a small surplus and in that same year nearly 5 percent of GDP had been shifted into the external sector (IMF, *Survey* 2/6/84:45). Hungary was pursuing an aggressive strategy to seek out new export markets in the West to offset its imports from that area (Tyson, *Economic Adjustment*, p. 66; IMF, *Survey* 12/13/82:407). The government was also successful in limiting economic growth in 1983 to only 0.5–1.0 percent, significantly below planned levels (IMF, *Survey* 12/13/82:407).

NEM reforms continued throughout the 1980s. A greater effort was made to increase the competitiveness of Hungarian firms after 1982 when new legislation increased the scope of small enterprise activity even further (IMF, *Survey* 1/24/83:25; Tyson, *Economic Adjustment*, p. 65). By 1983, 300 new firms had entered the Hungarian market. Kornai views this as a positive sign for the future of the market in Hungary as he believes that it is the small enterprises which are least affected by government intervention (p. 1714). There has also been some indication that the government intends to introduce elements of self-management into the socialist sector in hopes of increasing productivity and competition between firms (Comisso and Marer, p. 450).

Firms have obtained greater discretion over the use of their profits and now may grant trade credits to customers or jointly found new enterprises with other firms (Kornai, pp. 1696, 1712). A major innovation has been the introduction of a bond market which remains small but active (NYT 7/8/86; Kornai, p. 1712).

Reforms in Hungary to date have not created a free market economy in that country. Significant elements of the former central planning system remain. The central government retains control over numerous prices and over investment, either directly (Tyson, *Economic Adjustment*, p. 34) or through control over bank investment funds (Kornai, p. 1696; Tyson, *Economic Adjustment*, p.34). The Hungarian government continues to discriminate in its treatment of enterprises, protecting large enterprises in the socialist sector from many of the adverse effects of increased participation in the world economy (Kornai, p. 1699). In particular, the government is reluctant to permit large enterprises to enter bankruptcy (Kornai, p. 1698), much like Yugoslavia. As Comisso and Marer so aptly noted, the reform process in Hungary is "neither concluded nor unidirectional" (p. 454) and is likely to remain an experiment for some years to come.

Of all the members of the Soviet Bloc in 1982, Hungary was least threatened by the market-orientation of the IMF and IBRD. Its need for increased liquidity had already led to significant experimentation with market mechanisms and Fund and Bank membership supplied the funds to support Hungary's established path. Hungarian membership served a purpose for the IMF and IBRD as well since Hungary was a member in good standing of the Soviet Bloc and CMEA, unlike Romania.

Poland

In 1981 Poland submitted its application for reentry into the Bank and Fund after a 31 year absence. Poland's application came in the midst of one of the most serious political and economic crises in its history. The growth rate of Net Material Product for the 1976–1980 period registered only 1.2 percent and reflected a more general economic decline.[16] The foreign trade balance declined to a $10.6 billion deficit and borrowing to finance the deficit brought Poland's net debt to the developed market economies of the West to $22.1 billion in 1980, an increase of $14.5 billion since only 1975 (IMF, *Survey* 4/19/82:119; Poznanski, p. 460). Poland's net debt and debt service ratio were the highest in the Soviet Bloc in 1981 (IMF, *Survey* 4/19/82:119; Tyson, *Economic Adjustment*, p. 69), and by 1981 Poland had stopped payments on its debt principal and was late in meeting its interest payments on the accumulated debt (WSJ 5/19/81; Pissulla, p. 68; Schröder, p. 89).

The Polish crisis had widespread impact not only in Poland but in the rest of the Bloc as well. Western creditors, dismayed by the apparent unwillingness of the Soviet Union to come to the aid of its ailing ally and the seeming inability of the Bloc nations to implement effective adjustment strategies, promptly reduced or eliminated further credits to all Eastern European nations (WSJ 5/19/81; Majda, p. 85; Comisso and Marer, p. 430). This unofficial credit embargo immediately brought several of the Bloc nations into a liquidity crisis and exacerbated the existing crisis in Poland (Poznanski, pp. 474–475). Rapid economic decline and the consequent enactment of severe austerity measures triggered a serious political crisis in Poland which resulted in strikes, protests, the formation of the Solidarity movement, and the eventual imposition of martial law in December 1981.

There were several roots to the crisis, but the credit embargo was the catalyst which led to Poland's insolvency in 1981. Like many other Bloc members, Poland had resorted to international borrowing to finance its mounting debts. In part, the reluctance of the Soviet Union to provide additional assistance, and in fact its curtailing of existing subsidies to CMEA members, was a major factor in the decisions of Hungary and Poland to turn outward to the international economy for their needs (WSJ 5/19/81; Poznanski, p. 477; NYT 12/21/84). Soviet behavior also contributed to the loss of confidence by Western creditors and the resulting credit embargo.

The common root to Soviet and Polish behavior in the 1970s was the effects of the two oil price shocks. The precipitous price increases affected the price of imports to the Bloc and the terms of trade of these countries with the West. The Soviet Union was experiencing its own difficulties and was therefore unwilling to subsidize Poland any further (NYT 12/21/84). For its part, Poland, like Hungary and Romania, responded inappropriately to the 1970s price shocks by continuing its strategy of extensive growth financed by intense international borrowing (Poznanski, pp. 455–457).

As the situation in Poland slowly gravitated toward complete collapse, Polish authorities sought to stem the decline through the implementation of a strict austerity program similar to those the IMF would recommend for Hungary, Romania, and Yugoslavia in the 1980s. Planned rates of growth in Net Material Product, imports, and consumption declined sharply from previous plan periods and special attention was paid to strengthening the export sector (IMF, *Survey* 4/19/82:119; Poznanski, pp. 466–470). The Polish Government proposed reforms in the central planning system (scheduled for implementation on January 1, 1982) which would revitalize the non-state farming sector and reduce bureaucratic intervention in the economy as a whole (Poznanski, pp. 466, 477). These reforms were more discussions of future possibilities than actual policy changes, however, and resembled the reform process in Romania more than in Hungary (Poznanski, pp. 460–462).

Attempted Membership

Part of the changes enacted in Poland in the early 1980s entailed a reversal of its long-standing stance on the IMF. In November 1981, Poland applied for renewal of its membership in the IMF. One obvious benefit of Fund membership was the access to new credit lines which would accompany it. The amount of credit available through the Fund was larger than the amount to which Poland had access in any single country (WSJ 7/30/82); based on its probable quota in 1981, Poland would have had access to $3–4 billion in additional funds (NYT 8/3/84), approximately 17 percent of Poland's total requirements in 1981 (Majda, p. 83). Since IMF loans carried a lower than market interest rate, this additional liquidity would have been less costly than the strategy Poland had pursued in the 1970s.

Fund membership also had subsidiary benefits which would have given Poland access to additional credit through the IBRD and the private credit market (Majda, pp. 81–84). The Bank's classification of Yugoslavia in the developing category was a good indication that Poland would be given access to development project funding and would be able to bid on Bank projects in other member countries, thus increasing Polish access to Third World markets.

Poland's creditors were also pressuring that nation to affiliate with the IMF. These banks and governments credited Poland's crisis to policy errors and the lack of policy supervision (Pissulla, p. 68). They recognized that they had no authority to impose appropriate stabilization measures on Poland and that the IMF was already organized for that purpose and would be an ideal mediator of future debt restructuring agreements (WSJ 5/19/81, 7/30/86). Poland thus confronted a situation in which renegotiation of its debt became contingent on Fund membership (Pissulla, p. 68; Schröder, p. 89). Evidence of the Fund's willingness to act in the capacity of debt negotiations mediator came in September, 1981 when the IMF participated as an observer on debt rescheduling talks between Poland and its Western creditors, a new role for the Fund (Schröder, p. 89).

In addition, Poland could gain credibility for its policy actions if these were implemented under the auspices of a Fund stabilization program (Majda, p. 83). While Poland's creditors viewed Fund membership from the perspective of increasing their leverage over Poland's policies, Poland's view of the Fund altered as it found itself implementing several of the policies the Fund typically recommended in its stabilization programs. In effect, Poland demonstrated that it was willing to submit to Fund conditions even *without* Fund membership (Pissulla, p. 69; Majda, pp. 87–88). From Poland's perspective, Fund membership would not significantly alter the course of Polish economic policy initiated in 1979–1980 and would, in fact, provide Polish authorities with additional expertise in resolving its economic problems (Majda, p. 80; WSJ 7/30/86).

Poland was also attracted to the international character of IMF lending. Because of the IMF's character as an international organization and specialized agency of the United Nations, its lending did not convey the same political connotations as loans from Western governments and institutions. Poland was more likely to accept conditions demanded by the Fund than a Western government, and thus Poland could maintain cordial relations with its creditors (WSJ 7/30/86; Schröder, p. 89). The Soviet Union appeared to agree with Poland's reasoning on this issue and after extensive discussions consented to Poland's application (Schröder, p. 87).

Conditions in Poland deteriorated throughout 1981 and on December 13, 1981 Communist Party leader Jaruzelski imposed martial law on the country in an attempt to forestall complete collapse of the centralized political and economic systems. This action had immediate effects on Poland's application to the Fund. The United States, as part of its broader sanctions on Poland for its December actions, promptly expressed its opposition to Poland's application to the IMF and announced its intentions to vote against the application in the Board of Governors and in the Executive Directors. This in effect vetoed Poland's application (Poznanski, p. 476; NYT 12/16/84), although if the application had proceeded to an actual vote, Poland might have succeeded.[17] The U.S. accomplished its goal to punish the Polish Government for its suppression of Solidarity in direct contradiction to the Fund's *Articles of Agreement* which explicitly forbids discrimination against a country based on its economic or political system.[18] It is clear that the U.S. placed its foreign policy interests before its economic interests in this case, as several of Poland's U.S. creditors strongly supported its membership in the IMF.

There was additional concern about the impact of Poland's entrance on the Fund's already depleted resources (rectified in 1984). The severity of Poland's economic problems and the size of its credit need raised some concerns within the Fund membership that assistance to Poland would seriously reduce the amount of funding available to other members (Pissulla, p. 70; NYT 8/3/84; WSJ 2/10/86). Questions also arose about Poland's willingness to abide by the IMF's rules regarding provision of information, the quality of that information, and conditionality (Pissulla, p. 70; Schröder, p. 90).

Membership

With its application to the Fund stalled, Poland continued its austerity program. Continuing political conflict made the necessary comprehensive reforms almost impossible (WSJ 7/30/86), but Jaruzelski proceeded with the stabilization program he had begun before martial law. Solidarity was outlawed, wages and prices were controlled, and tentative reforms were instituted to increase the autonomy of enterprises and reduce the power of central ministries (Poznanski, p. 482; NYT 4/22/85).

These measures did result in a slight improvement in the Polish economy, but international creditors were suspicious of the authenticity of the reforms and remained wary of extending new commitments to Poland (Poznanski, pp. 482–484). Poland was successful in reopening debt negotiations in 1983 and rescheduled over $1.6 billion in its Western debt in March 1986 (WSJ 3/11/86; NYT 3/9/86, 8/6/84; Poznanski, p. 483). New credits remained elusive.

As the need for the restrictive measures of martial law receded, Poland's application to the IMF regained salience. In July 1984, Poland released 600 political prisoners, largely members of the outlawed Solidarity movement, and the release of two prominent Solidarity activists followed in early December 1984 (NYT 12/15/84). The U.S. responded immediately and announced its intention to withdraw its veto of Poland's application, conditional on no further repressive measures against Solidarity members (NYT 12/15/84, 8/3/84). The Western European nations, especially Great Britain, also encouraged the renewal of consideration of Poland's request for membership in the Fund (NYT 12/16/84).

Action on Poland's application proceeded according to the Fund's standard operating procedures, and a technical assessment of Poland's economy was prepared in time for the April 1986 meeting of the Interim Committee (WSJ 2/10/86; NYT 2/13/86). The Interim Committee forwarded the application to the entire Board of Governors in May, and on May 29, 1986 Poland's application to the Fund was approved by 125 votes out of a possible 149, a clear majority (WSJ 5/29/86; NYT 6/1/86).

The United States abstained on the Polish vote as it had indicated it would earlier in 1986. The U.S. Government was not pleased with recent developments in Poland's treatment of Solidarity members and had nearly renewed its veto (NYT 12/18/84; WSJ 5/23/86). Dissatisfaction with Poland's "slowness" in adopting adjustment reforms also contributed to the U.S. abstention (WSJ 5/29/86). Perhaps the most telling justification for the abstention was the Reagan Administration's fear that an affirmative vote on Poland's admission to the Fund would alienate the U.S. Congress and thus endanger Congressional approval for future funding for the IMF and other international banks (WSJ 5/23/86, 5/29/86). The U.S. did assure Poland that it would limit its consideration of any Polish request for a Fund loan to strictly economic criteria (WSJ 12/19/86).

Poland became the 151st member of the IMF on June 12, 1986 and was assessed a quota of approximately $800 million. This quota enables Poland to borrow a maximum of $2 billion from the IMF's various facilities under current Fund rules. Poland joined the IBRD soon after and began preparing project proposals for submission to the Bank (NYT 6/16/86). The IMF dispatched a mission to Poland in July, 1986 to investigate recent policy changes in Poland which included a new emphasis on profitability, increases in enterprise autonomy, curbs on some subsidies, and a moderate price reform (NYT 12/21/84; WSJ 6/1/86, 6/16/86). Polish authorities devalued the zloty 15 percent soon after the mission's visit (WSJ 9/2/86).

It is too soon to evaluate the effects of Fund and Bank membership on the Polish economic system. Poland's economy is still struggling; its trade surplus with the West had declined to $200 million by the beginning of 1986, and exports to the West decreased by 5.3 percent in the first half of 1986 as imports during the same period increased 1.2 percent (NYT 6/1/86; WSJ 9/2/86). The Chernobyl accident in the Ukraine and the subsequent EEC restrictions of Polish agricultural exports are likely to exacerbate these trends.

Poland's debt to the industrialized market economies reached $31 billion in 1985 (NYT 6/16/86; WSJ 7/30/86). Poland was again unable to service its debt in 1986 and was forced to reschedule $2.06 billion of its debt in June 1986 and its $1.7 billion debt to the United States in July 1986 (WSJ 6/13/86, 7/31/86). Although new credits were not forthcoming, the rescheduling agreements were a clear indication of a slight improvement in the West's confidence in a Polish economic recovery, or at least in the Fund's ability to ensure that Poland pursued policies which would not aggravate the problem.

Conclusion:
CMEA States in the IMF and the IBRD

The experiences of Hungary and Poland with the Fund and the Bank were strongly affected by changes in intra-CMEA relations. The two oil price shocks were felt within the CMEA and elicited similar reactions from its members. The financing of the extensive growth strategy by borrowing outside the CMEA ultimately led to liquidity crises in several CMEA members, including Poland and Hungary. What changed in the 1980s was the Soviet Union's willingness to subsidize its allies; the Soviets were experiencing their own economic difficulties and could not forego the income oil would bring on the world market (NYT 12/21/84). From the Soviets' perspective, Bank and Fund membership was one means of meeting the economic, and potential political, crisis in the Bloc (Schröder, p. 88).

Thus, both Hungary's and Poland's relations with other members of the Soviet Bloc provided a unique opportunity for integration into the international economic system. Concerns about the political costs of membership, voiced at Bretton Woods by the Soviet Union, faded when confronted by the successful experiences of Yugoslavia and Romania and when faced with impending economic crisis. Both Yugoslavia and Romania had secured Bank lending despite their rather high levels of per capita income and had received extensive assistance from the Bank and Fund without the coercive imposition of economic reforms. In particular, "the experience of Romania [showed] that the influence of the IMF, even when it does get involved in the economy of a particular country, remains moderate" (Schröder, p. 87). Although complaints from both Yugoslavia and Romania had surfaced by the 1980s, neither country's concerns had led to withdrawal from the Fund or the Bank.

Economic reform in Hungary preceded its membership in the Bank and Fund, and the direction of those reforms almost guaranteed that Hungary's relations with both organizations would tend toward cooperation. Like Yugoslavia, Hungary's combination of a market-orientation with elements of central direction had practically guaranteed the Fund's approval, and Hungary's intentions of closer integration into the international economy were nicely enhanced by the Bank and Fund's own goals. Popular support for the NEM in Hungary makes it likely that Hungary's economic direction will continue along its present course with or without assistance from the IMF (Tyson, *Economic Adjustment*, p. 38; Comisso and Marer, p. 439).

Future economic policy in Poland is more problematic. While Poland has pursued several Hungarian-type economic reforms in recent years, it is too early to evaluate their effects or longevity. The commitment of the government to these reforms is also questionable. It is possible that the IMF will be able to reinforce current trends, but this is contingent on the behavior of alternative lenders to Poland. Should Poland have access to alternative sources of funding, it would be plausible that Poland would avoid Fund loans and their attendant conditionality (WSJ 7/30/86).

Like Romania, Poland is a test case of Fund and Bank membership for other CMEA countries. The role of the United States in the course of Polish membership in both organizations is likely to be critical. It is entirely plausible that Poland may withdraw a second time if it feels that the costs of membership outweigh the benefits, and the voting power of the U.S. ensures that it will be a central actor in the disposition of Bank and Fund benefits to Poland. Whether the Fund can or does develop performance criteria specific to the conditions of its Soviet Bloc membership will depend on U.S. acquiescence in the process. Hungary and Poland make it necessary for the Fund to consider this alternative (Schröder, p. 90).

Unlike the early years of Romania's membership, to date Hungarian and Polish influence on Fund and Bank procedures has been minimal. The 1980s have seen a much different role for the Fund than the 1970s, and this has reinforced the Fund's traditional perspective on market-oriented conditionality. The debt crisis of the 1980s has placed the Soviet Bloc members in weaker positions than ever before while simultaneously strengthening the role of the Fund in the management of the crisis. With private and government creditors literally insisting on Fund membership as a condition for future credits, the IMF is virtually assured of near universality of membership. Until this situation changes, it is improbable that the Fund will alter its present emphasis on market solutions to economic problems.

Notes

1. Petra Pissulla, "The IMF and the Countries of Eastern Europe," *Intereconomics*, vol. 19, no. 2 (1984), p. 65.

2. Klaus Schröder, "The IMF and the Countries of the Council for Mutual Economic Assistance," *Intereconomics*, vol. 17, no. 2, p. 87.

3. Janos Kornai, "The Hungarian Reform Process: Visions, Hopes, and Reality," *Journal of Economic Literature*, vol. 24 (December 1986), pp. 1690, 1715; Schröder, p. 88; World Bank, *Hungary:Economic Developments and Reforms* (Washington, D.C.: IBRD, 1984); IMF, *Survey* 1/24/83:22. This document from the IMF *Survey* is an exerpt from an IMF Occasional Paper (No. 15) which served as the working document for the evaluation of Hungary's membership application.

4. IMF, *Survey* 1/24/83:22; Kornai, p. 1691; Ellen Comisso and Paul Marer, "The Economics and Politics of Reform in Hungary," *International Organization*, vol. 40, no. 2 (1986), p. 425. For a complete description of Hungary's New Economic Mechanism, see *Reform of the Economic Adjustment Mechanism in Hungary: Development 1968-1971*, edited by Otto Gadó (Budapest: Akademiai Kiado, 1972), especially Chapters IV: Foreign Trade, and V: Market and Domestic Prices; *Hungary: A Decade of Economic Reform*, edited by P.G. Hare, H.K. Radice, and N. Swain (London: George Allen and Unwin, 1981), especially Chapters 1: Introduction, 5: Investment, 8: Foreign Trade, and 9: Exchange Rate; World Bank, *Hungary: Economic Developments and Reforms*.

5. Laura D'Andrea Tyson, *Economic Adjustment in Eastern Europe*, R-3146-AF, prepared for the U.S. Air Force (Santa Monica: The Rand Corporation, 1984), p. 32.

6. See Tyson, *Economic Adjustment*, "Introduction"; Comisso and Marer, pp. 147-149; Kornai, p. 1721.

7. Schröder, p. 88; Tyson, *Economic Adjustment*, p. 65.

8. Kornai, p. 1704.

9. The planned growth rate for the 1981-1985 plan period was 2.6-3.2 percent. See IMF, *Survey* 4/19/82:119.

10. IMF, *Survey* 4/19/82:119; Tyson, *Economic Adjustment*, p. 69; *Wall Street Journal* (WSJ) 5/19/81; Pawel Majda, "L'importance du Fonds Monetaire International pour la Pologne et les autres pays d'Europe Orientale," *Revue d'études comparatives est-ouest*, vol. 13, no. 4 (1982), p. 91.

11. Pissulla, p. 67; Schröder, p. 88; *New York Times* (NYT) 5/16/82.

12. IMF, *Survey* 5/10/82:129; NYT 5/6/82.

13. IMF, *Annual Report 1982* (Washington, D.C.: IMF, 1982); IMF *Survey* 5/10/82:129; NYT 12/15/84.

14. IBRD, *Annual Report 1982* (Washington, D.C.: IBRD, 1982); Schröder, p. 89; Pissulla, p. 67.

15. These figures are taken from IBRD, *Annual Reports 1982– 1986*; NYT 7/12/86.

16. Kazimierz Poznanski, "Economic Adjustment and Political Forces: Poland Since 1970," *International Organization*, vol. 40, no. 2 (1986), p.477; IMF, *Survey* 4/19/82:119.

17. Membership decisions require a 51 percent vote of the membership of the Fund. At the time, the U.S. possessed approximately 20 percent of the Fund total voting power, and the fact that the Western European states were likely to join in the U.S. veto of Poland's membership application virtually assured that if Poland had pressed the matter, the application would have been denied. See Joseph Gold, *Membership and Nonmembership in the International Monetary Fund* (Washington, D.C.: IMF, 1974) and the 1982 *Annual Report* for discussion of this issue and the relevant voting strength of Fund members.

18. See the IMF, *Articles of Agreement* and Pissulla, p. 70.

8

The Soviet Bloc
in the IMF and the IBRD:
Conflict and Cooperation

The International Monetary Fund and the International Bank for Reconstruction and Development were designed in 1944 to facilitate the operation and growth of the international economy. When the organizations began operations in 1945, only three Soviet Bloc countries appeared on the membership roster, despite both institutions' professed goal of universal membership. By 1955, only one Communist country remained, Yugoslavia, and in 1979 total Soviet Bloc membership numbered only two. It was the purpose of this analysis to examine the experiences of the five Soviet Bloc states which have been members of the IMF and IBRD as examples of the operations of political factors in Bank and Fund policies and decisions to lend.

There are two conflicting claims in the literature on Bank and Fund policies and behavior regarding the possible political nature of Bank and Fund operations. The technocratic approach contends that Bank and Fund decisions, due to their technical nature, are strictly apolitical and are made with reference to established economic and technical criteria. The critics of the Bank and Fund disagree and assert that the dominant philosophy of Bank and Fund founders at Bretton Woods, laissez-faire capitalism, is reflected not only in the charters of the two financial institutions but in all aspects of their operations. These critics predict that members whose economic ideologies are inconsistent with, or hostile to, laissez-faire capitalism or the operation of the free market would encounter difficulties in obtaining assistance from the IMF and IBRD. In practice, therefore, the presence of political influences on decisions to lend by both organizations would increase both the potential costs and the uncertainty encountered by prospective borrowers. This could conceivably alter the potential borrower's behavior with respect to the lending organizations (e.g., result in a decision *not* to apply for a loan).

In order to examine the influence of political variables in Bank and Fund lending policies and operations, two arenas of decision-making were posited in which lending decisions by the IMF and IBRD may be located. Decisions to lend which are made solely with reference to technical or economic criteria would be located in the technical arena, whereas decisions made according to political factors such as foreign policy or ideology would be placed in the political arena. In reality, the boundary between the two arenas is not obvious and may shift in response to changing economic and political conditions.

Three types of influence on lending decisions are postulated in this analysis: ascriptive, leverage, and reverse. Ascriptive influences are characteristics of the borrower which the borrower cannot easily alter, such as regime type. Leverage influences take several forms: punishment, reward, inducement, and reinforcement through which the lender seeks to influence the behavior of the borrower. Reverse influences reflect the extent to which the borrower is able to influence the policies and operations of the lender. It is through these three types of inputs that the existence of the political arena can be traced.

Results

The fact that some states receive a level of Bank and Fund aid which is not consistent with their performance on selected economic variables does testify to the existence of a political arena, even a very small one, in both the IMF and IBRD. Decisions to lend to the five Soviet Bloc members of the Bank and Fund (Poland, Czechoslovakia, Hungary, Yugoslavia, and Romania) are located in the political arenas of both organizations by virtue of the fact that these countries either received no funds at all or received an above-average level of loans. Since 1960, Soviet Bloc states tended to receive a larger total amount of loans from the Bank and Fund than would be expected, given both their political and economic characteristics.

Confrontation

IMF and IBRD relationships with the Soviet Bloc can be classified into three periods: a period marked by caution and mutual suspicion (1945–1960); a period of relative cooperation (1960–1978); and a period of increasing tension resulting from economic crisis (1978–1985). Several factors determined the nature of the relationship between the Fund, the Bank, and their Bloc members, but each period contained examples of attempted leverage by the IMF and IBRD and efforts at reverse influence by the Soviet Bloc countries.

At the United Nations Monetary and Financial Conference at Bretton Woods, N.H., held in July, 1944, several concessions were made in the *Articles of Agreement* to accommodate potential Communist members. These provisions concerned primarily the provision of economic information to the IMF, the size of quotas, and the payments of subscriptions. Although the U.S.S.R. ultimately did not join either organization, the Soviet Bloc countries which entered the Bank and Fund did benefit from these concessions—some of the few examples of reverse influence discovered by this inquiry.

From the analysis of the experiences of all five Soviet Bloc members of the IMF and IBRD, it is clear that it was not ideology or economic structure but the status of the individual Soviet Bloc member's relations with the Soviet Union which most influenced Bank and Fund decisions to lend. Poland and Czechoslovakia had very close, positive relationships with the U.S.S.R. during their terms of membership and also received no assistance from either the Bank or the Fund; eventually each withdrew from both organizations. Although the conflicts between these states and the Bank and Fund were couched in terms of violations of their membership obligations, similar violations by members who were antagonistic to the Soviet Union were overlooked. Bank and Fund refusals to lend were, therefore, a punishment for the two states' reliance on Soviet assistance and support, both military and economic.

Other factors which contributed to the rather hostile relations between the Bank and Fund and their Soviet Bloc members in the early 1950s were the international political and economic environments of the time. The Cold War had reached a period of intense hostility, and trust between East and West was at a minimum. Bank and Fund reluctance to lend to Communist countries in the early 1950s had its roots, therefore, in the fear that since the Soviet Union was not a member of either organization, and consequently not bound by their rules and procedures, it would encourage its satellites to default on their obligations or otherwise disrupt Bank and Fund activities.

In addition, the IMF and IBRD were only in the first decade of their existence, and it is conceivable that this lack of experience and the experimental nature of the entire Bretton Woods system were manifested in an unwillingness to bend the rules (although there *were* cases during this period where regulations were suspended; see Chapter 3). Finally, at the time of the Bank's and Fund's disputes with Poland and Czechoslovakia, both countries were relatively isolated from the international economy; therefore, these countries' impact on the environment of the IMF and IBRD was minimal, and thus they were expendable.

There were no incentives, then, for the Bank and Fund to make allowances for the special needs of their Communist members during the 1946-1959 period. Indeed, during this time both organizations pursued an essentially confrontational policy with respect to their Communist members. Since this attitude was essentially in accord with the views of the dominant members of both organizations (the U.S., U.K., France, and Italy), as well as the majority of the membership *at that time*, and the potential impact of the Communist members on Bank and Fund operations was negligible, the costs of a confrontational policy were rather low for both the IMF and the IBRD. Consequently, both organizations were free to reduce the internal stresses caused by Communist membership (particularly by Czechoslovakia) and to pursue in an open manner their organizational goal of a market-oriented free trade system.

Cooperation

The first two countries with successful relationships with the Bank and Fund, Yugoslavia and Romania, were not "typical" Communist, Soviet Bloc states in the one area which had proven critical to Czech and Polish experiences in the two international organizations: relations with the Soviet Union. Yugoslavia began its independent, non-aligned foreign policy posture in response to the Soviet-induced Cominform break of 1948. Experimentation with a novel economic structure, workers' self-management and market socialism, began soon after. The latter concept incorporated many economic principles and policies which were consistent with the Fund's and Bank's organizational philosophy and rendered the Yugoslav economy more comprehensible to Bank and Fund staff.

As a result, Fund financial assistance to Yugoslavia gradually increased to a level above what would normally be expected for a country with Yugoslavia's economic characteristics. This occurred only after Fund officials were satisfied that post-1948 developments in the Yugoslav economy were not a ruse. The Fund's financial assistance to Yugoslavia during this period was primarily intended to reinforce existing developments in Yugoslav economic policy rather than to initiate new policy since concurrently developed economic thought in Yugoslavia was formulated with the advice and cooperation of the Fund and was also considered appropriate to the Fund's aims.

As can be seen from the preceding discussion, Bank and Fund policy with respect to Soviet Bloc countries followed a rather isolationist position during the 1960s. While the sole Soviet Bloc member of both organizations was cordially treated and accommodated, unlike other Bloc members in the previous decade, the IMF and IBRD did not actively solicit the membership of other members of the Soviet Bloc during this period. In fact, Yugoslavia's continued membership was partially due to the fact that it was no longer a member of the Soviet Bloc.

Mutual disregard characterized relations between the Bank and Fund and the Soviet Bloc during the 1960s, and no new efforts were made to accommodate centrally-planned economies (which Yugoslavia was *not*) until Romania's entrance in 1972. In addition, reforms in the Yugoslav economy, which brought it to full market socialism, required little alteration in IMF and IBRD rules and procedures. Yugoslavia's policy of non-alignment enabled both organizations to demonstrate their theoretical neutrality with respect to ideology without any significant effort on their part. The IMF and IBRD, therefore, were able to isolate Yugoslavia from the more general attitude of the major members of both organizations toward Soviet Bloc countries.

Romania's membership in the Bank and Fund after 1972 inaugurated a new period of cordiality in Bank and Fund orientations toward Communist membership. Romania's strained relations with the Soviet Union preceded its membership in the IMF and IBRD by several years, and therefore, there was little cause for concern in the Bank and Fund that the Soviets would have undue influence over Romanian economic policy. Though the structure of the Romanian economy was unfamiliar to Bank and Fund staff (and indeed, was antithetical to the market) and showed few signs of significant reform, Bank and Fund assistance to Romania was steady and generous. In this case, any concern or objection the Band and Fund might have had over Romania's centrally-planned economic structure was overridden by the organizational imperative of universal membership.

Universal membership once again became important to the Bank and Fund because Soviet Bloc states were no longer considered merely peripheral participants in the international economy, and the desire to integrate those economies more closely into world trade was expressed by both East and West. Potentially, active participation by the Soviet Bloc in the international economy could have a significant impact on Bank and Fund operations (as the early 1980s would prove); consequently, inclusion of those countries as members of the IMF and IBRD became an attractive, if not necessary, proposition. Integration of Soviet Bloc countries into the international economy was necessary in order to prevent the uncontrolled disruption of that system. Membership in the IMF and IBRD, theoretically, would give the Communist countries a stake in the preservation of the economic system which those institutions supported and would also enhance Fund and Bank management of that system.

As a consequence of this change in environment, Romania became a test case for the ease with which the Bank and Fund could accommodate traditional centrally-planned economic systems. Failure of the IMF and IBRD to retain Romanian membership would have had serious consequences for the future of the universal membership goal; loans to Romania, therefore, were extended to induce it to remain in both organizations. Thus, the Fund and Bank were eager to adapt to Romania's unusual circumstances, and as a result, Romania exerted reverse influence on the IMF and IBRD derived from the unfamiliar nature of its economy and the renewed emphasis of both organizations on the need for universal membership.

For the Bank and the Fund, the 1970s were, thus, a period of cooperation with Communist members, especially when the experiences of Yugoslavia during that period are considered in addition to Romania's. This change can be attributed to the fact that the environment of the IMF and IBRD had changed; the lessening of tensions brought about by détente had temporarily eclipsed the Cold War atmosphere of hostility between East and West, and the increased participation of Soviet Bloc countries in the international economy altered the incentives for the IMF and IBRD in favor of cooperation with communist members.

Experience was also a factor in the growing cordiality of the Bank and Fund toward Soviet Bloc members. The IMF and IBRD, by 1980, had had over 35 years' experience as financial assistance agencies, and their continued existence, for the most part, was assured; consequently, both organizations were less constrained by their regulations and the wishes of their memberships. Bank and Fund interactions with Yugoslavia and Romania had become increasingly amicable and prosperous, and the performance of Soviet Bloc states in terms of repayment of international debts had dispelled many of the two organizations' earlier apprehensions about the reliability of Communist states. The Bank and Fund were now willing to integrate Communist countries into their operations because they had learned that the political and economic systems of these countries were not a threat or barrier to either those organizations or the international economy as a whole.

In addition, perhaps the changes of the 1970s were also a consequence of an alteration in the goals of the IMF and IBRD. The relatively smooth integration of non-capitalist, non-market countries into a free-trade, capitalist international economic system and the reflection of this trend in IMF and IBRD membership may have altered the goal of the Fund and the Bank from one of a world populated only by market-type economies to a world which was at least familiar to IMF and IBRD staff and therefore, controllable. To speculate even further, it could be argued that the dominant goal of the Bank and Fund had always been one of maximizing control over an unpredictable environment, and thus, increasing Communist membership would be a rational response to changes in that environment; the fact that the Fund was created specifically to prevent the unpredictable and destructive actions which led to the Great Depression lends credence to this notion.

Tension

The debt crisis of the 1980s inaugurated a new era in Bank and Fund relations with the Soviet Bloc. The Bloc countries experienced the same economic problems which were afflicting many other developing countries, such as spiralling debt, declining terms of trade, balance of payments deficits, and decreasing growth. The Soviet Bloc's steadily increasing need for financing made the Bretton Woods organizations, especially the World Bank, at the same time more attractive and necessary. As the debt burdens of the Bloc grew, they could no longer avoid IMF conditionality as their creditors made further financing conditional on the conclusion of a Stand-by Arrangement with the IMF.

Both Yugoslavia and Romania relied on Fund and Bank assistance during the early portions of this difficult period but ultimately chose to reduce their reliance on the Fund. An IMF SBA was a necessary condition for negotiations with creditors on rescheduling, but the SBAs entailed strict austerity measures which required heavy sacrifices by their respective populations. Ultimately, Romania balked at imposing even harsher measures at the behest of the Fund and, risking a complete credit embargo, refused to draw on a newly-arranged SBA. Yugoslavia was reluctant to risk its credit rating in this manner but made it quite clear that further SBAs, and their attendant conditionality, were a last resort. Yugoslavia's creditors were satisfied with merely the promise that Yugoslavia would work closely with the Fund in formulating policies to deal with its economic problems.

Romania also reduced its borrowing from the IBRD in an effort to eliminate its foreign debt from all sources. Yugoslavia chose a different strategy to mitigate the effects of austerity on the standard of living and continued to rely on Bank lending to supplement its investment resources, particularly to the lesser developed republics.

The threat the debt crisis presented to domestic political and economic stability elicited different policy responses in Yugoslavia and Romania. Romania reacted by retreating into autarky and clinging as much as possible to its central planning formula. Ultimately, Romania rejected the market based advice of the Fund, avoiding the Fund's influence merely by refraining to borrow. Yugoslavia responded by once again examining market options within the framework of BOALS, social compacts and self-management agreements.

Hungary joined the organizations in the midst of the debt crisis. Hungary was also experiencing a short-term liquidity crisis and sought the direct and indirect financial benefits membership in the Bretton Woods organizations would bring. In addition, Bank and Fund membership enhanced its efforts to more closely integrate its market reform efforts with the international economy. To date, Hungarian membership in the Bank and Fund has been mutually beneficial.

It is too early to assess the tenor of Poland's relationship with the two international financial organizations. Much depends on the interest of the Polish Government in stabilization and possible economic reform. Poland's policies are likely to meet close scrutiny, particularly from the U.S., and whether Poland will submit to even harsher austerity measures than it has already implemented is problematical.

The political effects of austerity are already felt throughout the Bloc as domestic protest of the declining standard of living erupts in Poland, Romania, and Yugoslavia. The Bank and Fund have not yet made special concessions to the Soviet Bloc in terms of lending conditions; however, there is a limit to how much these states are willing to sacrifice in pursuit of stabilization. Whether the goal of universality outweighs that of uniformity will be a crucial question for both organizations if this threshold is exceeded.

Leverage and Prospects for the Future

It is difficult to prove that the Bank and the Fund use their leverage to coerce market-oriented economic reform in their Soviet Bloc members. When leverage is present in these cases, it appears as reinforcement or rewards. The Bank, in particular, has refrained from imposing sanctions on its Soviet Bloc members. Until the 1980's, the Bank did not possess the mandate and capabilities to impose conditionality on its members, and by Bank standards, the Soviet Bloc countries were attractive investment opportunities.

The IMF has also been reluctant to punish its Soviet Bloc members. Such an action has been counterproductive in the past when Poland and Czechoslovakia withdrew in response to the Fund's refusal to accommodate to the needs and circumstances of the Bloc countries. More recently, Romania also reacted negatively to Fund pressure. The Fund risks jeopardizing its norm of universality if it applies its criteria too stringently. The Soviet Bloc members could withdraw.

If membership in the Fund and Bank has had an impact on the economic reform process in their Eastern European members, it has been an indirect one. In Yugoslavia and Hungary, there was considerable momentum within both societies for the adoption of a market element in their economies prior to any extensive contact with the Bank and Fund. Hungary implemented the NEM well in advance of its application to the IMF. Poland also was seriously considering market type reforms before the imposition of martial law. It is more difficult to determine Fund influence in Yugoslavia's reforms. In the early period, it is clear that Workers' Self-Management was a genuine indigenous innovation. In the 1960s case it is also clear that there was considerable interest in market socialism stemming from an internal ideological debate within Yugoslav academic and party circles. The 1970s recentralization and emphasis on BOALS certainly did not resemble typical market prescriptions. In some aspects, the 1970 adjustments to market socialism represented a partial rejection of the market. By 1980, though, Yugoslavia had returned to reliance on market mechanisms to resolve its burgeoning economic problems.

Romania is perhaps the clearest example of the inability of the Fund and the Bank to force market reforms on their members. Romania has not adopted any fundamental economic reforms during its tenure in the Bank and the Fund. It remains almost a classic centrally planned economy. IMF attempts to increase the conditionality associated with a new SBA in 1984 resulted in Romania's refusal to utilize the Fund's facilities. As Romania demonstrates, then, the Soviet Bloc is therefore both politically and economically capable of countering Fund attempts at coercion.

Despite these differences and problems, the results of this analysis indicate that foreign policy position was the dominant attribute influencing World Bank and IMF actions toward their Soviet Bloc members from 1945 through 1985. Soviet Bloc countries which asserted their independence from the Soviet Union fared much better in terms of actual loan receipts from the IMF and IBRD than loyal Soviet Bloc members. The refusal of the Bank and Fund to lend to Soviet satellites was leverage used by these institutions to punish those countries for their close relations with the Soviet Union. As the 1950s show, the probability of repayment was a dominant concern in the decisions of the Bank not to lend to Poland and Czechoslovakia—a concern that was due to the hostile nature of the Soviets' attitude toward both organizations at the time, as well as the general level of tension between East and West during the immediate post-war period.

Leverage in the 1960–1980 period predominantly took the form of reinforcement of some desired activity. This responds to the independent nature of both Yugoslavia and Romania. The Fund and Bank attempted to reinforce the independent foreign policies of these countries. In the case of Yugoslavia, this was the reform of the economy toward market socialism. This orientation changes after 1980. Two loyal members of the Bloc, Hungary and Poland enter the two organizations. Their status in the Soviet Bloc still ensures placement in the political arena, but for different reasons. Some of the factors which suggest that these countries will receive favorable treatment from the Bank and Fund include the intention of the major Western powers to seduce these states from the Soviet Bloc, to reinforce whatever tendencies toward economic reform might exist in these countries, and to use the Bloc states as further examples of Bank and Fund universality.

The IMF and IBRD are now entering a new phase of their operations with respect to Communist membership and the needs of non-market economies. The Soviet Bloc countries, for their part, have become aware that, in most instances, the benefits of membership in the IMF and IBRD tend to outweigh the costs. The potential costs of membership, such as increased foreign debt, loss of secrecy, and increased vulnerability to fluctuations in the world economy, are very real, however, and may be insurmountable, depending on a Communist state's priorities.

The benefits are numerous. Membership in the IMF and IBRD eases interactions with other members of the international economic system, and these interactions are increasing at a rapid pace. As the experiences of Yugoslavia and Romania demonstrate, Bank and Fund facilities furnish a source of hard currency to finance participation in the international economy at a relatively low cost and also provide opportunities for access to new export markets. To date the effects of conditionality on the domestic economic structures of the Soviet Bloc have been minimal. Finally, membership in the IMF and IBRD offers relatively low cost assistance for many of the persistent economic problems present in many Eastern European nations, as well as a means of reducing financial dependence on the Soviet Union (a fact which must also appeal to the Soviets). This assistance provides valuable time for East European governments to create and consolidate new economic arrangements if they so choose.

The costs of membership for the Bloc have not greatly altered since Bretton Woods. The Fund is not likely to waive its requirements on the provision of information and conditionality. The possibility that Fund and Bank membership would be a threatening intrusion into sensitive economic information remains, therefore. For the members of the Soviet Bloc discussed here, this has not been an insurmountable problem since most of them already published such information. Additionally, these states are all relatively developed economies when compared to other non-European members of the Bloc, such as Vietnam, and as such have acquired a certain degree of economic and political independence and legitimacy which would enable them to withstand Fund and Bank pressures.

The treatment that new Bloc members are likely to receive, as this analysis demonstrates, will depend on the prevailing conditions in the environment of the IMF and IBRD. In the past, the tensions of the Cold War period significantly influenced relations of the IMF and the World Bank with their Soviet Bloc members. When tensions were especially high between East and West, the environment of the Bank and Fund was not conducive to extensive cooperation with their Soviet Bloc members. Poland and Hungary, however, are entering the Bank and Fund at a time when these organizations' environment significantly differs from that which Poland and Czechoslovakia encountered during the immediate post-war years. As stated above, the emphasis in the Bank and Fund's present (1986) environment seems to have shifted away from Cold War issues toward management of the international economy. This shift in emphasis also entails the recognition that the Soviet Bloc is an integral part of that economy and bodes well for the treatment of Bloc members in the Bank and Fund.

On the other hand, should conditions change and tensions between East and West once again come to dominate international political and economic relations, the Soviet Bloc countries could expect increasing tensions in their relations with the World Bank and the IMF as well. This could be exacerbated by increased economic difficulties within the Bloc. However, it is unlikely, even under conditions of renewed tensions, that the atmosphere within the Bank and Fund would make it difficult for Soviet Bloc countries to remain as members. Universal membership will continue to be an important goal for the IMF and the IBRD, and this goal will be reinforced by the desire of the Bank and Fund, formally embedded in the *Articles of Agreement*, to manage the international economy. Given these goals and the increasingly interdependent nature of the international economy, the Bank and Fund are unlikely to exclude deliberately the Soviet Bloc countries.

The nature of the relationship between the IMF and IBRD and their Soviet Bloc members in the near future, therefore, will most likely be a result of a combination of factors including the status of the Cold War and the Bank and Fund's assessment of priorities in their environment. Past successes and failures of the Bank and Fund in their relations with Soviet Bloc members will also surely influence future policy with respect to those members. It remains to be seen which of these factors the Bank and the Fund will select to guide their decisions in meeting the challenges confronting them in the next decade.

Bibliography

Antić, Zdenko. "Yugoslavia's New Foreign Currency Regulations." *Radio Free Europe Research: Communist Area*, no. 1251, January 3, 1971.

Assetto, Valerie J. and Ronnie J. Phillips. "Reagan, the IMF, and Eastern Europe." Unpublished paper presented at the annual meetings of the Allied Social Science Association, December 28–30, 1985.

Ayres, Robert L. *Banking on the Poor: The World Bank and World Poverty.* Cambridge, MA: The MIT Press, 1985.

Baldwin, David A. "The International Bank in Political Perspective." *World Politics* 18 (October 1965):68–81.

Baran, Paul A. "On the Political Economy of Backwardness." In *The Political Economy of Development and Underdevelopment.* Edited by Charles K. Wilbur. New York: Random House, 1973, pp. 82–93.

Bergsten, C. Fred. "Interdependence and the Reform of International Institutions." *International Organization* 30(2):361–372, Spring 1976.

Bićanić, Rudolf. "Economics of Socialism in a Developed Country." *Foreign Affairs* 44(4):633–661, July 1966.

Bird, Graham and Timothy Orme. "An Analysis of Drawings on the International Monetary Fund by Developing Countries." *World Development* 9(6):563–568, 1981.

Brada, Josef C. and Marvin R. Jackson. "Strategy and Structure in the Organization of Romanian Foreign Trade Activities, 1967–75." *East European Economies Post-Helsinki.* Washington, D.C.: U.S. Congress, Joint Economic Committee, 1977, pp. 1260–1276.

Brau, Edward. "The Consultation Process of the Fund." *Finance and Development* 18(4):13–16, 1981.

Burk, R. V. "The Political Hazards of Economic Reform." *Reorientation and Commercial Relations of the Economies of Eastern Europe.* Washington, D.C.: U.S. Congress, Joint Economic Committee, 1974, pp. 51–78.

Burkett, John P. *The Effects of Economic Reform in Yugoslavia: Investment and Trade Policy, 1959–1976.* Research Series No. 55. Berkeley: University of California, Institute of International Studies, 1983.

Cargill, I.P.M. "Efforts to Influence Recipient Performance: Case Study of India." *The World Bank Group, Multilateral Aid, and the 1970s.* Edited by John P. Lewis and Ishan Kapur. Lexington, MA: Lexington Books, 1973, pp. 89–95.

Cichock, Mark A. "Reevaluating a Development Strategy: Policy Implications for Yugoslavia." *Comparative Politics* 17(2):211–228, January, 1985.

Claude, Inis L., Jr. *Swords Into Plowshares: The Problems and Progress of International Organizations*. 4th edition. New York: Random House, 1971.

Clayton, Elizabeth M. "Economic Reforms in Bulgaria and Romania: Prospects for the 1980s." *Economic Reforms in Eastern Europe and Prospects for the 1980s*. NATO Colloquium, April 16–18, 1980, Brussels, Belgium. New York: Pergamon Press, 1980, pp. 141–148.

Cohn, Theodore H. "Politics in the World Bank Group: The Question of Loans to the Asian Giants." *International Organization* 28(3):561–571, Summer 1974.

Comisso, Ellen T. "Yugoslavia in the 1970's: Self-Management." *Journal of Comparative Economics* 4(2):192–208, June 1980.

Comisso, Ellen and Paul Marer. "The Economics and Politics of Reform in Hungary." *International Organization* 40(2):421–454, 1986.

Crawford, J.T. "Yugoslavia's New Economic Strategy: A Progress Report." *Economic Development in Countries of Eastern Europe*. Washington, D.C.: U.S. Congress, Joint Economic Committee, 1970, pp. 608–633.

Crockett, Andrew. "Issues in the Use of Fund Resources." *Finance and Development* 18(2):10–15, 1982.

Crowther, William. "Romanian Politics and the International Economy." *Orbis* 28(3):553–574, 1984.

David, Wilfred L. *The IMF Policy Paradigm: The Macroeconomics of Stabilization, Structural Adjustment, and Economic Development*. New York: Praeger Publishers, 1985.

Dell, Sidney. "Stabilization: The Political Economy of Overkill." *World Development* 10(8):597–612, 1982.

deVries, Margaret Garritsen. *The International Monetary Fund, 1966–1971: The System Under Stress*, Vol. 1: Narrative, Washington, D.C.: IMF, 1976.

Dubey, Vinod. *Yugoslavia: Development With Decentralization*. Baltimore, MD: The Johns Hopkins University Press, 1975.

Fischer-Galaţi, Stephen. *Twentieth Century Rumania*. New York: Columbia University Press, 1970.

Furtado, Celso. "The Brazilian Model." *Social and Economic Studies* 22(1):122–131, March 1973.

Gadó, Otto, editor. *Reform of the Economic Mechanism in Hungary: Development 1968–71*. Budapest: Akademiai Kiado, 1972.

Gamarnikow, Michael. "Balance Sheet on Economic Reforms." *Reorientation and Commercial Relations of the Economies of Eastern Europe*. Washington, D.C.: U.S. Congress, Joint Economic Committee, 1974, pp. 164–213.

Girvan, Norman. "The Development of Dependency Economies in the Caribbean and Latin America: Review and Comparison." *Social and Economic Studies* 22(1):1–33, March 1973.

Gold, Joseph. *Conditionality*. Pamphlet Series, no. 31. Washington, D.C.: IMF, 1979.

_____ . *Financial Assistance by the International Monetary Fund: Law and Practice*. Pamphlet Series, no. 27. 2nd edition. Washington, D.C.: IMF, 1980.

_____ . *Membership and Nonmembership in the International Monetary Fund*. Washington, D.C.: IMF, 1974.

_____ . "Political Considerations Are Prohibited By Articles of Agreement When the Fund Considers Requests for Use of Resources." IMF, *Survey*:146–148, 1983.

_____ . *The Stand-by Arrangements of the International Monetary Fund* (Washington, D.C.: IMF, 1970).

_____ . *Voting and Decisions in the International Monetary Fund*.Washington, D.C.: IMF, 1970.

Graham, Lawrence S. *Romania: A Developing Socialist State*. Boulder, CO: Westview Press, 1982.

Guitián, Manuel. "Fund Conditionality and the International Adjustment Process: The Early Period, 1950–70." *Finance and Development* 17(4):23–27, 1980.

_____ . "Fund Conditionality and the International Adjustment Process: The Changing Environment of the 1970s." *Finance and Development* 18(1):8–11, 1981.

_____ . "Fund Conditionality and the Adjustment Process: A Look into the 1980s." *Finance and Development* 18(2):14–17, 1981.

Haas, Ernst B. *Beyond the Nation-State: Functionalism and International Organization*. Stanford, CA: Stanford University Press, 1964.

Haas, Michael. "A Functional Approach to International Organization." *Journal of Politics* 47(3):498–517, August 1975.

Hare, P.G., H.K. Radice, and N. Swain, editors. *Hungary: A Decade of Economic Reform*. London: George Allen and Unwin, 1981.

Hauvonen, J.J. "Money and Banking in Yugoslavia, 1945–65". *Finance and Development* 8(4):24–30, 1971.

_____ . "Money and Banking in Yugoslavia: Since 1965." *Finance and Development* 9(1):40–47, 1972.

Hawlowitsch, Johann. "Yugoslavia: The Pioneer Still Leads." *Reforms in the Soviet and Eastern European Economies*. Edited by L.A.D. Dellin and Hermann Gross. Lexington, MA: D.C. Heath and Co., 1972, pp. 123–140.

Hayter, Teresa. *Aid As Imperialism*. Baltimore, MD: Penguin Books Ltd., 1971.

Hirsch, Fred. "Is There A New International Economic Order?" *International Organization* 30(3):521–531, Summer 1976.

Hoffman, Michael L. "The Challenges of the 1970s and the Present Institutional Structure." *The World Bank Group, Multilateral Aid, and the 1970s*. Edited by John P. Lewis and Ishan Kapur. Lexington, MA: Lexington Books, 1973, pp. 13–19.

Holly, Daniel A. "L'O.N.U., le système économique international et la politique internationale." *International Organization* 29(2):469–483, Spring 1975.

Horsefield, J. Keith and Margaret G. deVries. *The International Monetary Fund, 1945–1965*. Washington, D.C.: IMF, 1969.

Horvat, Branko. "Yugoslav Economic Policy in the Post-War Period: Problems, Ideas, Institutional Development." *The American Economic Review* 61(3, part 2):69–169, June 1971.

Horvat, Branko. *The Yugoslav Economic System*. White Plains, NY: International Arts and Sciences Press, Inc., 1976.

Horvat, Branko. "The Economic System and Stabilization." *Eastern European Economics* 23(1):66–91, 1982.

IBRD. *Annual Report*. Washington, D.C.: IBRD, 1950–1986.

IBRD. *Articles of Agreement*. Washington, D.C.: U.S. Treasury, 1944.

IBRD. *General Conditions Applicable to Loan and Guarantee Agreements*. Washington, D.C.: IBRD, 1969.

IBRD. *Statement of Loans, September 30, 1981*. Washington, D.C.: IBRD, 1981.

IBRD. *The World Bank: Policies and Operations*. Washington, D.C.: IBRD, 1960.

IBRD. *World Tables, 1976*. Washington, D.C.: IBRD, 1976.

IBRD. *Yugoslavia and the World Bank*. Washington, D.C.: IBRD, 1979.

IMF. *Articles of Agreement*. Washington, D.C.: U.S. Treasury, 1944.

IMF. *Annual Report of the Executive Board*. Washington, D.C.: IMF, 1950–1985.

IMF. *Balance of Payments Yearbook*. Washington, D.C.: IMF, 1961–1982.

IMF. *International Financial Statistics*. Washington, D.C.: IMF, 1960–1985.

IMF. *Technical Assistance Services of the International Monetary Fund*. Pamphlet Series, no. 30. Washington, D.C.: IMF, 1979.

Iota, V. "Main Bases of Romania's Domestic and Foreign Economic Policy." Translated by Leon Mindlin. *East European Economics* 15(4):100–110, Summer 1977.

Jackson, Marvin R. "Industrialization, Trade, and Mobilization in Romania's Drive for Economic Independence." *East European Economies Post-Helsinki*. Washington, D.C.: U.S. Congress, Joint Economic Committee, 1977, pp. 886–940.

Jackson, Marvin R. "Perspectives on Romania's Economic Development in the 1980s." *Romania in the 1980s*. Edited by Daniel N. Nelson. Boulder, CO: Westview Press, 1981, pp. 254–305.

Jha, L. K. "Comment: Leaning Against Open Doors?" *The World Bank Group, Multilateral Aid, and the 1970s*. Edited by John P. Lewis and Ishan Kapur. Lexington, MA: Lexington Books, 1973, pp. 97–101.

Johnson, A. Ross. *The Transformation of Communist Ideology: The Yugoslav Case, 1945–1953*. Cambridge, MA: The MIT Press, 1972.

Jovanović, Milan. "Changes in Yugoslavia's Economic System." *Review of International Affairs*, 35(March 5, 1984):24–28.

Jovović, Dejan. "Yugoslavia and the International Monetary Fund." *Review of International Affairs* 36(June 20, 1985):23–26.

Kaser, Michael. "Romania." *The New Economic Systems of Eastern Europe*. Edited by Hans-Hermann Hohmann, Michael Kaser and Karl C. Thalheim. Berkeley: University of California Press, 1975, pp. 171–197.

Kay, David A. "On the Reform of International Institutions: A Comment." *International Organization* 30(3):533–538, Summer 1976.

Killick, Tony, ed. *The Quest for Economic Stabilization*. New York: St. Martin's Press, 1984.

King, Robert R. *A History of the Romanian Communist Party*. Stanford, CA: Hoover Institution Press, 1980.

————. "Romania and the Third World." *Orbis* 21(4):875–892, Winter 1978.

Klarić, M. "Yugoslavia and the International Monetary Fund." *Review of International Affairs* 35(April 5, 1984):25–28.

Klemenčič, Vladimir. "Yugoslavia and Its External Debt." *Review of International Affairs* 36(1985):5–9.

Körner, Peter, Gero Mass, Thomas Siebold, Rainer Tetzlaff. *The IMF and the Debt Crisis.* Translated by Paul Knight. London: Zeb Books, Ltd., 1986.

Kornai, Janos. "The Hungarian Reform Process: Visions, Hopes, and Reality." *Journal of Economic Literature* 24(December 1986):1687–1737.

Krasner, Stephen D. "The International Monetary Fund and the Third World." *International Organization* 12(1):670–688.

Krause, Lawrence B. and Joseph S. Nye. "Reflections on the Economics and Politics of International Economic Organizations." *International Organization* 29(1):323–342, Winter 1975.

Lang, Rikard. "Yugoslavia." *The New Economic Systems of Eastern Europe.* Edited by Hans-Hermann Hohmann, Michale Kaser, and Karl C. Thalheim. Berkeley: University of California Press, 1975, pp. 223–250.

Lavigne, Marie. "The International Monetary Fund and the Soviet Union." *International Economics—Comparisons and Interdependence.* New York: Springer-Verlag, 1978, pp. 367–382.

Lewis, John P. and Ishan Kapur. "The World Bank Group, Multilateral Aid, and the 1970s." *The World Bank Group, Multilateral Aid and the 1970s.* Lexington, MA: Lexington Books, 1973, pp. 1–11.

Libby, Ronald T. "External Co-optation of a Less Developed Country's Policy Making: The Case of Ghana, 1969–1972." *World Politics* 29(1):67–89, October 1976.

Lindberg, Leon and Stuart Scheingold. *Europe's Would-Be Polity: Patterns of Change in the European Community.* Englewood Cliffs, NJ: Prentice-Hall, Inc., 1970, pp. 101–140.

Linden, Ronald H. "The Impact of Interdependence: Yugoslavia and International Change." *Comparative Politics* 18(2):211–234, January 1986.

Linden, Ronald H. "Socialist Patrimonialism and the Global Economy: The Case of Romania." *International Organization* 40(2):347–380, 1986.

Lipson, Charles. "The International Organization of Third World Debt." *International Organization* 35(4):603–631, 1981.

Lyons, Gene M., David A. Baldwin, Donald W. McNemar. "The 'Politicization' Issue in the UN Specialized Agencies." *Proceedings of the Academy of Political Science* 34(4):81–92, 1977.

Mačešić, George and Dimitrije Dimitrijević. *Money and Finance in Contemporary Yugoslavia.* New York: Praeger Publishers, 1973.

Mačešić, George. *Yugoslavia: The Theory and Practice of Development Planning.* Charlottesville: The University Press of Virginia, 1964.

Majda, Pawel. "L'importance du Fonds Monetaire International pour la Pologne et les autres pays d'Europe Orientale." *Revue d'études comparatives est-ouest* 13(4):79–100, 1982.

Mason, Edward S. and Robert E. Asher. *The World Bank Since Bretton Woods.* Washington, D.C.: The Brookings Institution, 1973.

Mayall, James. "Functionalism and International Economic Relations." *Functionalism: Theory and Practice in International Relations.* Edited by A.J.R. Groom and Paul Taylor. New York: Crane, Russak and Co., Inc., 1975, pp. 250–277.

Mitrany, David. *A Working Peace System: An Argument for the Functional Development of International Organization*. NPC Pamphlet, no. 40, 4th edition. London: National Peace Council, 1946.

Mittleman, James H. "International Monetary Institutions and Policies of Socialism and Self-Reliance: Are They Compatible? The Tanzanian Experience." *Social Research* 47(1):141–165, Spring 1980.

Mladek, J.V., E. Sture and M.R. Wyezalkowski. "The Change in the Yugoslav Economic System." *IMF Staff Papers* 11(3):407–438, November 1952.

Montias, John Michael. "Romania's Foreign Trade: An Overview." *East European Economies Post-Helsinki*. Washington, D.C.: U.S. Congress, Joint Economic Committee, 1977, pp. 865–885.

Moulton, Anthony D. "On Concealed Dimensions of Third World Involvement in International Economic Organizations." *International Organization* 32(4):1019–1035, Autumn 1978.

New York Times. Selected articles dating from 1950 to 1986.

Nichols, Patrick J. "Western Investment in Eastern Europe: The Yugoslav Example." *Reorientation and Commercial Relations of the Economies of Eastern Europe*. Washington, D.C.: U.S. Congress, Joint Economic Committee, 1974, pp. 725–743.

Nowzad, Bahram. *The IMF and Its Critics*. Essays in International Finance, No. 146 (December 1981). Princeton: Princeton University.

OECD. *Economic Surveys: SFRY*. Paris: OECD, 1966–1985.

Ohman, Carl I. "Comment: A Social Radicalism." *The World Bank Group, Multilateral Aid, and the 1970s*. Edited by John P. Lewis and Ishan Kapur. Lexington, MA: Lexington Books, 1973.

Payer, Cheryl. *The Debt Trap: The International Monetary Fund and the Third World*. New York: Monthly Review Press, 1974.

Payer, Cheryl. *The World Bank: A Critical Analysis*. New York: Monthly Review Press, 1982.

Pentland, Charles. "Functionalism and Theories of International Political Integration." *Functionalism: Theory and Practice in International Relations*. Edited by A.J.R. Groom and Paul Taylor. New York: Russak and Co., Inc., 1975, pp. 9–25.

Pinto, Aníbal and Jaan Kñakal. "The Center-Periphery System Twenty Years Later." *Social and Economic Studies* 22(1):34–89, March 1973.

Pissulla, Petra. "The IMF and the Countries of Eastern Europe." *Intereconomics* 19(2):65–70, March 4, 1984.

Polak, J.J. "Monetary Analysis of Income Formation and Payments Problems." *IMF Staff Papers* 6:1–40.

Polak, J.J. "Monetary Analysis of Income Formation and Payments Problems." *The Monetary Approach to the Balance of Payments*. Washington, D.C.: IMF, 1977, pp. 15–64.

Polak, J.J. and Victor Argy. "Credit Policy and the Balance of Payments." *The Monetary Approach to the Balance of Payments*, 1977, pp. 205–226.

Political Handbook of the World. Editied by Arthur S. Banks. Binghamton, N.Y.: CSA Publications, 1986.

Political Handbook of the World. Edited by Arthur S. Banks and William Overstreet. New York: McGraw-Hill, 1975, 1981.

Political Handbook of the World. Edited by Richard P. Stebbins and Alba Amoia. New York: Simon and Schuster, 1970.

Political Handbook of the World. Edited by Walter H. Mallory. New York: Harper and Brothers, 1960.

Poznanski, Kazimierz. "Economic Adjustment and Political Forces: Poland Since 1970." *International Organization* 40(2):455–488, 1986.

Proceedings and Documents of the United Nations Monetary and Financial Conference. Vol. 1 and 2. Department of State Publication 2866. Washington, D.C.: U.S. GPO, 1948.

Radio Free Europe. *Radio Free Europe Research: Communist Area.* October 22, 1969; October 16, 1970; January 3, 1971.

Ramet, Pedro. *Nationalism and Federalism in Yugoslavia; 1963– 1983.* Ch.6, "The Reform Crisis, 1963–71". Bloomington: Indiana University Press, 1984.

Remmer, Karen. "The Politics of Economic Stabilization: IMF Standby Programs in Latin America, 1954–1984." *Comparative Politics* 19(1):1–24, 1986.

Rohleder, Claus D. "Rumania: The Laggard." *Reforms in the Soviet and Eastern European Economies.* Edited by L.A.D. Dellin and Hermann Gross. Lexington, MA: D.C. Heath and Company, 1972, pp. 115–122.

Rusinow, Dennison. *The Yugoslav Experiment, 1948–1974.* Berkeley: University of California Press, 1977.

Scheetz, Thomas. *Peru and the International Monetary Fund.* Pittsburgh: University of Pittsburgh Press, 1985.

Schrenk, Martin, Cyrus Ardalan and Nawal A. El Tatawy. *Yugoslavia: Self-Management Socialism and the Challenges of Development.* Baltimore, MD: The Johns Hopkins University Press, 1979.

Schröder, Klaus. "The IMF and the Countries of the Council for Mutual Economic Assistance." *Intereconomics* 17(2):87–90, March–April 1982.

Sewell, James Patrick. *Functionalism and World Politics: A Study Based on United Nations Programs Financing Economic Development.* Princeton, NJ: Princeton University Press, 1966.

Sharkansky, Ira and Dennis L. Dresang. "International Assistance: Its Variety, Coordination, and Impact Among Public Corporations in Kenya and the East African Community." *International Organization* 28(2):207–231, Spring 1978.

Singleton, Fred and Bernard Carter. *The Economy of Yugoslavia.* New York: St. Martin's Press, 1982.

Smith, Alan H. "Romanian Economic Reforms." *Economic Reforms in Eastern Europe and Prospects for the 1980s.* NATO Colloquium, April 16–18, 1980, Brussels, Belgium. New York: Pergamon Press, 1980, pp. 35–57.

Smith, Fred L., Jr. "The Politics of IMF Lending." *Cato Journal* 4(1):211–241, Spring/Summer 1984.

Solomon, Robert. "The Politics of IMF Lending: A Comment." *Cato Journal* 4(1):243–247, 1984.

Stojanović, Radmila. *The Functioning of the Yugoslav Economy.* Armonk, NY: M.E. Sharpe, Inc., 1982.

Tajnikar, Maks. "The Coexistence of Market and Plan in the Development of Yugoslav Economic Thought." *Eastern European Economics* 16(1):74–101, Fall 1977.

Tsantis, Andreas C. and Roy Pepper. *Romania: The Industrialization of an Agrarian Economy Under Socialist Planning.* Washington, D.C.: IBRD, 1979.

Tyson, Laura D'Andrea and Gabriel Eichler. "Continuity and Change in the Yugoslav Economy in the 1970s and 1980s." *East European Economic Assessment, Pt. 1—Country Studies, 1980.* Washington, D.C.: U.S. Congress, Joint Economic Committee, 1981, pp. 139–214.

Tyson, Laura D'Andrea. *The Yugoslav Economic System and Its Performance in the 1970s.* Research Series, No. 44. Berkeley: Institute of International Studies, University of California, 1980.

Tyson, Laura D'Andrea. *Economic Adjustment in Eastern Europe.* R-3146-AF, prepared for the U.S. Air Force. Santa Monica: The Rand Corporation, 1984.

United Nations. *United Nations Statistical Yearbook.* New York: U.N., 1958–1978.

Vukmanović, Svetozar. *Economic Reform in Yugoslavia.* Belgrade: Confederation of Trade Unions of Yugoslavia, 1966.

Wall Street Journal. Selected articles dating from 1972 to 1986.

Williamson, John. *The Lending Policies of the International Monetary Fund.* Policy Analysis in International Economics. Washington, D.C.: Institute for International Economics, 1982.

Woodward, Susan L. "Orthodoxy and Solidarity: Competing Claims and International Adjustment in Yugoslavia." *International Organization* 40(2):505–54, 1986.

Index